Renas B'nai Yaakov

Presents

The Hadran Alach

A Project of The Daf Map
www.thedafmap.com

Renas B'nai Yaakov

Presents

The Hadran Alach

A project of The Daf Map
www.thedafmap.com

Cover Design by The Pro Doodler
www.theprodoodler.com

The Pro Doodler
www.thedafmap.com

Ordering Information:
Quantity sales: Special discounts are available on quantity purchases by corporations, associations, and others. For details, contact the publisher at the address above.
Printed in the United States of America

First Edition
14 13 12 11 10 / 10 9 8 7 6 5 4 3 2 1
ISBN #978-1-7360331-5-9

הַדְרָן עֲלָךְ מַסֶּכֶת ... וְהַדְרָךְ עֲלָן. דַּעְתָּן עֲלָךְ מַסֶּכֶת ...
וְדַעְתָּךְ עֲלָן. לָא נִתְנְשֵׁי מִינָךְ מַסֶּכֶת ... וְלָא תִתְנְשֵׁי מִינָן, לָא
בְּעָלְמָא הָדֵין וְלֹא בְּעָלְמָא דְאָתֵי

יְהִי רָצוֹן מִלְּפָנֶיךָ יְיָ אֱלֹהֵינוּ וֵאלֹהֵי אֲבוֹתֵינוּ שֶׁתְּהֵא תוֹרָתְךָ
אֻמָּנוּתֵנוּ בָּעוֹלָם הַזֶּה וּתְהֵא עִמָּנוּ לָעוֹלָם הַבָּא. חֲנִינָא בַּר
פָּפָּא, רָמִי בַּר פָּפָּא, נַחְמָן בַּר פָּפָּא, אַחַאי בַּר פָּפָּא, אַבָּא
[מָרִי] בַּר פָּפָּא, רַפְרַם בַּר פָּפָּא, רָכִישׁ בַּר פָּפָּא, סוּרְחָב בַּר
פָּפָּא, אַדָּא בַּר פָּפָּא, דָּרוּ בַּר פָּפָּא

הַעֲרֶב נָא יְיָ אֱלֹהֵינוּ, אֶת דִּבְרֵי תוֹרָתְךָ בְּפִינוּ וּבְפִיּוֹת עַמְּךָ
בֵּית יִשְׂרָאֵל, וְנִהְיֶה כֻלָּנוּ אֲנַחְנוּ וְצֶאֱצָאֵינוּ וְצֶאֱצָאֵי עַמְּךָ
בֵּית יִשְׂרָאֵל, כֻּלָּנוּ יוֹדְעֵי שְׁמֶךָ וְלוֹמְדֵי תוֹרָתֶךָ. מֵאֹיְבַי
תְּחַכְּמֵנִי מִצְוֹתֶךָ כִּי לְעוֹלָם הִיא לִי. יְהִי לִבִּי תָמִים בְּחֻקֶּיךָ
לְמַעַן לֹא אֵבוֹשׁ. לְעוֹלָם לֹא אֶשְׁכַּח פִּקּוּדֶיךָ כִּי בָם חִיִּיתָנִי.
בָּרוּךְ אַתָּה יְיָ לַמְּדֵנִי חֻקֶּיךָ. אָמֵן אָמֵן אָמֵן סֶלָה וָעֶד

מוֹדִים אֲנַחְנוּ לְפָנֶיךָ יְיָ אֱלֹהֵינוּ וֵאלֹהֵי אֲבוֹתֵינוּ שֶׁשַּׂמְתָּ
חֶלְקֵנוּ מִיּוֹשְׁבֵי בֵּית הַמִּדְרָשׁ, וְלֹא שַׂמְתָּ חֶלְקֵנוּ מִיּוֹשְׁבֵי
קְרָנוֹת. שֶׁאָנוּ מַשְׁכִּימִים וְהֵם מַשְׁכִּימִים. אָנוּ מַשְׁכִּימִים
לְדִבְרֵי תוֹרָה וְהֵם מַשְׁכִּימִים לִדְבָרִים בְּטֵלִים. אָנוּ עֲמֵלִים
וְהֵם עֲמֵלִים. אָנוּ עֲמֵלִים וּמְקַבְּלִים שָׂכָר וְהֵם עֲמֵלִים וְאֵינָם
מְקַבְּלִים שָׂכָר. אָנוּ רָצִים וְהֵם רָצִים. אָנוּ רָצִים לְחַיֵּי הָעוֹלָם
הַבָּא, וְהֵם רָצִים לִבְאֵר שַׁחַת. שֶׁנֶּאֱמַר: וְאַתָּה אֱלֹהִים
תּוֹרִדֵם לִבְאֵר שַׁחַת אַנְשֵׁי דָמִים וּמִרְמָה לֹא יֶחֱצוּ יְמֵיהֶם
וַאֲנִי אֶבְטַח בָּךְ

A Project of

THE DAF MAP

The Daf Map's mission is to provide a Gemara learning experience on all of *Shas* that empowers all who want to achieve their learning goals. The Daf Map achieves this aim through its unique audio *shiurim* in both English and Hebrew and marked *dapim* of Gemara that covers the entire Talmud Bavli.

The Daf Map system is an innovative method that uses geometric shapes and notes to structure the Gemara, thereby increasing understanding, retention, and effective *chazara*. Over forty years in development, this method is currently being used by thousands of people worldwide.

The Daf Map project itself uses the material from HaRav Yehonasan Berger, *Shlita*, who also gave one of the approbations herein. The material in this *sefer* is not from HaRav Berger, Shlita, however, it follows the same mission.

When I was growing up and beginning in the sea of the Torah, I often found myself drowning as there was no guide like The Daf Map to help me. When HaRav Berger introduced me to it, I was intrigued and decided to do what I could to spread the word and help others. In the same vein, I created Renas B'nai Yaakov to give you, my dear reader, some of the knowledge and background that it took me years to accumulate. My goal and hope is to help you so you will not have the same struggles that I had in my early years at Yeshiva.

THE DAF MAP

As the Mishnah says, "Our job is not to finish the work, but at the same time, we are not free to neglect it either.[1] We have to put in the effort and HaShem will guide and help us go from level to level.

We at The Daf Map wish you much success in your learning.

---

[1] Pirkei Avos 2:16

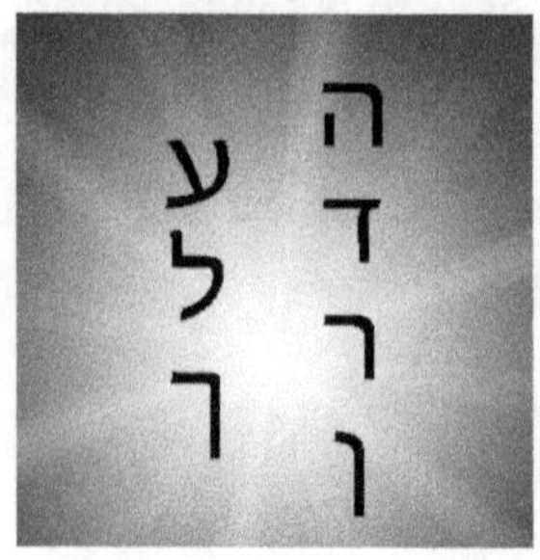

ACKNOWLEDGEMENTS

NO BOOK OF THIS MAGNITUDE would be complete without expressing thanks and appreciation to certain individuals.

First and foremost, I would like to humbly express my never-ending gratitude to the Big Boss, without whose help I would not be anything or have anything.

I would also like to thank my dear wife whose patience with me is unending. I thank her for allowing me the time and space to be able to write this book and bring it to the light of day.

Thank you to my honored parents and in-laws who have raised me and encouraged me and without whom I would not be the man I am.

Finally, I would like to say thank you to the following people:

HaRav Yehonasan Berger, Shlita, for his constant support and encouragement throughout this project and others. I also want to thank Rav Berger for instilling in me a love for learning Torah. In the same vein, I want to thank all my Rabbis, past and present for instilling in me a love for learning and growing in Torah. Their love for HaShem and His Torah is infused with everything they say and do.

HaRav Tzvi Mandel, Shlita, for his support for this project and encouragement in learning the Torah.

Simcha Langsam for his help with numerous suggestions to make this manuscript a much better *sefer*. Moreover, I want to thank him for his constant encouragement and friendship.

ACKNOWLEDGEMENTS

I want to thank Liz Marcus for her meticulous eye for detail and her help in editing this manuscript.

I would also like to express appreciation to several friends who wish to remain anonymous.

More resources for learning can be found on our website www.thedafmap.com.

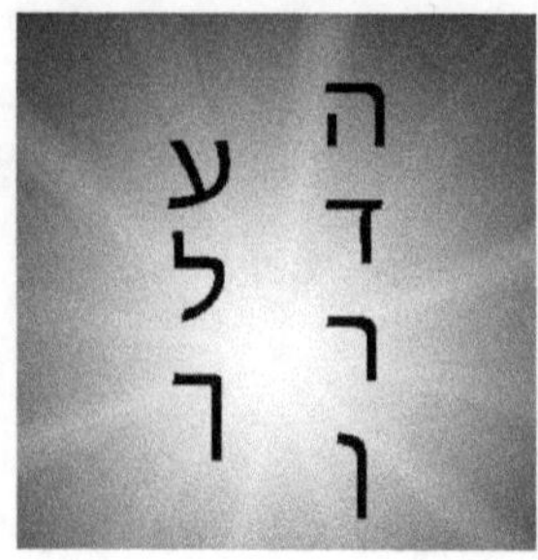

DEDICATION

I would like to dedicate this *sefer* to those who are protecting our people on a spiritual level. Meaning those who dedicate their lives to the Torah and serving our people through their complete dedication to the Torah. I am referring to the Rabbis, members of *Kollel*, and our *Gedolay* Yisrael, among others.

This *sefer* is also dedicated to the IDF soldiers and all the first responders in Israel who work so hard with such dedication to protect our people with the help of The Big Boss.

I also dedicate this *sefer* as a *tefillah* (heartfelt prayer) to HaShem, that He sends a speedy and complete recovery to all of Jewry who needs it: a healing in body, mind, and spirit.

SPONSORS

This *sefer* is sponsored in memory of Rabbi Pinchas Kemuel *ben* Benyamin Yaakov, ZT"L.

This *sefer* is sponsored in memory of Shmuel Yechezkel *ben* Benyamin Yaakov, Z"L

This *sefer* is sponsored in memory of Naftali ben Yisrael and Masha *bas* Avraham, Z"L.

This *sefer* is sponsored in memory of Hadassah *bas* Ephraim, Z"L.

APPROBATIONS

<u>מכתב ברכה</u>

שלום רב

נתבשרתי זה עתה מפי יקרי אהובי זה מכבר למעלה מחמישים שנה ר' בנימין יעקב שליט"א, שכוונתו להוציא לאור פירוש על ההדרן לרגל יום השנה לפטירת מר אביו החשוב הרב פנחס קמואל ז"ל. אמנם טרם ראיתי הדברים בכתב מכל מקום חזקה על חבר שאינו מוציא מתחת ידו דבר שאינו מתוקן.

ר' בנימין עוסק במרץ רב בהרבצת תורה לעם ה' ובחיבור הנ"ל מקיים יקרא דשכבי לכבוד אביו הגדול וכן יקרא דחיי מתוך רצונו להעניק נחת רוח לאמו, שתחי'. נשאר רק לברכו שיפוצו מעיינותיו החוצה ויעלה חיבורו על שלחנם של מלכים – מאן מלכי רבנן ושיראה נחת מכל חלציו ומכל פרי עמליו והכל מתוך אושר ועושר ובריאות איתנה.

המברכו ואוהבו
יהונתן הכהן ברגר
אייר תשפ"ד
ירושלים תובב"א

APPROBATIONS

Letter of Blessing

Warm greetings to all,

I have just been informed by my dear and beloved friend of over fifty years, Rabbi Ben Jakob, Shlita. His intention is to publish a commentary on the *Hadran Alach*, in memory of his late father, Rabbi Pinchas Kemuel *ben* Benyamin Yaakov, ZT"l.

Although I have not yet seen this *sefer* in its completion, it is assumed that someone as pious and observant as Rabbi Jakob would not publish something from under his hand that was not perfect and in line with Torah thought.

Rabbi Jakob is energetically engaged in teaching Torah to the people of God, and in the aforementioned *sefer*, he does so in memory of his great father and to bring satisfaction to his mother, may she live and be well.

All that remains is to bless him that he will continue to spread his wellsprings of Torah outward and that his work will be put on the table of kings – the kings of great Rabbis, and that he will see satisfaction from all his loins and all the fruits of his labors, all out of happiness, wealth, and sound health.

From one who blesses and loves him,
Yehonasan HaKohen Berger
From the Holy City of Yerushalayim

THE HADRAN ALACH

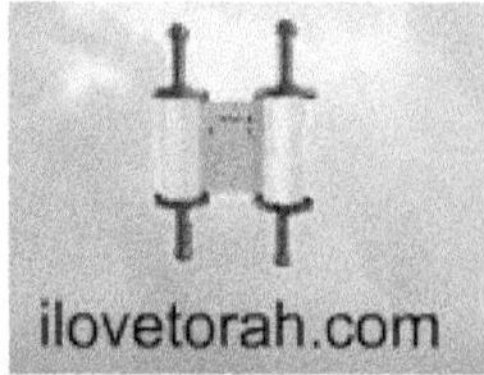

Haskamah for my dear friend Rabbi Ben Jakob:

We know that the entire *Torah*, written and oral, was given at *Har Sinai*; Since Shlomo HaMelech said that there is nothing new under the sun (Koheles 1:9).

We know that we aren't allowed to add to Hashem's praises beyond the words already given since that would imply that Hashem's greatness has a limit. Similarly, one might think that adding to the *Torah*, which is complete, would indicate a lack of appreciation for its perfection--but we see it's not this way. The greatness of *Torah* is revealed when someone seeks the *emes,* truth, and tries to uncover, through toil and arduous work, what is hidden inside. The true *Torah* of Moshe shines forth from the desire to reveal what is hidden and to clarify it, thereby sharing the detailed understanding the person acquired from their toil.

Even though the *Torah* is perfect, it was given in such a way that a human being can bring forth new insights, a fresh perspective to what is already given. The desire to reveal the *Torah* to others and illuminate it in practical ways through *chiddushei Torah* is what the oral *Torah* is about. I see Rabbi Jakob's desire to show people a way to find HaShem in our generation. Each soul at *Har Sinai* received its own revelation; no two have the same spiritual experience because no two people are exactly alike. Rabbi Jakob shares the experience through his *chiddushei Torah* and other *sefarim* that he has written and continues to write. I hope that Hashem gives him the strength to continue spreading to the world the holy words of *Torah* to inspire us to bring the best out of ourselves.

Rabbi Jakob is a *tomim* (pure-hearted one) in the most flattering sense of the word.

I wish Rabbi Jakob much success in all his endeavors.

With blessings,

APPROBATIONS

Rabbi Moshe Steinerman

Jerusalem, Israel

www.Ilovetorah.com

15

THE HADRAN ALACH

Rabbi Eliezer Parkoff
Rosh Yeshiva Medrash Chaim
Rehov Panim Meirot 4
Jerusalem, Israel 9442346

מכתב ברכה

17 Menachem Av, 5784

I was very pleased to receive a manuscript of Renas B'nai Yaakov, a peirush on the Hadran recited at a Siyum, by my dear talmid Ben Jakob of Maryland. The Hadran is very rich in meaning, but is cryptic and difficult to fully understand. My dear talmid has done a marvelous job of breaking down the Hadran into its various parts to make it more understandable. It is quite evident that he put a tremendous amount of thought and effort into this sefer to make it a useful aid to make a siyum much more meaningful.

I wish to give him my bracha that this sefer should be met with success and that it should be an important assistance to those beginners who wish to enter into learning Mishnayos.

With heartfelt bracha,

Rabbi Eliezer Parkoff

APPROBATIONS

הרב צבי מאנדעל

Rabbi Tzvi Mandel
Kashrus Division
Administrative Office
6 Alan Road
Spring Valley, NY 10977

718-813-5386

בס"ד

יום א פרשת לך לך ב חשון תשפה לפק

Dearest friend *Moreinu* Harav Benyamin, Shlita. An old friend always with new and exciting ideas. Rav Benyamin has written a sefer on the subject of Hadran with his creative *Neshama*.

The *sefer* Shasheles HaKabalah is quoted as having written that the mentioning of the children of Rav Papa the First (who lived during the era of Rav) is a *segula* to remember one's learning. The Tur Shulchan Aruch, Orach Chaim, siman 47, says that HaShem gave us the Torah that He Himself, "Joyfully studies daily." Our prayer and wish is that the Torah studying be a vehicle of feeling, pursuing, and adhering to connect to what is sweet to Him.

Tonight, 3 Chesvan is the Yahrtzeit of the Holy Rav Yisrael of Rizhen, ZYA. The sefer Ner Yisrael, Page 172 quotes a story about when the Rizhiner's visited his *mechuten* the Holy Rav Aharon of Karlin, ZYA in Sadiguer, in Jail, who was convicted to terrible suffering including being incarcerated in jail by the Russian government through the antagonists against Chasidus, he asked him, "Where are you holding (spiritually)?" To which he answered, "I am still holding by the word ‘שויתי’ (free translation would be "I am trying to be aware of; cognizant of") HaShem, but I have not yet reached the advanced level of ה"

The sweetness of being close to HaShem comes with knowing how far we are from true *d'veikus* and longing to attain his closeness. King David says, "From far, HaShem has been seen by me."

May HaShem give us all the humility to always toil in His Torah, His Sweetness through *Tefilah*, Torah, and *Maasim Tovim besimchah*.

With love and respect.

על שם הרה"ק יוסף משה בן הרב אלקנה זצוקללה"ה זיעועכי"א
תלמיד אש"ה הבעש"ט הקדוש זצללה"ה זיעועכי"א מ"מ זבאריב וזאלאזיץ

THE HADRAN ALACH

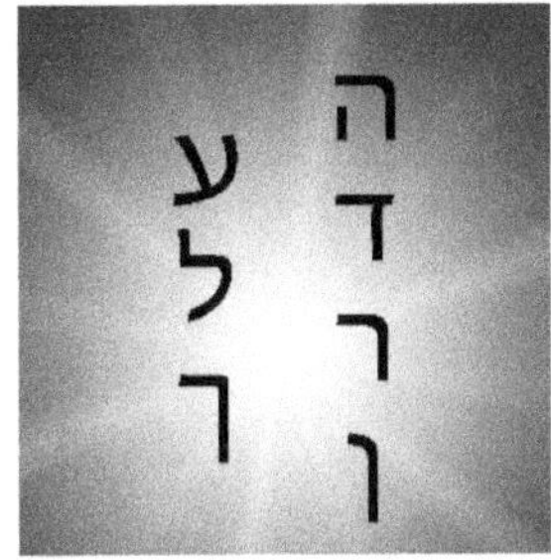

TABLE OF CONTENTS

TABLE OF CONTENTS

HOW TO USE THIS SEFER

I SPENT A SIGNIFICANT AMOUNT of time working on this *sefer* and I am thankful to the Big Boss for allowing me to bring this to the light of day and the Torah public. This *sefer* is unique and I would like to share some pointers with you on how to get the most out of your learning. This *sefer* assumes that you are already familiar with at least the basics of learning Mishnayos and Gemara. However, even a beginner should be able to glean much from this *sefer*.

Herein you will find much information about what is a *siyum*, what is a *Hadran*, and what the difference is between them. I will also cover some of the basics of the special *Kaddish* that is said at the end of the *siyum*. I have included extra prayers that are not typically said anymore at a *siyum*, in case you want to add them to your joyous occasion. Maybe in due course, these prayers and recitals will be added back in and then you will be a step ahead already knowing about them.

To make this *sefer* easier to navigate, I have broken it into four sections:
1. The first section contains different facts and information about the history and development of the *Hadran*.

2. The second section is broken down into parts of the *Hadran*, their translations, and their meanings.
3. The third section is the actual parts of the *siyum* prayers that are said. This section can be used at your *siyum* for the concluding prayers and *Kaddish* that you will be saying.
4. The fourth and final section is reference material.

As with most things having to do with the Torah, there are many clandestine and hidden explanations in the *Hadran* and they are just that, hidden, esoteric, deep, and most are beyond my knowledge and abilities. I often jokingly say that they are above my pay grade. A few of what I have been able to understand, I overtly reveal herein, and some I can only hint at. However, I am completely unaware of the existence of most of the hidden meanings of the *Hadran* and the *Kaddish*. I apologize for my ignorance and inability to comprehend the material of our ancients beyond the basics, and even most of the basics are above my abilities. The brilliance, comprehension, and understanding of the great Rabbis of yore are lightyears beyond my abilities to begin to fathom.

For your accommodation, when we get to parts that are to be recited as prayers, I have **bolded** the instructions and gray-highlighted paragraphs that are only said on special occasions. For the sections that contain the prayers and parts that we say, as opposed to the sections herein for study, I used a slightly larger font for your convenience.

Any mistakes, omissions, or errors are due to the limitations and sins of the author.

SECTION ONE

PREFACE

WHAT IS A *SIYUM*? I thought you would never ask. I know many people believe it is just another opportunity for us Jews to have a party and eat some food. In a sense, this is partially true, however, as with everything in Judaism, there are methods and reasons behind everything we do. Let us explore some of those together. However, before we begin, we need to learn what a *siyum* is, when we make one, and on what occasions. The word comes from the Hebrew word סים (*sayam*) which means to conclude. When we take on a major undertaking and finish it, that is an appropriate time to fete the milestone. When we are learning and then conclude a *Masechta* of Gemara (Bavli or Yerushalmi) or a *seder* of Mishnayos it is also an occasion to celebrate. We do so with special prayers that have special and cryptic meanings, and a festive meal to which we invite some participants. This ceremony of concluding the section of what we learned is called a *siyum* (conclusion). The prayers we recite are called the *Hadran* (after the first word of the prayers we say) and we add to that the special *Kaddish HaGadol* that is said at the conclusion of the *Hadran*.

You may have attended a *siyum* or two and had numerous questions but did not know where to turn or whom to ask for answers and explanations. For example, what do those prayers mean? Why do we mention Rav Pappa and his ten sons? Who were they? What is that long *Kaddish* that we say at the end? With the help from the Big Boss, I hope to answer these questions and share with you the little bit of knowledge I have gleaned on the subject over the years.

We know that no matter how well we studied any material, there is much more to learn and delve into; nevertheless, yours is still a major accomplishment that should be commemorated and celebrated with friends and family. We are going to discuss how to do it properly according to *halacha* so that it has a deeper spiritual meaning.

Typically, one makes a *siyum* after the completion of one of the following:

- When finishing the entire Chumash with at least one major commentary.[1]
- When completing one of the Nevi'im with the commentary of one of the Rishonim.[2]
- A *seder* of Mishnayos
- After completing the entire six Orders of Mishnayos
- A *Masechta* of Talmud Bavli
- A *Masechta* of Talmud Yerushalmi
- After completing the entire Talmud Bavli
- After completing the entire Talmud Yerushalmi
- After the completion of a complete section of Shulchan Aruch
- Learning the whole of Rambam's Mishnah Torah
- Reading through all the Zohar even if he did not understand it.

We have all heard about people around the world making or attending different *siyum* events for the conclusion of the *Daf Yomi* cycle every seven and a half years. I have had the honor of attending several of those wonderful events both in Israel and The United States.

My father, ZT"L, told me about a *siyum* where the person celebrating was an older gentleman who had never learned any Torah in his life. He became a *baal teshuvah* and started learning late in life. Eventually, with his rabbi, he started learning the first Mishnah in Berachos and continued with the Gemara. Because the gentleman was of limited background, it took them several years until they were able to get through the first *daf*. The man was so excited, that he decided to make a *siyum* and invited many people. My honored father told me it was a beautiful event, and the gentleman felt complete and happy, especially with many scholarly rabbis who took time from their busy schedules to attend this one-of-a-kind *siyum*.

---

[1] Iggros Moshe; Orach Chaim 1:157
[2] Ibid.

PREFACE

You have concluded a *Masechta* of Gemara, a *seder* of Mishnayos, or another great accomplishment in learning that should be lauded. That is fantastic! I and many others are so proud of you that I cannot even begin to describe how we feel. It is a fantastic accomplishment. May you have the strength and ability to begin and finish many more.

More importantly, you should know that HaShem is also proud of your accomplishments. This is a time to celebrate. However, the celebration is not for self-aggrandizement or adulation. It is a time to thank and praise the Big Boss for helping you and allowing you to attain this wonderful and spectacular occasion.

I have had the merit to make and attend a few *siyumim* in my life and until I started the research for this *sefer*, I never really understood much of what we say, or why. I firmly believe that the *siyumim* where the celebrant had a deeper understanding of what they were saying at the conclusion were more inspirational to me, even though I did not fully appreciate what was being said.

With this *sefer*, I hope to explain some of the meanings, reasons, and customs behind what we do and say at a *siyum*. I sincerely hope this helps you and encourages you to continue learning and advance from level to level.

Upon completion of one of the above-mentioned major works, a festive meal with a *minyan* of men should be arranged. If a meal is served, it has the status of a *seudas Mitzvah*. If ten men are not present, everything but the proceeding *Kaddish* should be said. There is a beautiful custom that since it is a *seudas Mitzvah*, some will light two candles at a *siyum*.

At a *siyum*, it is preferable to serve meat (or chicken) and wine. However, Rabbi Moshe Sternbuch, in his Teshuvos v'Hanhagos, rules that this is not obligatory. He writes that a *seudas Mitzvah* needs to be a meal that one would be happy to serve to important guests. Some of the reasons we invite guests to a *siyum* are to spread the Torah, bring glory to the Big Boss, and encourage others to learn the Torah and make their own *siyum*. Making a *siyum* is also a wonderful way to educate your children as they see how you show importance and honor to the Torah.

THE HADRAN ALACH

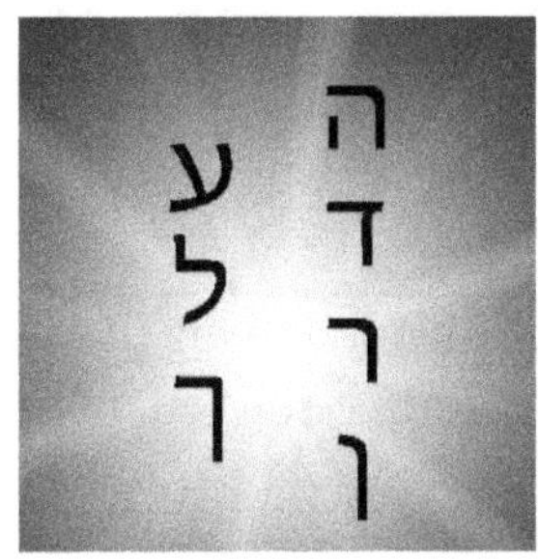

PRAYER BEFORE LEARNING

IT SAYS IN TUR SHULCHAN Aruch 110:8 that when one enters the Beis Midrash to learn, he should say the following before starting. This is a special prayer asking the Almighty for help in one's learning so that he should not make mistakes. When one says this prayer, he should do so with great humility before the Big Boss. Rav Nechunya *ben* Hakanah compiled this prayer and the following one.[3]

Both of these prayers have been incorporated into the *Hadran* and we will explicate them in their appropriate places.

Table 1 Prayer Before Learning

HEBREW	ENGLISH
יהי רצון מלפניך יהוה אלוהי ואלוהי אבותי	May it be Your will, Lord my God and the God of my ancestors
שלא יארע דבר תקלה על ידי ולא אכשל בדבר הלכה וישמחו בי חברי	May no mishap occur by my hand, and that I will not make a mistake in *halacha,* and that my friends should not rejoice in my mistake.

---

[3] Berachos 28b

לֹא אוֹמַר עַל טָמֵא טָהוֹר וְלֹא עַל טָהוֹר טָמֵא	I should not speak of impure being pure, nor of pure being impure
וְלֹא עַל מוּתָּר אָסוּר וְלֹא עַל אָסוּר מוּתָּר	Nor (shall I say) what is permitted is not allowed, and (what is) allowed is not prohibited,
וְלֹא יִכָּשְׁלוּ חֲבֵרַי בִּדְבַר הֲלָכָה וְאֶשְׂמַח בָּהֶם.	And my friends shall not fail in the matter of *halacha,* and I rejoice in their blunder.
וְתָאִיר עֵינַי בִּמְאוֹר תּוֹרָתֶךָ,	And enlighten me with the light of Your Torah,
וְתַצִּילֵנִי מִכָּל מִכְשׁוֹל וּטְעוּת הֵן בְּדִינֵי אִסּוּר וְהֶיתֵּר,	And save me from every obstacle and error both in the laws of prohibition and permissible,
הֵן בְּדִינֵי מָמוֹנוֹת, הֵן בְּהוֹרָאָה, הֵן בְּלִימּוּד.	Whether in civil laws, instruction or learning
גַּל עֵינַי וְאַבִּיטָה נִפְלָאוֹת מִתּוֹרָתֶךָ.	Lift my eyes and let me behold wonders from Your teachings
וּמַה שֶּׁשָּׁגִיתִי כְּבָר, הַעֲמִידֵנִי עַל הָאֱמֶת וְאַל תַּצֵּל מִפִּי דְּבַר אֱמֶת עַד מְאוֹד.	And what I have already achieved, let it stand by the truth and do not withhold any truth from my mouth at all.
כִּי יְהֹוָה יִתֵּן חָכְמָה מִפִּיו דַּעַת וּתְבוּנָה, גַּל עֵינַי וְאַבִּיטָה נִפְלָאוֹת מִתּוֹרָתֶךָ.	For the Lord will give wisdom from His mouth, knowledge and understanding, open my eyes and let me see the wonders of Your Torah.

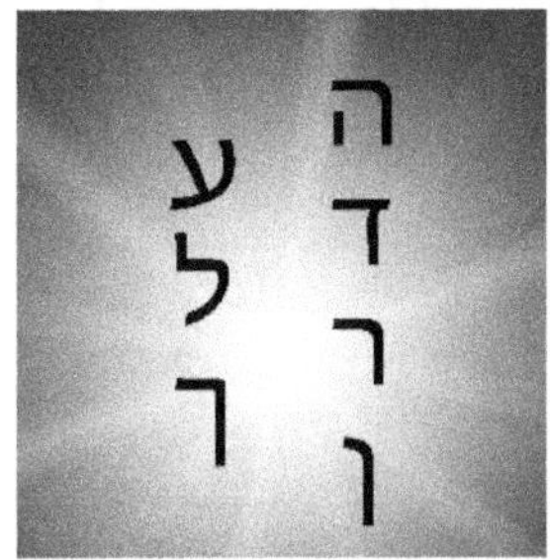

PRAYER AFTER LEARNING

AFTER ONE COMPLETES HIS LEARNING for the day, one should say the following prayer of thanks to HaShem. This is to thank Him for the opportunity to be one of those who merits the ability to learn the holy Torah. This is customarily said when one leaves the Beis Midrash for the day.

Table 2 Prayer After Learning

HEBREW	ENGLISH
מודה אני לפניך יהוה אלוהי ואלוהי אבותי	I acknowledge before You, my God and the God of my ancestors
ששמת חלקי מיושבי בית מדרש ולא שמת חלקי מיושבי קרנות.	You placed my portion among the members of the study hall and not among the members of the street corners.
שאני משכים והם משכימים. אני משכים לדברי תורה והם משכימים לדברים בטלים.	I wake up, they also wake up. I wake up for Torah study, and they wake up for idle matters.

אני עמל והם עמלים. אני עמל ומקבל שכר והם עמלים ואינם מקבלים שכר.	I work and they work. I work and receive a salary, while they work and do not receive a salary
אני רץ והם רצים. אני רץ לחיי העולם הבא והם רצים לבאר שחת	I run and they run. I run toward the afterlife, and they run toward destruction.
שנאמר ואתה אלוהים תורידם לבאר שחת אנשי דמים ומרמה לא יחצו ימיהם ואני אבטח בך.	As it says, And You, God, will bring them down to an empty well, men of blood and deceit will not cross their days, and I will trust in You.

SUGGESTIONS

YOU ARE IN YESHIVA. THAT is great! I wish you much success in your learning and growing in the Torah. I am sure that you have heard the expression, "This semester (זמן) we are learning this particular *Masechta*." This is not an uncommon refrain.

Generally speaking, this means that you are only going to learn a specific number of pages in that particular *Masechta* and you can practically set your watch by that. With this common practice, you will never make a *siyum,* and more importantly, you will not finish even one *Masechta*. In addition, most *Masechtos* will never see the light of day.

My opinion, which seems to be not a popular one, is that we need to consider changing this attitude and work on finishing *Masechtos*, from beginning to end. Of course, I would never disagree with *Rabbanim* or *Gedolim*, it is just a thought I hope they will consider in the near future.

At one time in my life, I had the merit to sit in front of the son of a *Gadol*[4] and leader of the generation. I listened in and watched the man learn, thinking maybe I could pick up some good habits. At that time, he said to me he had only been through half of *Shas Gemara*. Watching the way he learned each topic in the Gemara was amazing. He opened and studied other pages and sections in other *Masechtos* that were referred to by the section in which he was involved. He studied each section and segment for hours and sometimes days, delving into all the commentaries

---

[4] His grandfather was also a Gadol and leader of the generation.

in great detail. In my observations of the man for about six months, it was clear that when he said he had only been through half of *Shas Gemara*, he had been through all Gemara. That is the way one should learn.[5]

Another point I learned from observations of other's learning and the lectures I have attended is what I have come to understand is the proper way to learn. The Rav would explain the Gemara and say that this is how the Ran understands the Gemara, and he would bring significant proof from the Ran in other places to show and expound on the Ran and his way of thinking and understanding the Gemara.

After this, the Rav proceeded to explain the Gemara completely differently and said that this is how the Rif understood the Gemara and again brought numerous proofs accordingly.

The Rav would continue in this vein explaining the Gemara in different ways according to the different *Rishonim* and *Acharonim*.

One of the many things I learned from both points is that each and every Gemara is dependent one upon the other. You cannot separate one *Masechta* from another, they are all intertwined. This is especially so when learning Gemara for practical *halacha*.

The Steipler used to say that if you begin a *Masechta* of Gemara, you should finish it. He gave two reasons for this:[6]

1. It is a question of being similar to a promise that you made to the *Masechta*, that once you begin it, you should finish it.
2. It is a lack of respect for the Gemara if you do not finish it.

When you learn the Gemara in-depth, you will find it easier to understand if you have already learned it completely even superficially. The Gemara says, that Rava said a person should first learn and then go deeply into it. Rashi, explains that a person should go from one subject to the next and will ask questions and give appropriate answers.[7]

Table 3 Understand Learning

IT IS PROPER TO GAIN an understanding into an excellent method by which the Mishnayos may be learned and remembered. As helpful as a text in English may be, the primary

---

[5] I am lecturing myself and letting you read what I am saying to myself. However, this is how our *Gedolim* learn. One day I hope to attain that same level.

[6] Shalom Yerushalayim Page 26

[7] Avoda Zara 19a

goal must be for the student to tackle the material in its original Hebrew.

If the student cannot read Rabaynu Ovadyah from Bartenura fluently, he is advised to begin his study with Mishnah Mivueres (AKA Kahati) which is written in easy modern Hebrew and which presents the reader with a basic comprehension of the text. After the student has completed a given Tractate in such a manner, he should relearn the text and explain it to himself or a friend, out loud, so that he is sure that he comprehends the material. At this point, he should learn the Tractate again. This next time should be with the commentary of Rabaynu Ovadyah from Bartenura. This is the most basic explanation of the text available, and one cannot properly learn the material without his assistance. He should then review this material by reading the text and citing the commentary, in his own words, from memory.

At this point, the student is ready to commence with the building of a solid Mishnah edifice. He will now go through the text with Tiferes Yisrael. About seventy percent of the comments will be familiar to him as they amplify what has already been stated by Rabaynu Ovadyah. However, new information is added which gives insights into deeper meanings behind the words of the text and one's comprehension of the text is considerably enhanced. The student then reviews the text in the manner previously described.

This method is better than trying to learn all the commentaries simultaneously because the student is not then swamped with more data than he can digest, and the constant repetitive review ensures that he will more easily grasp and remember the material.

The third commentary that should be learned is Rambam (Maimonides). In most cases, this will echo what has already been learned. However, Rambam occasionally offers an entirely different explanation of the text.

The fourth commentary to be tackled is Tosefos Yom Tov. This is because the student will now be quite familiar with the basic interpretation of the text, and Tosefos Yom Tov will no longer be so difficult. The points he makes will give the reader new insights and a far deeper comprehension of the material. He will then become familiar with many of the Tosefos brought down in the Talmud.

> The next commentary should be the Meiri. Meiri not only explains the text in depth, but he also presents virtually all alternative explanations and disputes regarding a correct interpretation of the text.
>
> Meleches Shlomo adds the icing to the cake by supplying additional comments from the Talmud Yerushalmi.
>
> One who has learned all this material has a thorough background knowledge of the Tractate and it is highly advisable for a student in *Yeshiva* to so learn the Mishnah as preparation for the Gemara that he is to study that year.
>
> Of course, it would be ideal for a student to learn the entire Six Orders of Mishnayos in this fashion before embarking upon the sea of Talmud. In such an event, the student may find it expedient to begin his study with Mo'ed (Festivals) as he is most probably already familiar with many of the laws pertinent to the Holidays. It is preferable to learn this second volume (Mo'ed) before the first because these Tractates are both shorter and easier than those contained in the first volume. Furthermore, it is a psychological boon to finish a Tractate regardless of how small it is, and the twelve Tractates of Volume Two may give him a bigger moral boost than the eleven contained in the first Volume (Zeraim).
>
> After completing Mo'ed with the commentaries cited above in the manner previously described, he should begin Nashim (Women) or Nezikin (Damages). Zeraim (Agriculture) comes next as much of it is relevant nowadays in Israel. At this point, the student will have a good solid foundation in both material and understanding of the styles of the different commentators which will make it easier to understand the final two *Sedarim*. Kodshim (Sacrifices) will now follow easily as the student will already have learned quite a bit about this subject from Mishnayos in the Orders that he has already learned. The same is true of the final Order of Taharos (Purity).
>
> As HaRav Yaakov Kaminetzky ZT"L used to say, "Mishnayos is the key to *Shas*. Without them, one cannot hope to properly understand the Gemara."[8]

Review, Review, Review. Over the years I have spoken to several *Gedolim* and *Talmidei Chachamim,* and all agree that one must review

---

[8] Renas B'nai Yaakov on Mishnayos Chagigah P 23

their learning repeatedly and every review is in the category of learning Torah. One should never consider it a waste of time. The consensus is that without many repetitions of their learning, none of them would be who they are (or were). This is an essential part of their learning. I once heard that HaRav Yisrael Zeev Gustman, ZT"L (Rosh HaYeshiva and founder of Yeshivas Netzach Yisrael) had learned *Maseches* Bava Basra over 200 times. He was a *Gadol Hador* who was known for never wasting a second of his life. If he reviewed his learning so many times, so can we. Reviewing is one of the most important aspects of your learning, do not neglect it. You will thank me later for this advice.

THE HADRAN ALACH

STORIES

STORIES. STORIES ARE A GREAT way to pass on traditions and instructions to our children and students. They can be fun and informative while simultaneously conveying a wealth of knowledge to the listener in many ways. I hope these few stories can help relay to you the importance of learning, repetition, and making a *siyum*. I also hope this *sefer* can teach you how to properly conduct and understand what goes on beneath the surface of the texts.

The anecdotes below I have read in other *sefarim*, read on the Internet, or heard from others. I cannot vouch for the veracity of any of them. Regardless, they are all good stories that I would like to share with you.

A young man witnessed his mother wear a special brand-new dress for his *siyum* on Bava Kamma. She did not reserve it for *Shabbos* or *Yom Tov*, she saved it to wear for his *siyum*; in doing so she showed her son how important the Torah was to her. His mother's actions made such an impression on him, and he was so impressed that he grew up to become HaRav Yitzchak Hutner, Rosh HaYeshiva of Mesivta Rav Chaim Berlin.

There was another young man with special needs and when he finished learning the entire Chumash, the family made a *siyum* for the entire *shul* to celebrate the event. It had taken the young man several years, but for the family, it was a special occasion. They invited many great rabbis and even catered the event and had a live band.

There are numerous stories of *Gedolim* who effusively give out blessings to people especially just before and immediately after a *siyum*. They say that the time of a *siyum* is a special time of joy and closeness to HaShem. It is an especially auspicious time to give out blessings to people. Rav Chaim Kanievsky would give people to drink from the wine he used at a *siyum* saying that it had a special holiness. He said that at the time of a siyum, all the Tannaim and Amoraim would stand up to protect and support the person making the *siyum*.

I have heard stories of people from the Holocaust who risked their lives to get their hands on Gemaras, learn them, and finish them. After the destruction, some of these men held lavish parties to celebrate their having merited the ability to learn Gemara in that Torah wasteland and place of human destruction.

A Rebbi of mine told me that one time Rav Moshe Feinstein, ZT"L was especially joyous while making a particular *siyum*. His reason was that he was making a *siyum* for finishing *Shas* 101 times – for the second time! Can you imagine? He learned through all Gemara 202 times. It is beyond my comprehension, but that is why he was the Gadol Hador.

Someone asked HaRav Chaim Pinchas Scheinberg, ZT"L how many times he had learned through *Shas*. He refused to answer, but he did admit that he had learned *Maseches* Niddah over ninety times. The reason was that he would learn that *Masechta* on his numerous trips abroad for fundraising.

A Rav once told me that when he was a *bachur* in Yeshiva, he would learn Mishnayos while waiting. For example, when wrapping his *tefillin*, waiting for the Rebbi to start a *shiur*, while waiting for *minyan* to start, while waiting for his *chavrusah,* and more. When he finished all

Mishnayos, he made a big *siyum*. I happened to be at that *siyum*, it was one of the first I attended.

There is a famous story told about HaRav Moshe Feinstein, ZT"L that one of his students was a *baal teshuvah*. He was doing well and even influenced his father who started to keep *Shabbos* and kosher. The father saw that his son loved learning Gemara and asked his son about it. The son explained to his father about Gemara and how it worked, etc. The father told his son that he also wanted to learn Gemara.

The son explained that it was no easy thing to learn Gemara. Nevertheless, the father insisted, and the son started to teach his father about Mishnayos and some of the basic concepts of learning Gemara. They started with the *Alef-Beis*, progressed to Chumash, then to Mishnayos, and finally to the Gemara. It took them over a year until they were finally able to start learning Gemara.

Much later, they finished their first *daf* of Gemara and the father wanted to throw a party in celebration. The son said that as far as he knew, one only makes a *siyum* on a complete *Masechta*. But he would ask Rav Moshe what they should do.

Rav Feinstein said that not only should the father make the *siyum*, but that he would show up and speak. Of course, Rav Moshe Feinstein showed up and spoke at the *siyum* to the utter joy and delight of the father, son, and guests.

Unfortunately, that night, the father passed away. At the funeral, Rav Feinstein spoke and said that some acquired the Hereafter in one hour, this man acquired the Hereafter after one *daf* of Gemara.

HALACHOS

AS WITH EVERYTHING IN TORAH and Judaism, there is a method and reason behind all we do. One important facet of making a *siyum* is that the meal can become more than just a repast of delicious food and camaraderie. Under the proper circumstances, the food one consumes becomes more than a gastronomical feast and now becomes a holy meal – a *seudas Mitzvah* with which to honor HaShem. I would like to share some *halachos* involved so that your siyum has a much deeper meaning.

- If this "party" has fulfilled the *halachic* requirements to become a *siyum*, the *Hadran* can now be said with the final *Kaddish HaGadol*. This *seudas Mitzvah* is such that it can be used to fulfill the obligation of a firstborn fasting on the day before *Pesach*. In order for this to work, the *siyum* has to be on one of the appropriate books mentioned above.[9] If one wants to celebrate any accomplishment, that is not a problem, but it has to meet appropriate criteria for it to have any *halachic* value.
- Rav Elyashiv says that one can make a *siyum* on something even if he did not read it out loud. Including things learned by heart without even using a *sefer*. What this means is that if one knows the entire *Masechta* of Gemara Berachos by heart, and then thinks

---

[9] See page 28

about it, going over in his mind every word, he can make a *siyum*.[10]

- One can make a *siyum* on having learned a *Masechta* in any language.

- We have discussed above[11] the different works with which one can make a *siyum*.

- If a minor finishes an appropriate work and wants to make a *siyum* a *Rav* should be consulted. There are differing opinions, and they are also dependent on the occasion. For example, if it is for the fast of the firstborn, people tend to be lenient and allow this if no one else is prepared.

- If you finish the entire material before the planned party, it is not a *seudas Mitzvah*. However, if you leave a little bit over to conclude at the *siyum*, then you can make the *siyum* and it becomes a *seudas Mitzvah*.

- It is preferable to make the *siyum* as close as possible to the time when one finished the material. However, under extenuating circumstances, one can delay the *siyum* for a couple of months. Please consult your *Rav* for more information.

- One should say "Migdol" in *birchas hamazon* as the *Mitzvah* of the *siyum* brings a great light into the world.[12]

- It is customary to wish the person making the *siyum* a "Mazal Tov".

- One can also wish the person making the *siyum* that he merits to begin, learn, and conclude more *sefarim* and even all Gemara.

- It is also customary to sing songs of praise lauding HaShem and the Torah.

- Some great Rabbis would make a *siyum* on their birthday.

- Some say that *Tachanun* is not said in the davening before a *siyum*, while others disagree. As always, ask your *Rav* for guidance.

- At the end of the *Hadran*, we say a special *Kaddish*. While it is preferable that one who does not have parents say this *Kaddish HaGadol*, many permit this. Again, ask your *Rav* what you should do.

- The custom is to start the next segment of learning immediately after the *siyum* or begin anew what one has just completed. This is to give yourself the impetus to continue learning and not leave

---

[10] Ashrei Ha'ish, Volume 3, Orach Chaim 55:10
[11] Page 28
[12] Shulchan Aruch, Yorah Da'ah 246:26, Kaf HaCayim Orach Chayim 189:11

an opening to the Evil Inclination to try to entice you not to continue learning.

- Some start the *siyum* before the *seudas Mitzvah* and some during the meal. Both positions are acceptable.
- It is preferable to light two candles at the *siyum*.
- It is preferable to have a meal of meat or chicken, however, one can make a *siyum* over cakes and drinks.
- It is preferable to say the *birchas hamazon* over a cup of wine
- In addition to the words of the *siyum*, it is preferable to have a Rav speak words of the Torah.
- It is customary to serve wine at the *seudas Mitzvah*.

THE HADRAN ALACH

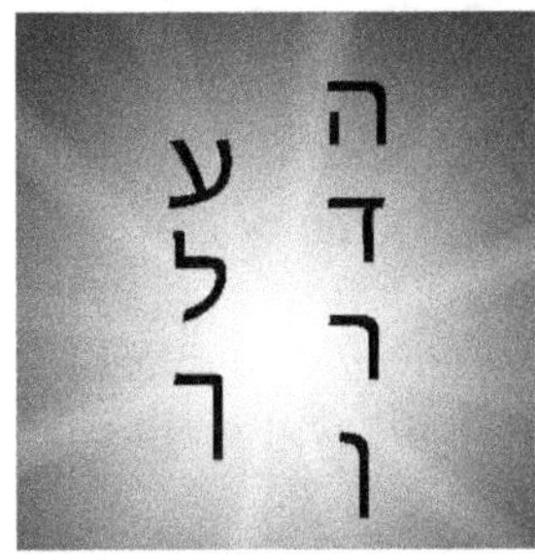

FUN FACTS

- *Maseches* Bava Basra seems like the longest *Masechta* because it has the most *dapim* at 176. However, *Maseches* Berachos is the longest having the most words.[13]
- HaRav Moshe Feinstein, ZT"l said that when a group of children finish a chapter of Gemara, they can make a *siyum*.
- Rav Meir Shapiro, ZT"l, Rosh HaYeshiva of Yeshiva Chachmei Lublin established the idea of the Daf Yomi. He suggested it at the Kenisiah Gedolah of Agudas Yisrael in 1923. He was encouraged by HaRav Moshe Feinstein and the Gerrer Rebbi, among others.
- *Maseches* Tamid is the shortest *Masechta* with only nine *dapim*.
- *Maseches* Horayos has thirteen *dapim*
- You can make a *siyum* on more than one *Masechta* at a time
- One can make a *siyum* on something learned in any language.
- The Steipler Gaon would make a *siyum* on a *seder* of Mishnayos every *Shabbos* morning.
- The Satmar Rebbi, Rav Yoel Teitelbaum learned the entire *Masechta* of Bava Basra on his wedding day.
- Several *Gedolim* used to make a *siyum* on a *Masechta* on their birthdays
- You can make a *siyum* on *Yom Tov*
- There are 2,711 *dapim* of Talmud Bavli (including Shekalim).

---

[13] Vilan Gaon

- There are thirty-six *Masechtos* in Talmud Bavli
- There are sixty-three *Masechtos* of Mishnayos in Bavli
- There are approximately 2,094 pages in Talmud Yerushalmi
- There are thirty-nine *Masechtos* in Talmud Yerushalmi
- Talmud Yerushalmi was compiled in the fourth century CE
- Talmud Bavli was compiled in the fifth century CE
- In the previous century, in Eastern Europe, a *siyum* would last for seven days. People would dress in their finest *Shabbos* clothing.

As mentioned above, there are thirty-six *Masechtos* in Bavli. There are thirty-six candles we light on Chanukah (not including the *shamash*). The Chanukah candles represent the Oral Traditions as does the Mishnayos. Thirty-six also has the numeric value of the word לו – his. This is to teach us that the Torah that one learns becomes his both in this world and the next. The *Hadran* mentions that his Torah should stand for him both in this world and the next. Numerous other connections to the word לו and thirty-six can be found in the Torah and other places.

סיום – THE SIYUM

THE WORD *SIYUM* IS COMPRISED of four letters on which we will expound briefly. Please keep in mind, that there is much more hidden here than I am discussing. I am just sharing with you a few minor points. There are dozens more hints and *gematrias* for the words *siyum* and *Masechta*, both full, partial, and other forms of *gematria*. Many *Rabbanim* have written about anachronyms, values, and more.

ס – THE SAMECH

THE NUMERIC VALUE OF THE *Samech* is sixty. There is a total of sixty-three *Masechtos* in Mishnayos. However, the three Bava's (Bava Kamma, Metziah, and Basra) were originally one large *Masechta* which brings our total to sixty-one. Since Avos is more *Agadic* in nature, many also discount that. This brings our total down to sixty.

The *Samech* is round which implies that when we finish one set of learning, we must continue onto the next stage of learning. It also hints at the need for constant review.

Sixty is also the age of becoming an elder. Certain foods are nullified in sixty parts. Dreaming is 1/60th of prophecy. Sleeping is 1/60th of death. Shabbos is 1/60th of the Hereafter.

י – THE YUD

AS WE WILL DISCUSS LATER,[14] the number ten plays an important role in the *siyum*, which is represented by the numeric value of the *yud* which is ten. It shows up in the ten Utterances with which HaShem created the world and the Ten Commandments.

Maybe it can represent the ten tests that Avraham Avinu had to go through. It is to tell us that as difficult as it is to finish a *Masechta* because of all the tests from the Evil Inclination we go through, HaShem helps us, just as He helped our Patriarch Avraham. *Nisayon* (test) has the numeric value of 176 which is the number of pages in the longest (number of pages) *Masechta* as Bava Basra.

ו – THE VAV

THE *VAV* REPRESENTS THE SIX Orders of Mishnayos.

In Kabbalah, there are seven divine emotive attributes, and the sixth one is Yesod, which represents completeness in morality, modesty, and areas of holiness. Participating in a *siyum* helps rectify sins of immorality.[15] See Appendix Four for more information about the Sefiros and what they stand for.[16]

The *vav* is the first letter of the sixth word in the Torah which has significant connections in Kabbalah. The *vav* is the main component of the first letter א in the alphabet which represents HaShem.

---

[14] Pages 58, 68, and 215, among others
[15] Ahavas Chaim, Volume 1 Parshas Bahaloscha page 115
[16] Page 213

מ – THE MEM

THE *MEM* WITH THE NUMERIC value of forty, stands for Moshe Rabaynu whose name starts with the mem and, spent forty days on Mount Sinai to receive the holy Torah. We spent forty years in the desert. Forty represents the concept of renewal and a new beginning.

A court can punish with forty lashes (less one) for the commission of certain crimes.

A *mikvah* contains forty *seah* (liquid measurement) of water, which corresponds to the number of days it rained in the times of Noah.

In Kabbalah, it talks about the four sides of the world, each side containing the ten *Sefiros*.

There are many other hints for all four of the above letters that I could expound upon for many more pages.

SECTION TWO

SIYUM

AS WE DISCUSSED ABOVE, AT the completion of a *Masechta* of Gemara, a *seder* of *Mishnayos,* or another major accomplishment of similar scope, it is customary to celebrate the occasion with a *seudas Mitzvah* and words of Torah. At this festive meal, he who is making the *siyum* reads the last few lines of the text and explains them to the assembled crowd so that all may rejoice with him at this opportune moment.[1] He should expound on the subject and make it understandable and interesting for those assembled. He should try to connect the end of what he is learning to either the beginning of what he is finishing or what he is about to embark upon.

An effort, moreover, should be made to invite at least ten adult males so that the special *Kaddish Hagadol* may be recited at the end.[2] At some point, the person who made the *siyum* should begin anew with the same *Masechta* or the next one on his agenda. This is to symbolize that learning is important to him and he will continue growing מחיל אל חיל[3] from level to level. It also shows that he plans to review his learning so that it will become second nature to him.

Notably, the "שהחיינו" is not said as the *Mitzvah* of Torah study is not one that comes at intervals, "You shall meditate in it (the Torah) by

---

[1] Shach: Yoreh Da'ah 246:26

[2] Ibid.

[3] Tehillim 84:8

day and by night."[4] [5] The שהחינו is only said for events or occasions that occur at specific events that happen on occasion. Torah study does not qualify as it is always time to study Torah and not something that has a time period that comes and goes.

Even the blessing of "שהשמחה במעונו" (The joy in his home) is omitted when making the *siyum* because not everyone in God's House is happy; the angels resent the fact that the Torah was given to man rather than to them.[6] This *bracha* is only said when the entire "universe" is happy with the occasion. For example, at a wedding under the wedding canopy and for *birchas hamazon* at the same.

When one completes the section of his learning for the *siyum*, it is customary to deliver a Torah discourse that ties the end of the *sefer* to its beginning to demonstrate that one must always review that which he has already learned and that no matter how often he has reviewed it, there is no limit to its eternal depths. A Tractate is called "מסכת", which also means weaving, as it is like the weaving loom. With each motion or review, more thread (wisdom) is added to the item of clothing (one's learning).[7]

This same lesson is underscored by the fact that no Tractate of the Babylonian Talmud has a *Daf aleph*. Every *Masechta* starts with *daf beis*. One is likewise reminded not to become haughty with his accomplishment as he has not yet learned "*daf aleph*", the first piece of information for this *Masechta* (you do not even know what is on *daf aleph*).[8]

One must end his Torah discourse with the wish that Yerushalayim be rebuilt with the speedy arrival of the Messianic Era so that one is not so carried away with his jubilation that he forgets about the destruction of the Temple.[9] This is similar to the reason we break a glass under the wedding canopy – to remind us that at the pinnacle of our happiness and celebrations, we have to remember that our happiness cannot be complete until the Holy Temple is rebuilt in Yerushalayim. May that wonderous and spectacular event occur speedily in our days.

I found that the Yabia Omer[10] holds that *Tachanun* is not recited at the *tefillah* immediately preceding or proceeding a *siyum*. He bases his opinion on the Mishnah[11] that talks about the *Kohanim* who made a party on the fifteenth of Av because people finished for the season the *Mitzvah*

---

[4] Yehoshuah 1:8

[5] Hadar Yitzchak Pages 10 – 11

[6] Ibid. Page 10

[7] Ta'amay Haminhagim: Likutim #92

[8] Ibid.: Rosh HaShanah #529

[9] Ibid. 903:3

[10] Yabia Omer 4:13

[11] Taanis 31a

of chopping wood for the Beis HaMikdash. I am not sure why the custom of not reciting *Tachanun* prior to a *siyum* is not universally accepted and fell into disuse.

SEUDAS MITZVAH

AT THE CONCLUSION OF THE *Hadran* and the *Kaddish HaGadol*, it is customary for the celebrant to welcome the guests to join him for something to eat in honor of the occasion. This is not just a meal, but a *seudas Mitzvah*, a meal in tribute to a *Mitzvah* honoring the Torah.

After the *siyum*, the invitees should enjoy a repast that should preferably include chicken or meat and wine. Since this is not always possible, drinks and cake are also acceptable. The *siyum* can be made before or after the meal has started.

One reason why we make a *siyum* is to commemorate the feast that King Solomon made after he realized that God's promise to make him a wise man had been fulfilled. King Solomon had prayed for an understanding heart to be a good ruler for his people. When he woke from sleep, he discovered he could understand the language of animals and birds. Just as he celebrated when his wisdom was "completed", so did it become customary for us to rejoice at the completion of a major phase of learning.[12]

As mentioned in the previous section, another source for this custom is a celebration made on the fifteenth of the month of Av when the necessary wood for the Temple Altar fires had been collected for the forthcoming year. Just as they rejoiced upon completing the preparations for the Altar fires, so too must one rejoice when finishing a portion of learning.[13]

Since you have invited ten or more men to be able to say the *Kaddish HaGadol*, when you finish eating the *seudas Mitzvah*, you should have ten men for the *birchas hamazon*.

---

[12] Hata'amim V'haminhagim: Ta'amim Nifradim #44
[13] Maharshal

THE TEN SONS OF RAV PAPA

AT SOME OF THE *SIYUMIM* you have attended, during the *Hadran*, you have heard the celebrant make mention of a bunch of the sons of Rav Papa. There are ten names mentioned in this enigmatic list as the sons of Rav Papa. Have you ever wondered why during the *Hadran* one mentions the ten sons of Rav Papa? I know I sure have, and I have found that few people know the reasons for this cryptic custom. Why are they only mentioned at some *siyumim* and not others? Who were they? Why did they merit mention at many concluding ceremonies? What was so special about these individuals? Rav Pappa lived during the fifth generation of Amoraim, and as you will see shortly, this is important to our discussion.

For clarification purposes, we will list the names of the ten sons of Rav Papa as they appear for a *siyum* of the Gemara. However, as we are about to learn, they may not all be the sons of the same Rav Papa. Our Rav Papa could also have had sons by the same names as other people.

Table 4 Rav Papa's Sons

חֲנִינָא	Chaninah
רָמִי	Rami
נַחְמָן	Nachman
אַחָא	Acha
אַבָּא מָרִי	Aba Mari
רַפְרָם	Rafram
רָכִישׁ	Rachish
סוּרְחָב	Sorchav
אַדָּא	Ada
דָּרוּ	Daru

Mentioning the ten sons of Rav Papa was first brought down by Rav Hai Gaon, who said that not all the names were sons of Rav Papa, but that tradition held reciting the names of these great men was a *segulah* against forgetting one's Torah learning.[14] Some of the names mentioned could refer to people who lived in earlier generations; for example:

- As mentioned, Rav Papa was a fifth-generation Amorah

---

[14] Sefer HaEshkol: Hilchos Sefer Torah 14

- Rafram *bar* Papa was a contemporary of Rav Chisda[15] a third-generation Amorah
- Rachish *bar* Papa was a student of Rav (Abba Aricha), a first-generation Amorah
- Acha, Aba Mari, and Ada *bar* Papa are mentioned in the Talmud with the title "Rabbi" which was the appellation given to scholars from the Land of Israel but not from Babylonia which is where Rav Papa lived.[16]
- Surchav *bar* Papa was a student of Ze'iri[17] who was a second-generation Amorah

There were seven or eight generations of Amoraim over about three hundred years.

For succinctness, we will continue to refer to them as the ten sons of Rav Papa, since that is how most people know and refer to them.

One of the reasons we mention their names is they represent the ten Utterances of the Lord with which the Universe was created, and Creation began with Torah which is called "ראשית".[18] Let us now explore how the ten sons of Rav Papa represent the ten Utterances with which everything came into existence. Please see Appendix Five[19] for more details about the Ten Utterances that HaShem used in the creation of the universe.

בְּרֵאשִׁית בָּרָא אֱלֹהִים אֵת הַשָּׁמַיִם וְאֵת הָאָרֶץ:
In the beginning, God created the Heavens and the earth.[20]

The Creation (בראשית) began with the establishment of mercy: the world would not be able to function upon the attribute of justice alone. Mercy was to be added as the world would not be able to exist without HaShem's attribute of Mercy. It is His Mercy that sustains the world and

---

[15] Shabbos 82a

[16] Bava Kamma 80b

[17] Kesuvos 17b

[18] Hata'amim V'haminhagim: Ta'amim Nifradim #45

[19] See page 215

[20] Beraishis 1:1

shows patience to the sinner waiting for him to repent. The first son of Rav Papa, Chanina, symbolizes this as "חנינא" which means mercy.[21]

וַיֹּאמֶר אֱלֹהִים יְהִי אוֹר וַיְהִי־אוֹר: וַיַּרְא אֱלֹהִים אֶת־הָאוֹר כִּי־טוֹב וַיַּבְדֵּל אֱלֹהִים בֵּין הָאוֹר וּבֵין הַחֹשֶׁךְ:

God said, "Let there be light"; and there was light. God saw that the light was good, and God separated the light from the darkness.[22]

The Lord divided the light and set aside a portion of the light, called the *Ohr Hagenuzah*, for the righteous in Gan Eden. Rav Papa's second son was called "רמי" (divided) as an allusion to this event of the divisions of the lights.[23]

וַיֹּאמֶר אֱלֹהִים יְהִי רָקִיעַ בְּתוֹךְ הַמָּיִם וִיהִי מַבְדִּיל בֵּין מַיִם לָמָיִם:

God said, "Let there be an expanse in the midst of the water, that it may separate water from water."[24]

God divided waters into separate realms. The waters that were designated to remain in the spiritual plane rather than in Heaven, however, were saddened to be removed from their lofty heights until God informed them that they would be poured upon the Altar as a Libation-Offering during *Sukkos*. Thus were the waters soothed. Rav Papa's third son, "נחמן", which means "condolences", hints at this incident of separation, division, and consolation.

וַיֹּאמֶר אֱלֹהִים יִקָּווּ הַמַּיִם מִתַּחַת הַשָּׁמַיִם אֶל־מָקוֹם אֶחָד וְתֵרָאֶה הַיַּבָּשָׁה וַיְהִי־כֵן:

God said, "Let the water below the sky be gathered into one area, that the dry land may appear." And it was so.[25]

Thus were the land masses and seas formed so that the latter might act as boundaries to the former. "סורחב", Rav Papa's fourth son alludes to this confinement and gathering. There are hints in Kabbalah of massive

---

[21] Hata'amim v'haminhagim: Ta'amim Nifradim #45

[22] Beraishis 1:3 – 4

[23] Ibid.

[24] Beraishis 1:6

[25] Beraishis 1:9

subterranean pools of water that may have come from the flood of the time of Noach.

וַתּוֹצֵא הָאָרֶץ דֶּשֶׁא עֵשֶׂב מַזְרִיעַ זֶרַע לְמִינֵהוּ וְעֵץ עֹשֶׂה־פְּרִי אֲשֶׁר זַרְעוֹ־בוֹ לְמִינֵהוּ וַיַּרְא אֱלֹהִים כִּי־טוֹב:

The earth brought forth vegetation: seed-bearing plants of every kind, and trees of every kind bearing fruit with the seed in it. And God saw that this was good.[26]

This event took place when the dew, rejuvenated (אד) them and caused the trees to blossom and bloom. "אדא", Rav Papa's fifth son, highlights the rejuvenation of this event.

וַיֹּאמֶר אֱלֹהִים יְהִי מְאֹרֹת בִּרְקִיעַ הַשָּׁמַיִם לְהַבְדִּיל בֵּין הַיּוֹם וּבֵין הַלָּיְלָה וְהָיוּ לְאֹתֹת וּלְמוֹעֲדִים וּלְיָמִים וְשָׁנִים:

God said, "Let there be lights in the expanse of the sky to separate the day from the night; they shall serve as signs for the set times — the days and the years;[27]

Originally there were supposed to be two luminaries – the sun (Jewry) and the moon (Gentiles) corresponding to the brothers Yaakov and Esav. The constant battle of good versus evil (Yaakov vs. Esav) results in a constant bloodbath. "אחא" (brother), the sixth son of Rav Papa symbolizes the two brothers being in constant rivalry to this day. This also alludes to the final war of Gog and Magog.

וַיֹּאמֶר אֱלֹהִים יִשְׁרְצוּ הַמַּיִם שֶׁרֶץ נֶפֶשׁ חַיָּה וְעוֹף יְעוֹפֵף עַל־הָאָרֶץ עַל־פְּנֵי רְקִיעַ הַשָּׁמָיִם:

God said, "Let the waters bring forth swarms of living creatures, and birds that fly above the earth across the expanse of the sky."[28]

Fish are mentioned first and regarding living creatures, as they multiply faster than all other forms of life. Rav Papa's seventh son "רפרם" (procreation) illuminates this scenario.

---

[26] Beraishis 1:12
[27] Beraishis 1:14
[28] Beraishis 1:20

וַיֹּאמֶר אֱלֹהִים תּוֹצֵא הָאָרֶץ נֶפֶשׁ חַיָּה לְמִינָהּ בְּהֵמָה וָרֶמֶשׂ וְחַיְתוֹ־אֶרֶץ לְמִינָהּ וַיְהִי־כֵן:
God said, "Let the earth bring forth every kind of living creature: cattle, creeping things, and wild beasts of every kind." And it was so.[29]

Thus, workers were created for man's benefit – beasts of burden to carry his wares. "דרו" (carry), Rav Papa's eighth son symbolizes this event of creating animals who would assist man in carrying things for him.

וַיֹּאמֶר אֱלֹהִים נַעֲשֶׂה אָדָם בְּצַלְמֵנוּ כִּדְמוּתֵנוּ וְיִרְדּוּ בִדְגַת הַיָּם וּבְעוֹף הַשָּׁמַיִם וּבַבְּהֵמָה וּבְכָל־הָאָרֶץ וּבְכָל־הָרֶמֶשׂ הָרֹמֵשׂ עַל־הָאָרֶץ:
And God said, "Let us make humankind in our image, after our likeness. They shall rule the fish of the sea, the birds of the sky, the cattle, the whole earth, and all the creeping things that creep on earth."[30]

Mankind was created as the ultimate being who would be like a father to all God's creation that was produced to serve man. Rav Papa's ninth son, "אבא מרי" (Father, Teacher) represents this achievement.

וַיֹּאמֶר אֱלֹהִים הִנֵּה נָתַתִּי לָכֶם אֶת־כָּל־עֵשֶׂב זֹרֵעַ זֶרַע אֲשֶׁר עַל־פְּנֵי כָל־הָאָרֶץ וְאֶת־כָּל־הָעֵץ אֲשֶׁר־בּוֹ פְרִי־עֵץ זֹרֵעַ זָרַע לָכֶם יִהְיֶה לְאָכְלָה:
God said, "See, I gave you every seed-bearing plant that is upon all the earth, and every tree that has seed-bearing fruit; they shall be yours for food.[31]

These, the plants, are man's property – his possessions "רכיש" (belongings), Rav Papa's tenth son alludes to plants being available to man for his food and other needs.

Others say that Rav Papa, (פפא) himself symbolizes the greatness of Moshe *Rabaynu* as the letters 'פ, 'פ, and 'א stand for the words "פה אל פה" – mouth to mouth – the Almighty spoke to Moshe face to face. The first two letters of his name could also be referring to the words (פקד

---

[29] Beraishis 1:24
[30] Beraishis 1:26
[31] Beraishis 1:29

(פקדתי)[32] that Moshe Rabaynu said, "I have surely remembered," to inform the Jewish people that he was the one sent by HaShem to redeem the Nation from bondage in Egypt. It is quite interesting to note that the double language of פקד פקדתי is referring to physical and spiritual redemption. At a *siyum*, we do both physical and spiritual activities – the meal and the words of the Torah. The word פפא (removing the second פ since it is duplicated) is numerically equivalent to 81 (אנכי) so that Rav Papa's name represents the first statement of the Decalogue: "I Am, (אנכי) the Eternal, Your Almighty."[33] In fact, Rav Papa and his ten sons are a symbolic representation of the Ten Commandments and it is thus quite appropriate to mention their names at the conclusion of a Tractate of Talmud.[34] We will discuss shortly why they are not mentioned at a *siyum* of Mishnayos.

As mentioned, the letter [35]פ represents the word פה (mouth) and our purpose in life is to use our mouths to praise HaShem. The Pesikta Rabbasi 2 quotes from Tehillim (115:17), "The dead do not praise God," however, the living do praise Him. The א stands for HaShem in that its numeric value is one and HaShem is one. In Kabbalah, all parts of the א allude to God's sacred name. Even the name Aleph, which is related to the word *aluph* (master) alluding to the sovereignty of God.

Let us now discuss the connection between Rav Papa's sons and the Ten Commandments.

לֹא־יִהְיֶה־לְךָ אֱלֹהִים אֲחֵרִים עַל־פָּנָי

You shall have no other gods besides Me.[36]

Jewry is commanded to have no mercy regarding idolatry. Such icons are to be utterly destroyed. However, regarding God, mercy and compassion are the order of the day. Just as He is merciful and compassionate, so too must all Jews act similarly. "חנינא" (mercy), Rav Papa's first son alludes to this fact of showing mercy to all.

---

[32] Shemos 3:11
[33] Shemos 20:2
[34] Responsa of Rav Moshe Isserles
[35] It is also the spelling of the letter פ and this leads to several other deep meanings
[36] Shemos 20:3

לֹא־תַעֲשֶׂה־לְךָ פֶסֶל וְכָל־תְּמוּנָה אֲשֶׁר בַּשָּׁמַיִם מִמַּעַל וַאֲשֶׁר בָּאָרֶץ מִתַּחַת וַאֲשֶׁר בַּמַּיִם מִתַּחַת לָאָרֶץ: לֹא־תִשְׁתַּחֲוֶה לָהֶם וְלֹא תָעָבְדֵם כִּי אָנֹכִי יְהֹוָה אֱלֹהֶיךָ אֵל קַנָּא פֹּקֵד עֲוֹן אָבֹת עַל־בָּנִים עַל־שִׁלֵּשִׁים וְעַל־רִבֵּעִים לְשֹׂנְאָי: וְעֹשֶׂה חֶסֶד לַאֲלָפִים לְאֹהֲבַי וּלְשֹׁמְרֵי מִצְוֹתָי:

You shall not make for yourself a sculptured image, or any likeness of what is in the Heavens above, or on the earth below, or in the waters under the earth. You shall not bow down to them or serve them. For I your God HaShem am an impassioned God, visiting the guilt of the parents upon the children, upon the third and upon the fourth generations of those who reject Me. but showing kindness to the thousandth generation of those who love Me and keep My commandments.[37]

A promise exists that he who turns to idols for comfort will ultimately be disappointed and regret fabricating and relying on these powerless images. "נחמן" (remorse), Rav Papa's second son symbolizes this regret of this manufacture.[38]

לֹא תִשָּׂא אֶת־שֵׁם־יְהֹוָה אֱלֹהֶיךָ לַשָּׁוְא כִּי לֹא יְנַקֶּה יְהֹוָה אֵת אֲשֶׁר־יִשָּׂא אֶת־שְׁמוֹ לַשָּׁוְא:

You shall not swear falsely by the name of your God HaShem; for HaShem will not clear one who swears falsely by God's name.[39]

It is dishonorable to swear in the Name of God as His Name is too great to be used as the object of an oath. Rav Papa's third son, "רמי" (lofty) hints at this lesson as the Name of God is to be kept holy and great, and taking His Name in vain is the polar opposite.[40] We have to keep the holy Name of HaShem in the highest of esteem and use it only at appropriate times and places, such as when we *daven* and say *brachos*.

זָכוֹר אֶת־יוֹם הַשַּׁבָּת לְקַדְּשׁוֹ: שֵׁשֶׁת יָמִים תַּעֲבֹד וְעָשִׂיתָ כָּל־מְלַאכְתֶּךָ: וְיוֹם הַשְּׁבִיעִי שַׁבָּת לַיהֹוָה אֱלֹהֶיךָ לֹא־תַעֲשֶׂה כָל־מְלָאכָה אַתָּה וּבִנְךָ־וּבִתֶּךָ עַבְדְּךָ וַאֲמָתְךָ וּבְהֶמְתֶּךָ וְגֵרְךָ אֲשֶׁר בִּשְׁעָרֶיךָ: כִּי שֵׁשֶׁת־יָמִים עָשָׂה יְהֹוָה אֶת־הַשָּׁמַיִם וְאֶת־הָאָרֶץ אֶת־הַיָּם וְאֶת־כָּל־אֲשֶׁר־בָּם וַיָּנַח בַּיּוֹם הַשְּׁבִיעִי עַל־כֵּן בֵּרַךְ יְהֹוָה אֶת־יוֹם הַשַּׁבָּת וַיְקַדְּשֵׁהוּ:

---

[37] Shemos 20:4
[38] Ibid.
[39] Shemos 20:7
[40] Ibid.

Remember the Shabbos *day and keep it holy. Six days you shall labor and do all your work, but the seventh day is a* Shabbos *of your God HaShem: you shall not do any work — you, your son or daughter, your male or female slave, or your cattle, or the stranger who is within your settlements. For in six days HaShem made Heaven and earth and sea — and all that is in them — and then rested on the seventh day; therefore, HaShem blessed the* Shabbos *day and hallowed it.*[41]

Rav Papa's fourth son, אדא, alludes to this Torah precept because the letters of "אדא", have a numerical value of six hinting at the six days of the week when labor is permitted, that lead up to *Shabbos.*[42]

כַּבֵּד אֶת־אָבִיךָ וְאֶת־אִמֶּךָ לְמַעַן יַאֲרִכוּן יָמֶיךָ עַל הָאֲדָמָה אֲשֶׁר־יְהֹוָה אֱלֹהֶיךָ נֹתֵן לָךְ:
Honor your father and your mother, that you may long endure on the land that your God HaShem is assigning to you.[43]

One way to honor a father is to call him, "My father, my teacher," which is, in fact, a loose translation of Rav Papa's fifth son's name, "אבא מרי".[44]

לֹא תִּרְצָח:
You shall not murder.[45]

Mankind must treat each other as brothers and sisters and thereby avoid bloodshed. "אחא" (brother) hints at this lesson in the name of Rav Papa's sixth son.[46]

לֹא תִּנְאָף:
You shall not commit adultery.[47]

---

[41] Shemos 20:8
[42] Ibid.
[43] Shemos 20:12
[44] Ibid.
[45] Shemos 20:13
[46] Ibid.
[47] Ibid.

Prostitutes beckon a person with winks and bodily gyrations. "רפרם" (winks) thus reminds Jewry of their obligation to remain true to their spouses. This can be found in the seventh son of Rav Papa, Rafram.

לֹא תִּגְנֹב:

Do not kidnap.[48]

The function of all forms of theft (including kidnapping which most of the time leads to a ransom demand) is to sell the item for money to increase one's possessions. "רכיש" (property), the name of Rav Papa's eighth son reminds one to conquer his baser tendencies.[49]

לֹא־תַעֲנֶה בְרֵעֲךָ עֵד שָׁקֶר:

You shall not bear false witness against your neighbor. [50]

Rav Papa's ninth son, "סורחב", is an allusion to "סרח בת אשר" (Serach *bas* Asher) who informed her grandfather Yaakov that Yosef was still alive, an allusion to the *Mitzvah* of giving truthful testimony.[51]

לֹא תַחְמֹד בֵּית רֵעֶךָ: לֹא־תַחְמֹד אֵשֶׁת רֵעֶךָ וְעַבְדּוֹ וַאֲמָתוֹ וְשׁוֹרוֹ וַחֲמֹרוֹ וְכֹל אֲשֶׁר לְרֵעֶךָ:

You shall not covet your neighbor's house: you shall not covet your neighbor's wife, or male or female slave, or ox or ass, or anything that is your neighbor's.[52]

In particular, Jewry was admonished not to hanker after another man's wife. "דרו" (home), Rav Papa's tenth son testifies to us the Gemara often refers to a man's wife as his home.[53]

---

[48] Ibid.
[49] Ibid.
[50] Shemos
[51] Ibid.
[52] Shemos 20:14
[53] Ibid.

The awesomeness of these men and their merit is so great that the mere recital of their names helps prevent one from forgetting that which he has learned. It is hence customary to recite their names in the *Hadran* for Gemara. [54]

According to the Pnei Yehoshuah, the particular sons mentioned in the *Hadran* were all children of the same father and most of them were students of Rava.[55]

As mentioned, however, others contend that these ten sons were from many different people who had the same name as Rav Papa who lived in many time eras, and that the ten selected sons were chosen as they were the greatest *tzadikim* of the group and a quorum of ten was mentioned to allude to the fact that a *minyan* should be present at a *siyum*.[56] This may be why they are all listed individually with their father's name and not all together with mentioning Rav Papa once at the end. I have heard that there are also significant Kabbalistic reasons behind these particular names and why they are specifically mentioned at a *siyum*.

No fewer than twelve different Rav Papa's are mentioned in Shas:

Table 5 Other Rav Papas

רב פפא בר אבא[57]	1
רב פפא בר אבא רישבא[58]	2
רב פפא בריה דרב אחא בר אדא[59]	3
רב פפא בריה דרב חנין[60]	4
רב פפא בריה דרב חנן[61]	5
רב פפא בריה דרב חנן מבי כלוחית[62]	6
רב פפא בריה דרב יוסף[63]	7
רב פפא בר יעקב[64]	8

---

[54] Sefer Ha'eshkol: Sefer Torah, Section #19

[55] Ibid.

[56] Hadar Yitzchok p. 149

[57] Yevamos 21b, 46a; Bava Metzia 91a

[58] Chullin 54a

[59] Berachos 29b

[60] Menachos 28b

[61] Bava Basra 153a

[62] Kesuvos 40b

[63] Bava Metzia 113a

[64] Chagigah 14a

רב פפא בריה דרב נחמן[65]	9
רב פפא סבא[66]	10
רב פפא בר שמואל[67]	11
רב פפא תוראה[68]	12

THE LEGACY OF RAV PAPA

RAV PAPA, A *TALMID MUVHAK* of Abayay,[69] and Rava,[70] was raised by his righteous mother אושפרתי (Ushparty) to become a great *talmid chacham*.[71] Rav Papa who was born in Rome, was also nurtured by other Rebbes, notably, Rav Idi bar Avin,[72] Rav Hamnuna,[73] and Rav Acha *bar* Yaakov.[74]

His lifelong friend and associate was Rav Huna the son of Rav Yehoshua.[75] His first wife was the daughter of a *Kohen*.[76] After she passed away, he married the daughter of Rav Abba Surrah who was from an aristocratic family.[77]

When Rav Papa and Rav Huna began studying together under Rava, they were both extremely poor.[78] Rav Papa later became wealthy selling poppy seeds and date beer.[79] He attributed his great wealth to having married the daughter of a *Kohen*.[80]

---

[65] Bava Metzia 113a

[66] Kiddushin 71b, Sanhedrin 49b, Menachos 33b

[67] Shabbos 54b, Pesachim 47b, Rosh HaShanah 27a, 34b

[68] Gitten 19a

[69] Berachos 20a, Pesachim 78a, Sukkah 46a

[70] Menachos 71a; Tosefos: Shabbos 93a – ד"ה אמר רב זביד; Rashi: Eruvin 26a – ד"ה אמר רב פפא; Tosefos: Avodah Zora 59b – ד"ה להרע

[71] See Taanis 24b, Aruch – ד"ה אושפרתי

[72] Pesachim 35a, Yevamos 85a

[73] Niddah 27a

[74] Chullin 33a

[75] Berachos 58a, Shabbos 136a, Pesachim 111b, Yevamos 85a, Kiddushin 32b, Bava Basra 22a

[76] Pesachim 49, Chullin 132

[77] Kesuvos 8, 52

[78] Horios 10

[79] Gittin 73a

[80] Pesachim 49a

After the death of Rava, his *Yeshiva* was split into two branches: Rav Nachman *bar* Yitzchak headed the branch in Pumpedisa while Rav Papa took over the Narish branch which was near Sura.[81] Both were great Torah centers in Bavel.

Rav Papa had a huge *Yeshiva* and among his notable students one must mention the following great individuals:

Table 6 Rav Papa's Students

רב אדא בר אהבה[82]	אמימר[83]
רב אשי[84]	רב הונא בריה דרב נתן[85]
רב יוסף בריה דרב סלא חסידא[86]	רב יוסף בריה דרב סלא חסידא[87]
רב יוסף בריה דרבא[88]	רב יוסף בר שמעיה[89]
רב כהנא[90]	רב יימר בר שלמיא[91]
מר בר רב אשי[92]	מר זוטרא[93]
רב מרי[94]	רב משרשיא[95]
רב פנחס[96]	רב נתן אבוה דרב הונא[97]
רב בר שבא[98]	רב בר שרביא[99]
רמי בר אבא[100]	רבינא[101]

---

[81] See Berachos 57a, Bava Metzia 93b, Chullin 127a

[82] Chullin 133b

[83] Ibid. 8b

[84] Avodah Zara 40a

[85] Pesachim 17b, Bava Metzia 66b

[86] Pesachim 73b, Chullin 74b

[87] Pesachim 73b, Chullin 74b

[88] Gittin 40a

[89] Eruvin 41b, Menachos 9b

[90] Kesuvos 86a, Gitten 89b

[91] Menachos 31a

[92] Sanhedrin 77b

[93] Yevamos 75b, Kesuvos 91a

[94] Berachos 24a

[95] Eruvin 48a

[96] Yevamos 22b

[97] Pesachim 117b

[98] Eruvin 33b

[99] Shavuos 30b

[100] Megillah 26b

[101] Bava Metzia 74b, Zevachim 2b

רב שמן בר אבא[102]	רב שימי בר אדא[103]
רב שימי בר רב אשי[104]	רב שימי בר זירי[105]
רב ששת בריה דרב אידי[106]	רב סמא בריה דרב ייבא[107]
רב שמואל בר אחא[108]	רב שמואל בר אידי[109]
	רב שמואל בר שימי[110]

Rav Papa served as the Rosh Yeshiva in Narish from 4112 (352 C.E.) until he died in 4131 (371 C.E.).[111]

---

[102] Pesachim 59b

[103] Nazir 50b

[104] Eruvin 3b, Nazir 26b

[105] Temurah 24a

[106] Bava Metzia 65a, 109a, Bava Basra 8a

[107] Bava Basra 9a

[108] Menachos 34a, Nazir 51b

[109] Taanis 9a

[110] Kerisos 27b

[111] Iggeres Rav Sherira Gaon 3:3, Hyman edition, P. 75

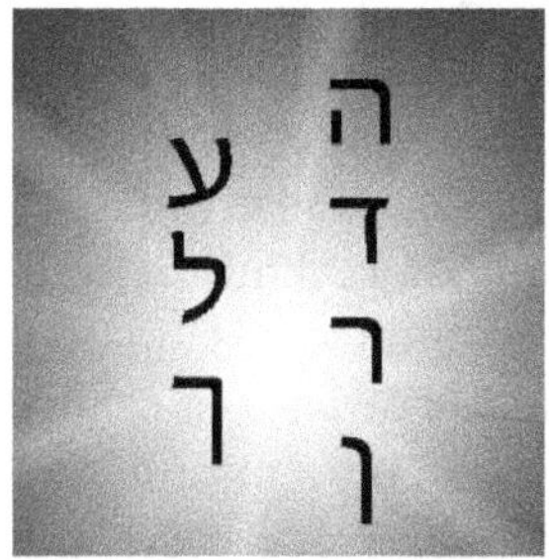

HADRAN

OVER THE GENERATIONS THERE HAVE been several versions of the *Hadran*. However, there are currently two versions in use. Many people are not aware that there are two renditions as the two versions in use today are almost identical, the slight difference is if the *siyum* is being made for a *seder* of Mishnayos or a *Masechta* of Gemara. Both are included herein with their explanations and commentaries. The exact origin and author of the *Hadrans* are not known, but it is universally recited at the conclusion of the different major works that we mentioned above. The third version included is for the completion of TaNaCH, one can possibly use it for the basis of the ceremony for other *siyumim*. We will discuss this in more detail further.

The text of the prayer gives thanks to God for allowing the reciter to learn the *seder* or *Masechta* and expresses the desire to return to the text for continued study in the future. There are many deep esoteric meanings behind the reasons for the words and phrases used in the *Hadran* and *Kaddish*, we will only be discussing a scant few. Throughout this volume, we will mention just a few hints at some of the deeper subjects and if you want to explore them, you may explore on your own.

The Gemara[112] says that someone who says, "I will return to this *Masechta*" is considered a promise that must be fulfilled. The question is why do we not say "not a *neder* (בלי נדר)" at a *siyum*? The answer is that

---

[112] Nedarim 8a

since one clearly does not have the intent to make a vow, he is not obligating himself to do so. Additionally, what we say on *Erev Yom Kippur* in Kol Nidrei, cancels what could possibly be considered a vow.[113] Because everyone at the celebration knows that the celebrant may not be able to return to the *Masechta*, the *Hadran* cannot be construed as a binding promise to return to the *Masechta* just learned. Technically, one may think that it is a *shevuah* and not a *neder*, however, since it is unlikely that one will return to the same *Masechta* within three Festivals, it cannot be considered a *shevuah* either. See Appendix One for more information on the difference between a *shevuah* and a *neder*.[114]

The Sefer HaChaim[115] says that the word *Hadran* means to show honor as in *hiddur Mitzvah*. We are the only people who show honor and respect to the Oral Traditions (Gemara, Midrashim, etc.), and therefore the Torah shows respect to those who have acquired Torah wisdom – והדרת פני זקן.[116]

The *Hadran's* origin can be traced back almost one thousand years.[117] It presents the *Hadran Alach*, *Yehi Ratzon*, and Rav Pappa's family passages. It did not have the *Ha'arev*, *Modim*, or second *Yehi Ratzon* commonly found in Gemaras today. We will break down each of these paragraphs one at a time further on.

Much of the commentary of the *Hadran* spawns from the differing potential interpretations of the word. Some say it comes from the word *hadar* (meaning "glory") and tells of the glory one experiences in finishing a *Masechta* or other major accomplishment, and the glory that awaits with further completions.

Perhaps the most elemental understanding is based upon the Aramaic translation of *Hadran Alach*, "We will return to you," meaning that the completion of the *Masechta* is not the end of the journey but just another step.

When reciting the *Hadran* and bidding farewell to our *Masechta*, we do so in a respectful and sorrowful way. While saying goodbye, we understand that we want to return to learning this particular *Masechta* or

---

[113] Minchas Shlomo 91:20, Shlaymas Chaim: Orach Chaim 231
[114] See page 207
[115] Chapter 2
[116] Vayikra 19:32 – and show respect to the old (wise).
[117] ספר האשכול in Hilchos Sefer Torah 14

seder, and our hope and prayer is that its teachings will always be with us (both in this world and the next).

Interestingly, the word *Masechta* can be interpreted as the object weavers use to tighten threads together (a weft that is propelled by hand or by a shuttle).[118] (From the *Passuk*, "Then Delilah said to Samson, 'You have been deceiving me all along; you have been lying to me! Tell me, how could you be tied up?' He answered her, 'If you weave seven locks of my head into the web.'" The word for web is מסכת).[119] Accordingly, every time one completes a *Masechta* they are akin to a weaver, throwing the *Masechta* around his understanding one more time, strengthening the bonds and adding to its durability, usefulness, and longevity. Further, the same way each weave helps create something new, every time one completes a *Masechta* again, they will come across new teachings and lessons they missed the first time around. With proper study and review, this will happen every time one delves into the material again. He should learn it as if he has never seen the material previously so that he will be able to find new and deeper meaning in what he is learning.

I have often joked with my Rav saying that I believe Rashi is still alive. My proof is that every year when I review the weekly *sedra* with Rashi, I find new material inside the famous commentary that was not there in the previous year (Rashi must be coming around and writing additional comments in my Chumash). (Separately, my brother contends the same thing for the same reasons.) My Rav responded that there is no true learning without coming up with a new understanding. אין בית מדרש בלא חידוש.[120]

Importantly, a *siyum* for a *Masechta* or *seder* is cause for a *seudas Mitzvah* (festive meal) and although some disdain the frivolity often accompanying wine imbibition, wine does have a place at the *siyum*.[121] Accordingly, one should eat meat and drink wine at this meal! Additionally, the *siyum* serves a dual purpose of inspiring others to undertake a journey of learning and discovery on the same path as the one who completes the *Masechta*.

---

[118] Taamei Minhagim, Sefer Chasidim #928
[119] Shoftim 16:13
[120] Chagigah 3a
[121] Otzer Dinim U'Minhagim, see Bava Kamma 37, Shach, Yoreh De'ah 246:37

SOURCE OF SIYUM

THE NOTION OF HAVING SOME form of celebration upon the completion of some section of Torah learning comes from the *Gemara*.[122] There, Abaye states that when he saw a Rabbinic student who had completed a tractate of the Talmud, he would make a holiday for the Rabbis in honor of the occasion. We have previously mentioned several other sources for this wonderful custom. However, I have not been able to find an actual source for the origin of the *siyum*, just what people have said or done at a *siyum*. It should be noted that it is important to say words of Torah at a *siyum* and not just the final couple of lines of the conclusion and the *Hadran*. Nor is this a party for frivolity! It is a celebration in honor of the Torah and the perfect opportunity to bring honor and glory to the Big Boss. There should be singing and dancing to enhance the beautiful event. If possible, a Rav should be invited and asked to speak about something relevant.

PARTS OF THE HADRAN

AS MENTIONED ABOVE, THERE ARE two different *Hadran's*: one for when one concludes a *seder* of Mishnayos and the other when one finishes a *Masechta* of Gemara. They are quite similar, however, there are some pertinent differences between the two. The following chart highlights the differences; we will break them down and elucidate them as we continue in this section. Further on, we will put everything into their respective places to make reading them easier and more cohesive. We will discuss the *Kaddish HaGadol* separately.[123]

---

[122] Shabbos 118b
[123] Page 101

Table 7 Parts of the Hadran

MISHNAH	GEMARA
Hadran	Hadran
Haarev Na	Yehi Ratzon Milfanecha
Modim	Haarev Na
Yehi Ratzon Lefanecha	Modim
Lehodos	Yehi Ratzon Lefanecha
Last Mishnah of Tamid	
Kaddish	Kaddish

Additionally, other parts are typically not said any more, however, I have included them in this section in a later chapter for your education. Some say them, but most do not.

HADRAN ALACH

THE FIRST SECTION FOR BOTH a *siyum* on a *seder* of Mishnayos and a *Masechta* of Gemara, begins with the words "*Hadran Alach*," which, according to most opinions, is Aramaic for, "We will return to you." It underlines the concept that when completing a Tractate or *seder*, we do not regard it as having been learned in its entirety, because the Torah is infinite. Therefore, the *Hadran* opens with the declaration "*Hadran Alach*" — that we intend to return to you. In effect, it is not farewell, but, rather, it is *au-revoir*!

Another meaning of the word *hadran* is "glory" (from the word *hadar* in Hebrew). We are stating that any glory we may have achieved comes from the Torah, and we request from God that the Torah pour down its glory upon us.

The custom is to recite the entire first section three times consecutively. The number three is significant in Jewish thought as it represents the establishment of a particular aspect (חזקה). Here it establishes our desire to return at some point in the future to further study the material that has just been completed. Additionally, you have just learned the material once and you are saying three additional times that you will return to it. This makes it four times and we will discuss later how important this number is.

FOR MISHNAYOS

הדרן עלך סדר ...

We shall return to you Order…

The word "הדר" means to review or repeat.[124] All learning is but a review, a recounting of the Torah taught to each Jew while in his mother's womb. We are taught that everything that a person is capable of learning is taught to him by his angel while yet in his mother's womb, and as he is about to be born, the angel strikes him over his upper lip (philtrum), and he forgets everything he learned. After that, a person's job is to relearn and remember everything he had been taught by the angel.[125]

The importance of constantly relearning and reviewing what one has studied is amply demonstrated by the Sages:

- Rabbi Chiya son of Abba, reviewed his learning every thirty days in the presence of his teacher, Rabbi Yochanan.[126]
- Raish Lakish repeated his studies forty times as a memorial to the Torah which was given to Moshe *Rabaynu* over a period of forty days,[127]
- Rav Ada son of Ahava, restudied it twenty-four times as an allusion to the twenty-four books of the TaNaCH upon which Talmud is founded.[128]

The Talmud,[129] states that one must sharpen the erudition of his studies through constant review. He must be able to answer questions without stumbling for a reply.

Torah is, moreover, compared to a mother's nipples: the more the child sucks (studies), the more he gets. New insights are borne through

---

[124] Berachos 13b, 51b; Sukkah 10b, Kesuvos 70b, Nedarim 41a, Bava Metzia 65a, Chullin 113a, Niddah 65b

[125] Niddah 30b

[126] Berachos 38b, Chullin 86b, Kerisos 27a

[127] Taanis 8a

[128] Ibid.

[129] Kiddushin 30a

constant labor.[130] Another allusion to this fact is the datum that he who learns the text one hundred times cannot be compared to one who reviews it one hundred and one times as each additional learning session adds new insight.[131]

To further emphasize this relevant fact, it is customary to begin to relearn the Tractate or *seder* afresh during the *siyum*.

Finally, there is an allusion to the absolute necessity to learn a section a minimum of four times – the four wide lines of Rashi and Tosefos found at the top of almost every page of Talmud.[132]

והדרך עלן

And you shall return to us

Another translation is, And I have thereby been rejuvenated by it.

Torah study rekindles a person's attachment to God if it is lacking and strengthens the bonds already created.

דעתן עלך סדר ...

Our thoughts are on you, the order of ...

I have totally immersed myself in the studies of this Order.

The term "דעת" refers to intense concentration to the total exclusion of all extraneous matters.[133]

It is important for a person to fully comprehend that which he learns because wisdom in the Torah leads to a stronger bond with God.[134]

In a similar vein, it is reminiscent of a conversation I had with HaRav Hagaon Rav Chaim Pinchas Scheinberg, ZT"L. He said, "If you want to make me happy, talk to me in Torah or ask me a question about something you have learned."

The Talmud therefore recommends that a person should study, "standing and sitting" *i.e.,* he should learn the material (standing) quickly to gain an overview of the subject and should then restudy it in depth (sitting).[135] In a similar vein, "The reward is that *bekius* yields profundity,"

---

[130] Eruvin 54b, Rashi: Ibid. 21b, - ד"ה - כל ההוגה בהן

[131] Chagigah 9b

[132] See Eruvin 54b

[133] Rabaynu Chananel: Eruvin 54b - ד"ה אף ד"ת כו'; Rashi: Megillah 28b – ד"ה צילותא; Rashi: Chagigah 12a – ד"ה דעת

[134] Avos D'Rabbi Nasan 4:1

[135] Megillah 21a

as one cannot delve into a matter and examine it critically until he first gains a superficial comprehension thereof.[136] Finally, he who wishes to become wise must study diligently and explore all facets of learning in their minutest detail in great depth[137] because each extra time that a matter is studied adds new insights.[138]

ודעתך עלן

And your thoughts are on us.

I have therefore become enlightened by the material I have studied.

Through intense study, a person's eyes are opened to the deep secrets of the Torah and the Big Boss mercifully aids that individual so that he will retain this knowledge without forgetting it.[139] And since true understanding is, in reality, a gift from God, one should pray for it with all his heart.[140] If one does this properly, it is humbling to realize that HaShem has allowed him to learn and remember the Torah.

... לא נתנשי מינך סדר

(Consequently), I shall not (easily) forget the Order of ...

He who has studied the matter thoroughly and reviewed it numerous times has indelibly printed the Torah material in his mind and shall therefore remember it for quite a spell, hopefully the rest of his life into the next.[141]

Still, since the gift of memory is a present from God, one should constantly pray to the Lord that He freely bestow upon him this favor.[142]

A person can develop a near-perfect memory with relatively little effort. If the studious individual will set aside fifteen minutes a day – every day – to memorize *Mishnah* or Talmud word for word, he will find that both his memory, speed, and retention will gradually increase until he can eventually read an item a single time and be able to repeat it back verbatim.

---

[136] Berachos 6b, Shabbos 63a, Eruvin 21b, Gitten 6b, Kiddushin 30a
[137] Niddah 70b
[138] Chagigah 9b
[139] Berachos 5a, Nedarim 38a
[140] Niddah 70b
[141] Talmud Yerushalmi: Berachos
[142] Megillah 6b

HADRAN

- ולא תתנשי מינן

Nor will it forget me –

The Torah a person learns will stand in his stead to always protect him. This applies in this world and the Hereafter. The Torah protects a person on several levels: physically, mentally, emotionally, and more. Have you ever noticed that the word Gemara (גמרא) has four letters? Of course you have, but what is the deeper meaning?

- ג stands for Gavriel (protector)
- מ stands for Michael (guardian)
- ר stands for Refael (healer)
- א stands for Uriel (salvation)

These are four *Malachim* (angels) who protect us on many levels. Because of our learning Gemara and reviewing it, we will be protected by these four angels with HaShem over them. Compare this to the prayer one says before going to sleep at night. There are numerous connections and comparisons between these points.

לא בעלמא הדין

Neither in this world,

Learning will help prevent a person from making an erroneous *p'sak din* (and other forms of decisions) and will moreover mold an individual's personality and imbue him with exemplary traits so that all men will be happy to be his friend and constant companion.[143]

ולא בעלמא דאתי:

Nor in the Hereafter.

What a person has studied in this world, he will be permitted to study in the Yeshiva of Gan Eden.[144]

For this reason, some people have the custom of reading through *Shas* even by means of an English language translation of the text – so that they will not come to the next world empty-handed because they have

---

[143] Berachos 28b

[144] Moed Katan 28a, Pesachim 50a, Kesuvos 77b, Bava Basra 10b; Maharshal: Shabbos 31a

79

learned *Shas*, however superficially. Of course, it is far better to understand what one learns and many so-called "*ba'alay batim*" who have learned *Daf Yomi* for many years are better versed in *bekius* than many *Yeshiva* students and *Kollel* men.

הדרן עלך סדר ... וההדרך עלן. דעתן עלך סדר... ודעתך עלן. לא נתנשי מינך
סדר... ולא תתנשי מינן, לא בעלמא הדין ולא בעלמא דאתי

We return to you, the Order of ... and you shall return to us. Our thoughts are on you, the Order of ... and your thoughts are on us. (Consequently,) we shall not (easily) forget the Order of ...; nor will it forget us – neither in this world nor in the Hereafter.

Another interpretation: there are three types of individuals whose attachment to the Torah differs from one another. One person loves Torah with all his heart and soul and devotes every second of his life to studying its precepts and fulfilling its *Mitzvos*. A second individual is involved in business and hence cannot use all his time for Torah instruction. Nevertheless, he does utilize his free moments to enhance his Torah knowledge by attending *shiurim*. A third individual does very little actual learning. Instead, he uses his money to support *Yeshivos* and Torah scholars, as well as the poor and needy.[145]

The first clause of the *Hadran*, "You have reviewed," refers to the first group of individuals who are constantly reviewing their Torah since their every waking moment is devoted to its study. The second phrase, "You have totally immersed yourself in your studies," is an allusion to the businessman whose love of Torah is so great that he forgets about his financial worries in his free moments so that he can submerge himself in the sea of Talmud. "You shall not easily forget it, nor will it forget you" refers to the tycoon who is too busy to learn regularly but does remember the little that he has learned and is constantly protected because he supports learning.[146]

All these individuals will be admitted to the Heavenly *Yeshiva* as each of them has learned the Torah in this world and has earned the right to learn it in the Hereafter, as well.[147]

The text cited above is repeated three times by the one reciting the *Hadran* to create a *chazaka* – a status quo of the continuance of this type of behavior. Similarly, the Torah is concluded to the thrice shouted *chazak*

---

[145] Sefer Charuza, Margolios
[146] Ibid.
[147] Ibid.

i.e., Chazak, Chazak, Venishazaik. Furthermore, the word חזק is numerically equal to 115; and 115 x 3 = 345, the numerical value of משה (Moshe *Rabaynu*) to indicate that one must learn his subject well before teaching it to others, which is what Moshe Rabaynu did.[148]

FOR GEMARA

MUCH OF THIS IS REPEATED from the previous section on the Mishnah because if you are making a *siyum* for Gemara, you may have skipped the part above.

...הדרן עלך מסכת

We have reviewed the Masechta *of...*

The word "הדר" means to review or repeat.[149] All learning is but a review, a recounting of the Torah taught to each Jew while in his mother's womb. We are taught that everything that a person is capable of learning is taught to him by his angel while yet in his mother's womb, and as he is about to be born, the angel strikes him over his upper lip (philtrum), and he forgets everything he learned. After that, his job is to relearn and remember everything he had been taught by the angel.[150]

The importance of constantly relearning what one has studied is amply demonstrated by the Sages:

- Rabbi Chiya, son of Abba, reviewed his learning every thirty days in the presence of his teacher, Rabbi Yochanan.[151]
- Raish Lakish repeated his studies forty times as a memorial to the Torah which was given to Moshe *Rabaynu* over a period of forty days[152]

---

[148] Hadar Yitzchak pp. 18 – 20; Eruvin 97a, Bava Kama 24a, 82a; Bava Basra 28a, 29a; Niddah 63a

[149] Berachos 13b, 51b; Sukkah 10b, Kesuvos 70b, Nedarim 41a, Bava Metzia 65a, Chullin 113a, Niddah 65b

[150] Niddah 30b

[151] Berachos 38b, Chullin 86b, Kerisos 27a

[152] Taanis 8a

- Rav Ada, son of Ahava, restudied it twenty-four times as an allusion to the twenty-four books of the Bible upon which Talmud is founded.[153]

The Talmud,[154] states that one must sharpen the erudition of his studies through constant review. He must be able to answer questions without stumbling for a reply.

Torah is, moreover, compared to a mother's breasts: The more the child sucks (studies), the more he gets. New insights are borne through constant labor in the study of the Torah.[155] Another allusion to this fact is the datum that he who learns the text one hundred times cannot be compared to one who reviews it one hundred and one times as each additional learning session adds new insight.[156]

To further emphasize this relevant fact, it is customary to begin to relearn the Tractate or *seder* afresh during the *siyum*.

Finally, there is an allusion to the absolute necessity to learn a section a minimum of four times – the four large lines of Rashi and Tosefos found at the top of almost every page of Talmud.[157]

This leads us to an interesting point about the beginning of the *Hadran* which we repeat the first line three times. According to the Steipler, ZT"l, one cannot begin to understand what he learned until he has studied it a minimum of four times. Since you are making a *siyum*, you have already learned it once. In the *Hadran*, we are repeating three additional times that we are going to go back and learn the material three more times for a total of four times. Then we have the four times of studying the Gemara or Mishnayos or whatever has brought you to this wonderful occasion. Of course, every time you finish the work or material you are studying, you make another *siyum*.

והדרך עלן

And you shall return to us

Another translation is, And I have thereby been rejuvenated by it.

---

[153] Ibid.
[154] Kiddushin 30a
[155] Eruvin 54b, Rashi: Ibid. 21b, - ד"ה כל ההוגה בהן
[156] Chagigah 9b
[157] See Eruvin 54b

HADRAN

Torah study rekindles a person's attachment to God if it is lacking and strengthens the bonds already created.

... דעתן עלך מסכת

Our thoughts are on you Maseches ...

I have totally immersed myself in the studies of this *Masechta*.

The term "דעת" refers to intense concentration to the total exclusion of all extraneous matters.[158]

It is important for a person to fully comprehend that which he learns because wisdom in the Torah leads to a stronger bond with God.[159]

The Talmud therefore recommends that a person should study, "standing and sitting" *i.e.*, he should learn the material quickly to gain an overview of the subject and should then restudy it in depth.[160] In a similar vein, "The reward is that *bekius* yields profundity," as one cannot delve into a matter and examine it critically until he first gains a superficial comprehension thereof.[161] Finally, he who wishes to become wise must study diligently and explore all facets of learning in their minutest detail in great depth[162] because each extra time that a matter is studied adds new insights.[163]

ודעתך עלן

And your thoughts are on us.

I have therefore become enlightened by the material I have studied.

Through intense study, a person's eyes are opened to the deep secrets of the Torah and the Lord mercifully aids that individual so that he will retain this knowledge without forgetting it.[164] And since true understanding is a gift from God, one should pray for it with all his heart.[165]

---

[158] Rabaynu Chananel: Eruvin 54b - ד"ה אף ד"ת כו'; Rashi: Megillah 28b – ד"ה צילותא; Rashi: Chagigah 12a – ד"ה דעת

[159] Avos D'Rabbi Nasan 4:1

[160] Megillah 21a

[161] Berachos 6b, Shabbos 63a, Eruvin 21b, Gitten 6b, Kiddushin 30a

[162] Niddah 70b

[163] Chagigah 9b

[164] Berachos 5a, Nedarim 38a

[165] Niddah 70b

THE HADRAN ALACH

לא נתנשי מינך מסכת ...

(Consequently), you shall not (easily) forget the Masechta ...

He who has studied the matter thoroughly and reviewed it numerous times has indelibly printed the Torah material in his mind and shall therefore remember it for quite a spell.[166]

Still, since the gift of memory is a present from God, one should constantly pray to the Lord that He freely bestow upon him this favor.[167]

A person can develop a near-perfect memory with relatively little effort. If the studious individual will set aside fifteen minutes a day – every day – to memorize *Mishnah* or Talmud word for word, he will find that both his memory, speed, and retention will gradually increase until he can eventually read an item a single time and be able to repeat it back verbatim.

ולא תתנשי מינן -

Nor will it forget you –

The Torah that a person learns will stand in his stead to constantly protect him. This applies in this world and the Hereafter. The Torah protects a person on several levels, physically, mentally, emotionally, and more.

לא בעלמא הדין

Neither in this world,

Learning will help prevent a person from making an erroneous *p'sak din* (also applies to non-Torah issues) and will moreover mold an individual's personality and imbue him with exemplary traits so that all men will be happy to be his friend and constant companion.[168]

ולא בעלמא דאתי:

Nor in the Hereafter.

---

[166] Talmud Yerushalmi: Berachos
[167] Megillah 6b
[168] Berachos 28b

What a person has studied in this world, he will be permitted to study in the Yeshiva of Gan Eden.[169]

For this reason, some people have the custom of reading through *Shas* even by use of an English language translation of the text – so that they will not come to the next world empty-handed because they have learned *Shas*, however superficially. Of course, it is far better to understand what one learns and many so-called *"ba'alay batim"* who have learned *Daf Yomi* for many years are better versed in *bekius* than many *Yeshiva* students and *Kollel* men.

הדרן עלך מסכת ... והדרך עלן. דעתן עלך מסכת ... ודעתך עלן. לא נתנשי מינך מסכת ... ולא תתנשי מינן, לא בעלמא הדין ולא בעלמא דאתי

We return to you, the Masechta *of ... and you shall return to us. Our thoughts are on you,* Masechta *of ... and your thoughts are on us. (Consequently,) we shall not (easily) forget the* Masechta *of ...; nor will it forget us – neither in this world nor in the Hereafter.*

Another interpretation: There are three types of individuals whose attachment to the Torah differs from one another. One person loves Torah with all his heart and soul and devotes every second of his life to studying its precepts and fulfilling its *Mitzvos*. A second individual is involved in business and hence cannot use all his time for Torah instruction. Nevertheless, he does utilize his free moments to enhance his Torah knowledge by attending *Shiurim*. A third individual does very little actual learning. Instead, he uses his money to support *Yeshivos* and Torah scholars, as well as the poor and needy.[170]

The first clause of the *Hadran*, "You have reviewed," refers to the first group of individuals who are constantly reviewing their Torah since their every waking moment is devoted to its study. The second phrase, "You have totally immersed yourself in your studies," is an allusion to the businessman whose love of Torah is so great that he forgets about his financial worries in his free moments so that he can submerge himself in the sea of Talmud. "You shall not easily forget it, nor will it forget you" refers to the tycoon who is too busy to learn regularly but does remember the little that he has learned and is constantly protected because he supports learning.[171]

---

[169] Moed Kotten 28a, Pesachim 50a, Kesuvos 77b, Bava Basra 10b; Maharshal: Shabbos 31a
[170] Sefer Charuza, Margolios
[171] Ibid.

All these individuals will be admitted to the Heavenly Yeshiva as each of them has learned the Torah in this world and has earned the right to learn it in the Hereafter, as well.[172]

The text cited above is repeated three times by the one reciting the *Hadran* to create a *chazaka* – a status quo of the continuance of this type of behavior. Similarly, the Torah is concluded to the thrice shouted *chazak* i.e., *Chazak, Chazak, Venishazaik.* Furthermore, the word חזק is numerically equal to 115; and 115 x 3 = 345, the numerical value of משה (Moshe *Rabaynu*) to indicate that one must learn his subject well before teaching it to others.[173]

When we repeat the word חזק thrice at the conclusion of a book of the Torah, it is similar to the reason we repeat the words הדרן thrice. It is the same concept of repetition and establishment of a status quo and permanence that we have learned something well and plan to return to it.

HAAREV NA

THIS SECTION IS SAID FOR both the completion of a *seder* of Mishnayos and a *Masechta* of Gemara.

הערב נא ,ה' אלוקינו ,את דברי תורתך בפינו

Eternal, our Almighty, make the teachings of Your Torah pleasant in our mouth

He who enjoys learning the Torah will immerse himself in its studies and will find that not only will he remember what he learns, but he will also be granted Heavenly aid to comprehend the innermost secrets of the Torah.[174]

ובפיפיות עמך בית ישראל

And in the mouth of Your Nation – the House of Israel.

---

[172] Ibid.

[173] Hadar Yitzchak pp. 18 – 20; Eruvin 97a, Bava Kama 24a, 82a; Bava Basra 28a, 29a; Niddah 63a

[174] Aitz Yosef; Berachos 5a, Megillah 19b, Chagigah 16b, Gitten 60b, Kerisos 8a

HADRAN

A person should not only pray for himself; he should also *daven* for others. He must beseech the Lord to induce all Jewry to study Torah diligently – even if the individual was raised in a non-observant environment – for through it the world is sustained and shall be redeemed.

ונהיה כולנו – אנחנו ,וצאצאינו ,וצאצאי צאצאינו ,וצאצאי עמך בית ישראל - כולנו יודעי שמך ולומדי תורתך לשמה.

May all of us – we, our children, our children's children, and the offspring of Your Nation, the House of Israel – be cognizant of Your Name and disciples of Your Torah for its own sake.

Through intense study of the Torah for its own sake without any ulterior motives, a person will come to understand the nature of each Name of God and how it affects the world, and he will likewise be privy to the esoteric secrets of mystical knowledge and reach a level where he can surmount the original destiny decreed for him.[175]

The reason why this prayer mentions three generations of learners is because such a tradition of Torah study in a family helps ensure that all future generations of that family will likewise study Torah and never forsake its ways.[176]

מאובי תחכמני מצותך ,כי לעולם היא לי.

Your precepts made me wiser than my enemies as they are always with me.[177]

A person who never reads any literature other than the Torah is guaranteed that this very learning will protect him from harm just as Yosef became Viceroy over Egypt and Daniel achieved renown during the reign of Nevuchadnezzer even though many sought to destroy them.[178]

Furthermore, he who learns from all people and all events becomes wise and does not easily stumble. And these lessons make one wiser than his adversaries so that he can always vanquish them.[179]

---

[175] Aitz Yosef, Iyun Tefillah
[176] Bava Metzia 85a
[177] Tehillim 119:98
[178] Hadar Yitzchok p. 22
[179] Rashi, Metzudas David

THE HADRAN ALACH

יהי לבי תמים בחוקיך למען לא אבוש ,לעולם לא אשכח פקודיך כי בם חייתני.
Cause my heart to be pure regarding Your statutes so that I will not be ashamed,[180] I will never forget Your precepts for through them You have given me life.[181]

One should always perform *Mitzvos* with a clear heart so that later he does not have pangs of conscience. He should always consciously realize that only Torah and *Mitzvos* give life meaning or value.[182] These need to be prayed for as they are not attributes easily acquired. Only through HaShem's Mercy will we be able to succeed in our efforts.

ברוך אתה ה' ,למדני חוקיך.
You are blessed, Eternal; teach me Your statutes.[183]

The reward comes to he who recognizes that God is the source of all blessings by granting him Torah knowledge to observe His precepts properly.[184]

אמן .אמן .אמן.
So be it. So be it. So be it.

This triple affirmation alludes to one's three-pronged obligation in learning: study TaNaCH, Mishnah, and Talmud daily. For this reason, it is customary to recite *Karbonos* every morning which contains Scriptural verses, Mishnah, and a short Talmudic discourse.[185] It also establishes in us a repetitive pattern of three and therefore gives us a precedent that we will always be able to continue our learning.

סלה ועד.
Forever.

---

[180] Tehillim 119:80
[181] Ibid. 119:93
[182] Metzudas David
[183] Tehillim 119:12
[184] Even Ezra
[185] Avudraham, Kiddushin 30a

This phrase is an allusion to the truth that he who is meticulously careful to respond, "Amen", opens the Gates of Heaven and guarantees himself a portion in the World-to-Come.[186] Since this prayer is one we are also offering for all of Jewry, we are asking HaShem to grant all of us a portion in the Hereafter.

YEHI RATZON MILFANECHA

THIS SECTION IS SAID ONLY for the completion of a *Masechta* of Gemara.

This next section is intriguing! As mentioned above, it lists by name the ten sons of a great Talmudic scholar named Rav Pappa. Rav Pappa was very wealthy, and each time he completed a tractate he would make a magnificent festive meal to which he would invite, among many others, his ten sons. So great was the glory that he brought to Torah scholarship that his sons followed in his path, and each one became an esteemed Torah scholar in his own right. And that is another reason why they are mentioned at each *siyum* of Gemara — to underline the potential for each of us that Torah learning carries with it.

There is another, somewhat esoteric, explanation regarding Rav Pappa and his ten sons that we mentioned above: Rav Pappa symbolizes Moshe Rabaynu, and his ten sons symbolize the Ten Commandments.

יהי רצון מלפניך ה' אלקינו ואלוקי אבותינו שתהא תורתך אמנותנו בעולם הזה

May it be Your will, Eternal, our Almighty, and the Almighty of our Patriarchs, that Your Torah shall be our (life's) work in this world

A person should strive to reach a level of faith where he is certain both intellectually and emotionally that the Lord will supply his every need just as He does for the wildlife, and that he does not need to pursue a livelihood but can instead devote his time to Torah and *Mitzvos* knowing that God will succor and protect him.[187]

---

[186] Shabbos 119b
[187] Kiddushin 82a

ותהא עמנו לעולם הבא.

And that it shall remain with us in the Hereafter.

Because a person learns the Torah in his lifetime, he is assured that he will be permitted to learn it in the Heavenly *Yeshiva*, as well.[188] He will not forget his learning done in this world when he gets to the Hereafter.

חנינא בר פפא ,רמי בר פפא ,נחמן בר פפא ,אחאי בר פפא ,אבא מרי בר פפא ,
רפרם בר פפא ,רכיש בר פפא ,סורחב בר פפא ,אדא בר פפא ,דרו בר פפא:

(The ten sons of Rav Papa:) Chanina, Rami, Nachman, Achoi, Aba Mari, Rafram, Rachish, Surchav, Ada, and Daru.

These sons sacrificed everything to learn the Torah. Anyone who puts up with hardship to learn the Torah is guaranteed a bright future in the World-to-Come.[189] One of the reasons we mention these holy individuals is so that by doing so, it will also influence us.

MODIM ANACHU LEFANECHA

THIS SECTION IS SAID FOR both the completion of a *seder* of Mishnayos and a *Masechta* of Gemara.

The ensuing section contains four comparisons of a life that is imbued with Torah learning and a life that is not. The penultimate comparison reads, "We toil and they toil. We toil and receive reward, and they toil and do not receive reward." The Chofetz Chaim explains that normally a person receives a reward for the finished product. For example, a tailor is paid for the suit that he sews, but if the tailor never finishes the garment, he will not receive any payment for his time and toil. This is not the case, says the Chofetz Chaim, when it comes to learning the Torah. Every word of Torah that we learn brings with it a reward for the effort and toil involved, even if we never actually finish the entire tractate.

---

[188] Sanhedrin 92a
[189] Sanhedrin 100a

HADRAN

The final comparison states, "We run, and they run. We run to a life in the World to Come, and they run to the 'Well of Destruction.'" If, however, each comparison is made up of two opposites, then the last part should seemingly read, "We run, and they run. We run to a life in the World-to-Come, and they run to a life in this world." Surely the opposite of the World to Come is this world, and yet it reads, "We run to a life in the World-to-Come and they run to 'Well of Destruction.'" Why? Because Judaism teaches that this world is not the opposite of the World-to-Come. Rather, this world can be used as the vehicle that brings us to the World-to-Come. Of course, if a person loses sight of that fact, then this world becomes a bottomless pit of emptiness and nothingness.

מודים אנחנו לפניך ה' אלקינו ואלקי אבותינו ששמת חלקנו מיושבי בית המדרש,
ולא שמת חלקנו מיושבי קרנות.

We offer thanks to You, Eternal, our Almighty, and the Almighty of our Patriarchs, for assigning me to a place among those who sit in the Beis Hamidrash rather than among those who stand (and gossip) at street corners.

A person should strive to be the first one in the *Yeshiva* or Beis Midrash each day because such an individual is given credit for all learning that takes place that day in that place![190]

Even though supporting institutions and individuals who learn Torah is extremely praiseworthy, and any such individual is given credit for all the learning that results from his financial support, actual learning is still more important. It is therefore preferable to be a Torah scholar rather than a successful business tycoon.[191]

שאנו משכים והם משכימים

We get up early and they get up early.

Jews and non-Jews alike find it expedient to get up early to start their day. Most people find that getting up early helps their day be more productive.

---

[190] Berachos 47b
[191] Shabbos 118b

"

THE HADRAN ALACH

אנו משכים לדברי תורה

We arise to fulfill the Torah

Any Jew who devotes every moment of his time to serving God faithfully is given credit for such service even while asleep.

Moreover, Torah study and raising children who observe the Torah are among the six items in which a person receives interest payments for his *Mitzvah* in this world while the principle remains for the Hereafter.[192]

והם משכימים לדברים בטלים.

But they get up early for vanities.

The life of the non-Jew who fails to observe the seven Noahide Precepts or even the life of a Jew who is non-observant are wasted, for although these individuals may live many years, they have accomplished nothing and have few, if any, *Mitzvos* to show the Heavenly Court. Such people inevitably are doomed to Gehinnom.

These thoughts are echoed throughout Shas. Rav Papa bemoaned the fact that he was not to die at the hands of the Romans for any worthwhile cause while Rabbi Akiva would give his life as a martyr who taught Torah in public against the wishes of his oppressors.[193]

Failure to study the Torah may result in the death of a person's children,[194] physically, spiritually, or both.

אנו עמל והם עמלים

We work and they work.

All mankind works for a livelihood, but as discussed above, wages are not guaranteed. The amount of time one spends working for a living still does not guarantee remuneration.

אנו עמלים ומקבלים שכר

We labor and receive recompense

---

[192] Shabbos 127a
[193] Berachos 61b
[194] Shabbos 32b

The Jew who learns Torah will benefit as this Torah protects him in his old age to give him increased vitality, and even the mere effort to study is rewarded even though the individual may have reached erroneous conclusions from his studies.[195]

Although all men were created to perform labor, a Jew's function in life is to learn the Torah.[196] Nor is this statement a contradiction to Rabbi Meir who states that a person who fails to teach his son a trade is abjudged to have taught him to commit a crime.[197] Although Rabbi Nehorai states that a man should only instruct his son in the Torah[198] and although Rabbi Nehorai was an alias of Rabbi Meir,[199] even these statements are in agreement with one another. A person who feels he must do his share is required to earn a livelihood and yet recognize that his earnings are not the result of his efforts but rather a gift from God. However, the ultimate goal is for a person to know that he can place his complete trust in God and devote all his waking hours to Torah and *Mitzvos* and be certain that the Lord will support him as He does all His creatures.

והם עמלים ואינם מקבלים שכר

But they toil and do not (always) get paid.

They do not receive compensation for a botched job; their earthly employers reward them only for work that was completed. Furthermore, this work which garners them money for sustenance yields no dividends when compared to the Hereafter; in that world, only Torah and *Mitzvos* are assigned values.

אנו רצים והם רצים

We run and they run.

The observant Jew rushes about from one *Mitzvah* to the next while others dash about from one vanity to another in a hopeless attempt to find joy and satisfaction in life.

---

195 Kiddushin 82a
196 Sanhedrin 99b
197 Kiddushin 29a
198 Ibid. 82a
199 Eruvin 13b

אנו רצים לחיי העולם הבא, והם רצים לבאר שחת. שנאמר: ואתה אלקים תורדם
לבאר שחת אנשי דמים ומרמה לא יחצו ימיהם ואני אבטח בך

We sprint toward life in the World-to-Come. They plunge into the depths of Hell. As stated, "You, Almighty, cast them into the abyss of Hell. They are a blood-stained dishonest horde who do not live out even half their days." But I place my trust in You.[200]

Those whose lives have been spent in sin – lying, cheating, and even killing – to get ahead, are predoomed to Gehinnom. Only he who has refined his *middos* through the Torah and has repented of his iniquities can look forward to Gan Eden.[201]

YEHI RATZON LEFANECHA

THIS SECTION IS SAID FOR both the completion of a *seder* of Mishnayos and a *Masechta* of Gemara.

This is a heartfelt plea that we should be able to continue learning more Torah and that we merit to complete many more tractates and holy works. Not just to finish them but to implement their lessons in our lives and to be able to transmit those sacred lessons to others. Contained in this paragraph is a poignant supplication that the Torah that we learn will not just remain with us but will continue and remain with our children and grandchildren forever.

The next nine segments of the text comprise the prayer uttered by Rabbi Nechunya the son Hakana, each time he left the study hall in the evening at the conclusion of his learning for that day as a form of thanks to the Lord. The quotation from the Scriptures, however, was added by those who finalized the text of the liturgy as it stands today.[202]

---

[200] Tehillim 55:24
[201] Bava Metzia 33a – b, Ta'anis 11a
[202] Berachos 28b

HADRAN

יהי רצון מלפניך ה' אלוקינו ואלוקי אבותינו, כשם שעזרתני לסיים סדר או מסכת ..., כן תעזרני להתחיל מסכתות וספרים אחרים ולסיימם.

May it be Your will, Eternal, our Almighty, and the Almighty of our Patriarchs, that just as You have enabled me to complete the (Order of ...,) (Masechta of ...) so too may You help me to begin other books, and finish them.

Since all Jews – whether they are rich or poverty-stricken, healthy or sickly, strong or weak, bright or dull – are duty-bound to learn the Torah to the best of their abilities, it is appropriate for a person to beseech God to help make this possible.[203]

ללמד וללמד מתוך הרחבה

May you also make it possible for us to learn and teach from a position of prosperity

Anyone who is duty-bound to study Torah is likewise obligated to instruct others in its intricacies as well.[204] Moreover, he who learns Torah, but does not disseminate its lessons to others is like a wild plant growing in the desert; he benefits no one.[205]

On the other hand, one who teaches Torah to a child is looked upon in Heaven as if he had given birth to that child; he is that lad's spiritual father.[206]

לשמר ולעשות ולקים את כל דברי תלמוד תורתך באהבה

So that we may observe, perform, and uphold Your Torah (in its minutest details) out of love.

The term "לשמר" is always an allusion to Negative Precepts[207] while the term "לעשות" is always a reference to Positive Precepts.[208] The goal of man is to perform all *Mitzvos* out of love for God *i.e.,* without any ulterior motives.[209]

---

[203] Shulchan Aruch: Yoreh Da'ah 246:1

[204] Kiddushin 30a

[205] Rosh Hashanah 23a

[206] Sanhedrin 19b, 99b; Kesuvos 103b

[207] Eruvin 96a, Rosh HaShanah 6a

[208] Berachos 14b, Rosh Hashanah 6a

[209] Nedarim 62a, Avos 4:5

וזכות כל התנאים ואמוראים ותלמידי חכמים יעמוד לי ולזרעי שלא תמוש התורה מפי ומפי זרעי עד עולם.

May the merit of all Tannaim *and Sages (enumerated herein) and in all the other* seforim *which I have learned, stand in my stead and protect my children and their descendants and prevent they and I from ever forsaking the study of the Holy Torah (God forbid).*

A person prays that his children will "inherit" the genius of great Torah scholars and he can ensure this to some degree by creating a three-ply cord (*i.e.,* three generations of Torah scholars), as the descendants of such illustrious parents, grandparents, and great-grandparents will most likely become scholars themselves.[210] And even though it is a well-known principle that Torah cannot be "bequeathed" to one's descendants; they themselves must immerse themselves in its studies to become Torah giants,[211] the potential to become a Torah giant may be transmitted.[212]

ויתקיים בי: "בהתהלכך תנחה אתך בשכבך תשמר עליך והקיצות היא תשיחך."

May all of us become a personification of the following Scriptural verse, "Wherever you walk, it shall lead you; when you lie down, it shall protect you; and when you awaken, it will converse with you."[213]

The Torah will defend a person in this life (wherever you walk), in the grave (when you lie down), and in the World-to-Come (when you awaken) and provide eternal guidance for him.[214] Torah will direct a person in the correct path, protect him from thieves lurking in the night, and act as a constant companion providing limitless invigorating discussions.[215]

"כי בי ירבו ימיך ויוסיפו לך שנות חיים."

"Through me, you shall be granted longevity and meaningful years of life."

---

[210] Bava Metzia 85a

[211] Nedarim 81a

[212] Ediyos 2:9

[213] Mishlei 6:22

[214] Avos 6:9

[215] Metzudas David

This verse is a paraphrase of, "It (Torah) will give you longevity and meaningful years of life and serenity."[216] Certainly, it intends to point out the fact that a lengthy life is not necessarily a desirable one. Each day must be jam-packed with *Mitzvos* and good deeds plus a significant amount of time learning.[217]

Moreover, a person seeks to live rather than be a zombie, "Who is dead? He who makes himself alive! Who is alive? He who kills himself!" This cryptic statement from the Talmud means to say that a person who permits his Yetzer Hara to run amok; though alive, he is in reality dead, and his life has no meaning.[218] He who has subjugated his Evil Inclination is alive. And this too is the interpretation of, "Avraham was old, well advanced in age,"[219] which literally means, "Avraham was old. He came with his days" *i.e.,* not a moment of his life was wasted; it was all devoted to fulfilling God's will.[220]

"...ארך ימים בימינה בשמאולה עשר וכבוד."
"In her right hand is longevity, in her left is wealth and honor..."

If a person studies the Torah for its own sake (symbolized by the right hand), he will merit to live a long life and will certainly gain prosperity and fame. If, however, he learns Torah for ulterior motives (symbolized by the weaker left hand), will still be granted his just reward of prestige and financial security, but will not necessarily live a long life.[221]

"ה' עוז לעמו יתן: ה' יברך את עמו בשלום."
"The Eternal gives strength to his Nation and blesses His People with peace."[222]

The term "עוז" (strength) symbolically refers to the special gift of Torah which God gave to Jewry; as it is Torah that constantly strengthens Jewry and enables her to survive in the face of her enemies.[223]

---

[216] Mishlei 3:2
[217] Avos 6:7
[218] Tamid 32a
[219] Beraishis 24:1
[220] Kiddushin 4:14
[221] Rashi: Avos 6:7, Metzudas David: Mishlei 3:16
[222] Tehillim 29:11
[223] Zevachim 116a; Rashi: Tehillim 29:11 – ד"ה עוז

And the vessel that contains all blessings that a person receives from the Lord – health, wealth, and longevity – and gives them value, is peace.[224]

LEHODOS

THIS SECTION IS SAID ONLY for the completion of a *seder* of *Mishnayos*.

להודות, להלל, לשבח, לפאר, לרומם, להדר, לברך, לעלה, ולקלס, על כל דברי שירות ותשבחות דוד בן-ישי עבדך משיחך.

(It is the obligation of all Creation) to offer thanks (to You) and to laud (You); to praise, glorify, and exalt (You); to extol (You) and make (You) illustrious even more than all the word of the songs and adulations of David, the son of Yishai, Your anointed servant.

A person's primary goal is to thank God by lauding His Name *i.e.,* a person's appreciation of the good that God has bestowed upon him is manifested through his actions. If he fulfills God's commands, he lauds Him; if Heaven forbid, he acts as he pleases irrespective of the Almighty's wishes, he demeans His Name.

However, it is not enough to merely observe the Torah in all its myriad details and to reach a level where one is incapable of even thinking of sinning; his every action must serve to praise, glorify, and exalt God's Name. He must attain a level of spiritual greatness where he takes from this world only that which is essential to his service to God. Anything that can be construed as a luxury – an item with which he could do without – is scorned by such a person because each move of his serves only one purpose: to exalt God's Name.

Even this accomplishment, however, is insufficient to extol Him and make Him illustrious in the eyes of all humanity. He must actively impel others to reach their spiritual height until every living thing in the universe is dedicated to the wholehearted service of God.

Even though King David did all these things in great measure and even wrote an entire book of praises to God – Tehillim – a person must do

---

[224] Uktzin 3:12

more. His obligation can never be adequately fulfilled, and one is obliged to realize that he will always be in debt to the Lord. Nevertheless, he must do all that is in his power to thank God for His constant favors.

THE REMAINDER OF THIS SECTION is for a *seder* of Mishnayos. It contains nine adulatory verses that are said prior to the final Mishnah from *Maseches* Tamid and then followed by the *Kaddish*.

(1) "בעצתך תנחני ואחר כבוד תקחני".
1) *"You have guided me with Your counsel so that I could consequently be honored."*[225]

The Torah is a roadmap to guide a person in the way in which he should go, and he who adheres to it has been effectively monitored by God and will hence be deserving of the greatest honor of an unbiased accurate comprehension of all events.[226]

(2) "והוא רחום יכפר עון ולא־ישחית והרבה להשיב אפו ולא־יעיר כל־חמתו".
2) *"He is compassionate, forgiving iniquity. Consequently, He did not annihilate (them). He, instead, often subdues His anger and keeps the majority of His wrath dormant."*[227]

God is compassionate and, therefore, mixes strict judgment with mercy so that an individual need not be punished immediately. Instead, he is given an adequate length of time to repent of his iniquity and if his *teshuva* is sincere, he is forgiven. In this fashion, the world is saved from destruction and given a chance to improve.

And even when the person is subject to chastisement, these punishments are kept at a minimum because the Lord knows that man easily falls prey to his Evil Inclination.[228] This verse contains thirteen

---

[225] Tehillim 73:24
[226] Metzudas David
[227] Tehillim 78:38
[228] Rashi: Ibid.

words as an allusion to the Thirteen Attributes of Mercy.[229] Since man has sinned, he needs to appeal for Divine mercy constantly.[230]

(3) "אשרי הגבר אשר־תיסרנו י-ה ,ומתורתך תלמדנו".

3) "Fortunate is the man who is admonished by You, the Eternal, and whom You teach Your Torah."[231]

The righteous are fortunate because the Lord can punish them for their slightest fault and thus encourage them through this process of behavioral modification to reach the highest levels of spirituality where their entire lives are a personification of everything that is written in the Torah.

(4) "ואני בחסדך בטחתי יגל לבי בישועתך אשירה לה כי גמל עלי".

4) "But I have placed complete trust in Your mercy. My heart shall (therefore) rejoice in Your salvation. I will sing to the Eternal because he has showered me with His favor."[232]

Man's trust in God tends to surface in three situations:
a)   When he is in trouble
b)   When he seeks help
c)   After he has been helped, especially if it seemed miraculous

When a man is powerless to defend himself and recognizes that only God can help him, he places his complete trust in God's mercy. If a person sees danger ahead and realizes that he needs outside assistance to surmount the difficulties that lie ahead, his heart rejoices in the forthcoming salvation of the Almighty. And finally, when the man has survived the danger, he profusely thanks the One above and sings his praises to the Eternal for favoring him with His Divine help.[233]

A person who has been reduced to poverty because his livelihood is in shambles and emergency expenditures have overwhelmed him is forced to place his trust in the Almighty because only the Lord stands

---

[229] See Exodus 34:6 – 7

[230] Machzor Vitri

[231] Tehillim 94:12

[232] Tehillim 13:6

[233] Siach Yitzchak

between him and starvation. Consequently, such a person is compelled to recognize the fact that all his puny efforts are worthless and do not determine his financial status.

When such a person is yet kept alive through open miracles of the Lord, he rejoices with the intellectual and emotional knowledge that his station in life is completely dependent upon the Will of the Almighty and he can then truly rejoice in this salvation as he now knows that he need never worry about his finances again as all is predetermined by God. He can devote his life to Torah and *Mitzvos* without worry.

When this level of trust has been achieved at the conscious level, a person can sing his praises to God and thank Him with all his heart because this favor from Above is worth so much – he can now be happy and content in life and is hence wealthy as serenity is more valuable than all the gold and silver of the universe.

(5) "שוש אשיש בה ותגל נפשי באלקי. כי הלבישני בגדי־ישע, מעיל צדקה יעטני ;כחתן יכהן פאר וככלה תעדה כליה".

5) *"I will greatly rejoice in the Eternal (and) my soul will be ecstatic in my Almighty because He has clothed me with the garment of salvation and wrapped me in the cloak of righteousness just as a bridegroom beautifies himself with the splendor and a bride adorns herself with her jewelry."*[234]

When a person is brought before the Heavenly Court to give an account of his life, both his body and soul greatly rejoice. The body is grateful to God for being cleansed in this world via hardships to thus avoid tasting Gehinnom – a mercy by which a person suffers a lesser punishment in this world to avoid a greater one in the Hereafter. The soul, however, is ecstatic for it will now return unsullied to its Source because it can be judged by the Almighty through His attribute of Justice since it is strong enough to undergo a rigid decontamination process that the body could not endure. Both the body and soul beam with joy because the punishments they have suffered have cleansed them so that they may be clothed in the salvation of the *Mitzvos* and wrapped in the cloak of their good deeds like a bride and groom on their wedding day resplendent in their attire anticipating this great moment in their life. So too do the body and soul look forward to the Eternal bliss of the World-to-Come where the *Shechinah* itself will rest upon them.

---

[234] Yeshayahu 61:10

(6) "ויבטחו בך יודעי שמך כי לא־עזבת דרשיך ה'"

6) *"Therefore, those who are cognizant of Your Name shall place their trust in You because You, Eternal, have never forsaken those who seek You."*[235]

When a person takes an honest look at the world, he will conclude that the righteous who suffer are being given their Gehinnom in this world so that they may enter Gan Eden immediately already purged of any taint. He will likewise realize that the wicked who seem so gay and carefree are getting paid off for their few *Mitzvos* so that they can ultimately arrive as paupers in the World-to-Come and thus forfeit any merit in the Hereafter. Instead, they will be sent to Gehinnom for purification and ultimately be ground into dust so the righteous may be provided with a floor upon which to tread. Thus, the righteous are not forsaken by the Lord. This realization will cause one to become cognizant of God and enable him to repent to such a degree that he too can join the ranks of the righteous.

(7) "שמחו בה' וגילו צדיקים והרנינו כל־ישרי־לב."

7) *"Let the righteous be glad with the Eternal and rejoice, and let the upright in heart shout for joy."*[236]

A righteous individual is not only familiar with the labyrinthine code of Jewish law but upholds these precepts to such a degree that he has become incapable of even thinking about sinning. He is a person who would be just as nauseated at the thought of speaking slander as he would be by a snack of worm cake washed down with a spicy cup of warm blood. Such a person can be glad about this life and rejoice in the next as he need not suffer in either since he has been faithful to the Lord.

The upright has attained the even loftier spiritual plenitude of going beyond the strict requirement of the law and observing its spirit, as well. They are careful not to benefit from this world unless such bounty is essential in their service to God. These rare individuals can surely jump for joy because their portion in Gan Eden is exceedingly great.

(8) "נר לרגלי דברך ואור לנתיבתי."

8) *"Your word is a lamp to my feet and a light to my path."*[237]

---

[235] Tehillim 9:11
[236] Tehillim 32:11
[237] Tehillim 119:105

The Torah prevents a person from stumbling in *halacha* and lights up his path in life; it helps prevent him from sinning by illuminating the correct actions to take.[238]

(9) "אודך כי עניתני ותהי־לי לישועה."
9) *"I will give You thanks because You have answered me and become my salvation."*[239]

When a man develops complete faith in the Lord, he knows that the Lord is always there to help him and that He will find a way of answering all his questions so that the Lord may indeed be his salvation in all times and all places.

These nine verses represent "truth" which is the *mispar katan* of "אמת" (nine) which means truth. *Mispar Katan* is where one reduces the value of each letter to one digit, dropping the zeros. The *mispar katan* of the Hebrew word for truth is nine and these scriptural golden nuggets outline a person's road map to success in all areas.

LAST MISHNAH OF TAMID

THIS SECTION IS SAID ONLY for the completion of a *seder* of *Mishnayos*.

At this point in the *siyum,* it is customary to recite the last Mishnah of *Maseches* Tamid. See further on page 133 where I explicate it in detail. Some say that this is said in place of the list of the sons of Rav Pappa who were during the time of the Gemara which was after the Mishnah.

---

[238] Rashi: Metzudas David
[239] Tehillim 118:21

KADDISH

AT THE CONCLUSION OF THE *Hadran*, we recite a special *Kaddish* that is only said on two occasions. Under normal circumstances, one does not say *Kaddish* unless one or both of his parents have already passed away. When someone is leading the services in the synagogue *(shul)* he says all but the mourner's *Kaddish* and the *Kaddish deRabanan*. According to many opinions, the person who is making the *siyum* can recite this *Kaddish HaGadol*, even if his parents are still alive (which hopefully they are).

The main difference between this *Kaddish* and the one you normally hear in *shul* is the second paragraph that talks about some of the wonderous events that will take place in the Messianic era. There are many Kabbalistic and esoteric meanings behind every single word. In the next chapter, we will briefly discuss some of these connotations.

KADDISH

IF TEN ADULT MEN ARE present at a *siyum*, the *Hadran* is concluded with a special *Kaddish*. This *Kaddish* is typically called *Kaddish HaGadol* (The Great *Kaddish*), but sometimes in literature, it is called *Kaddish De'ischadeta* (Renovate). This second name is based on the fifth word of the addition to the *Kaddish*.

The Gemara[240] talks about the holiness of the *Kaddish* and says that in the merit of saying the *Kaddish*, the world is blessed and sustained. It is specifically referring to the central expression of *"Yehai Shemei Rabbah..."* that is said after the public study of Gemara.

ORIGINS OF KADDISH

RAV YEHUDA SAID: IN THE case of a deceased person who has no comforters, *i.e.*, he has nobody to mourn for him, ten people should go and sit in his place and accept condolences. The Gemara relates the story of a certain person who died in Rav Yehuda's neighborhood who did not have any comforters, *i.e.*, mourners; every day of the seven-day mourning

---

[240] Sotah 48a – 49b

period, Rav Yehuda would take ten people, and they would sit in his place, in the house of the deceased. After seven days had passed the deceased appeared to Rav Yehuda in his dream and said to him: Put your mind to rest, for you have put my mind to rest.[241]

Rabbi Abbahu said: Everything people say before the deceased, he knows and hears until the tomb (grave) is sealed. Rabbi Chiyya and Rabbi Shimon, the son of Rabbi Yehuda HaNasi, disagreed regarding the meaning of this statement. One said that the deceased is aware until the tomb is sealed with the dirt covering the grave (*Tosefos*). And one of them said that it is until the flesh decomposes.[242]

The Legend of Rabbi Akiva (As told by various tenth through fourteenth-century Midrashim):

Rabbi Akiva once saw (what he thought was) a man struggling with a heavy burden on his shoulders and bemoaning his lot in (what Rabbi Akiva thought was) life. Concerned that this might be an overworked slave deserving to be freed, Rabbi Akiva asked the man his story. The oppressed laborer replied that he was the soul of a person who committed every conceivable sin and that if he stopped to talk, he would get in even more trouble.

The punishment for this sinner was that he had to gather the wood which was used to burn him every day. Rabbi Akiva asked if there was any way to free this soul, and the deceased replied that the only way was if he had a son who would stand in front of the congregation and say "*Barechu es HaShem hamevorach*" or "*Yisgadal v'yiskadash…*," after which the congregation would reply, "*Baruch HaShem hamevorach l'olam voed*" or "*Yehai Shemei Rabbah…*," respectively. These are the prayers of *Barechu* and *Kaddish*, in which the leader of the service calls upon the congregation to praise God, which they then do.

Finally, Rabbi Akiva asked the man, if he had a son who had survived him; the spirit replied that his wife had been pregnant when he died. Rabbi Akiva recorded the name of the deceased man's wife, and his hometown so that he might investigate the matter.

Hurrying to the man's city, Rabbi Akiva discovered that the deceased was particularly reviled by the townspeople. He had been a corrupt tax collector who took bribes from the rich and oppressed the poor. Among his more notorious deeds, the man had violated a betrothed girl on Yom Kippur! Rabbi Akiva located the widow, who had given birth to a son. So despised was her husband that no one had even circumcised the

---

[241] Shabbos 152a – b
[242] Ibid.

child. Rabbi Akiva took care of this grievous omission and, when the child was old enough, he taught him Torah and how to *daven* in *shul*, including the prayers the man had specified.

As soon as the boy recited the appropriate prayers, his father's soul was relieved of its harsh punishments. The man's spirit reappeared to Rabbi Akiva in a dream to thank the scholar for saving him from the tortures of Gehinnom.

The *Kaddish* is an intensive and deep declaration of our faith. It is one of the most beautiful, deeply significant, and spiritually moving prayers in Jewish liturgy. It is said that the *Kaddish* is the echo of Iyov in the prayerbook: "Though He slay me, yet will I trust in Him."[243] It is a call to God from the depths of catastrophe, exalting His name and praising Him, despite the realization that He has just wrenched a human being from life. Like the *Kol Nidre* prayer of the Day of Atonement, the significance of *Kaddish* is usually taken for granted. It is a response from the depths of the soul an almost primitive, mesmerized response to the sacred demand to sanctify Almighty God. Its passionate recitation has inspired many people in a time of deep sorrow.

The *Kaddish* appears in the daily prayers no less than thirteen times. It is recited at the conclusion of all the major prayers and after the service. It also serves as a transition recital at every minor turning point in the service. It is recited after a Talmud study period, at the cemetery after burial, at services during the year of mourning, every *yahrzeit,* and more. These sages said that one who recites the *Kaddish* with all his inner power and conviction will merit the abolition of any severe Divine decree directed against him. They contended that the whole world itself, as it were, is maintained because of its recital and that it redeems the deceased, specifically from perdition.

The *Kaddish* was considered so vital to the religious life of the Jew that it was recited in Aramaic (just as Yiddish was in the European *shtetl*), the spoken tongue of the Jewish masses in ancient times, so that every individual would understand it. In testimony to its continuing power, it is recited in that language to this day.

Another reason suggested for the use of the common Aramaic language is that it functioned as an educational device. It taught that daily, secular life must be infused and interpenetrated by holiness, the epitome of which is expressed in the *Kaddish*. Inevitably, the *Kaddish* became so popular that the sages had to forewarn the people lest they come to rely on

---

[243] Iyov 13:15

it as some magical power, and lest they increase the number of recitations, possibly leading to the undesirable consequence that a prayer for the dead might become central to the worship service.

For all its majesty, grandeur, and importance, the origins of the *Kaddish* are beclouded in the obscurity of our ancient religious tradition. From the sparse, brief, yet emphatic, references to the *Kaddish* in the Talmud, it is evident that the recitation of the essence of the *Kaddish*, *Yehai Shemei Rabbah*, "May His great name be blessed," was so well-established a custom that its origin and significance were taken for granted. It is probable that the *Kaddish* was formulated after the destruction of the first Temple and was recited primarily after a lecture or discourse on a Torah theme. It then slipped easily into the worship service into which its themes and responses fitted admirably.

There arose five variations of the basic *Kaddish* which embodied the *Yehai Shemei Rabbah*, the central core of every *Kaddish*:

1. The abbreviated form, called the "Half *Kaddish*," is used as a transitional theme following minor portions of the service. This is only the first half of the *Kaddish*.
2. The "Complete *Kaddish*" is used to terminate major parts of the service and, thus, includes the prayer, *tiskabel*, and asking God to accept the heartfelt prayers just uttered.
3. The "Rabbi's *Kaddish*" is used as an epilogue to the study of rabbinic literature, and contains the rubric *al Yisrael*, a prayer for the welfare of students of Torah and of all Israel – in the hope that they may devote themselves uninterruptedly to their sacred tasks.

Until this point in its history, the *Kaddish* was considered highly important, but its significance was appreciated only by scholars and students who understood the deeper meaning of the prayers. In the tractate Soferim, an early medieval *geonic* document, we are told that it soon came to be used as a solemn recitation at the end of the *Shiva* period, when mourning the death of a scholar. The *Kaddish* began to ride the crest of popularity when to avoid embarrassing distinctions between scholar and layman, it came to be used for all who died and by all, especially youngsters, who did not know how to recite the prayers or study the Oral Law. It then began to engage the minds of all Jews, knowledgeable or illiterate, and it was recited at the closing of every Jewish grave.

4. Thus, a fourth form of *Kaddish* arose, the "burial *Kaddish*," which adds one paragraph referring to the resurrection of the dead and the restoration of the Temple. It thus became associated with the

deepest emotions of man. This is also the *Kaddish* that is said at a *siyum*.

5. The service itself soon incorporated a fifth form of *Kaddish*, the "mourner's *Kaddish*," which was recited for the first year after interment, making it the primary prayer for the Jewish bereaved of every age. While there remains nothing explicit in the mourner's *Kaddish* that refers to the grave, the dead, or life after death, the recitation of the *Kaddish* was so well patterned to the mood of the mourner that it became a cherished part of the Jewish people, regardless of denominational attachment.

THE KADDISH

NOW LET US EXPLORE SOME of the deeper meanings of the *Kaddish*.

יתגדל ויתקדש שמה רבא.

May His great Name be renowned and sanctified

The opening line of *Kaddish* is a paraphrase of, "In this fashion, I will exalt Myself and sanctify Myself and I will make Myself known in the eyes of numerous nations and they shall know that I am the Eternal"[244] which speaks of the final war of Gog and Magog when the nations of the world unite in an attempt to destroy the Jewish People. These war-mongers shall themselves be annihilated and the survivors will then truly perceive the greatness of God and His Name will be exalted and enhanced in that all acknowledge His greatness, and His Name will be sanctified because all will pay homage to Him. Therefore, the Scriptures proclaim, "On that Day the Eternal will be One and His Name will be One."[245]

In more general terms, the initial phrase of *Kaddish* is a plea that the Almighty cause His own Name to become enhanced and sanctified by always destroying the wicked in all places. When the world witnesses the punishment of the iniquitous, they are compelled to admit that God is indeed guiding destiny and, in this way, His Name is enhanced because more people recognize His existence. His Name is then sanctified because

---

[244] Yechezkel 38:23
[245] Zechariah 14:9. Aitz Yosef, Yechezkel 38:1 – 23

people (both Gentiles and Jews) perform the Will of the Omnipotent One by observing His commandments.[246]

One must not mistakenly assume that the terms, "Renown and sanctified" imply, Heaven forbid, that He will eventually be greater and holier than He is now as such a thought is pure heresy. Man's pleas that God be renowned and sanctified is that people will become cognizant of God's unchanging greatness as personified by His deeds and that they will recognize His eternal holiness by becoming more familiar with His Essence. In this manner, God's Name will be enhanced and sanctified in the hearts of men as they will now perceive Him as He has always been.[247]

His great Name which would appear to refer to the tetragram – Eternal Lord of Mercy – may in this instance allude to His attribute of Creator because the word רבא (great) may be rearranged to form the word ברא (create).[248]

There are opinions that the text should be translated (not read) as written:

יתגדל ויתקדש שמ י-ה רבא

i.e., "May His Name of "Yud-Hay" be exalted and sanctified by being made great," meaning may the Name Yud-Hay which forms the first half of the Tetragram be completed to Yud-Hay-Vav-Hay (Eternal) during the Messianic Era when the iniquitous will be subdued, and the descendants of Amalek will be wiped off the face of the earth. Until then, Scripture comments, "Because the Eternal (י-ה) has sworn by his Throne (כס) that the Eternal will wage war with Amalek from generation to generation."[249] The Name, Eternal, was written defective (minus the final ו-ה) and even the word throne was inscribed lacking the final א' – an allusion to the truth that, "The Eternal's Name cannot be whole nor His Throne be whole until the name of Amalek is erased."[250]

However, when Amalek is finally exterminated, the Lord's Name and throne will become complete as stated, "The enemies (Amalek) will have come to an end in perpetual ruin and their cities will have been demolished so that no memorial remains of them. Then the Eternal (Yud-

---

[246] Iyun Tefillah, Rashi: Shemos 14:1; Mechilta: Shemos 15:1
[247] Dovair Shalom
[248] Aitz Yosef
[249] Shemos 17:16
[250] Rashi: Ibid.

Hay-Vav-Hay) will endure forever; He has prepared His Throne כסא with the 'א for judgment."[251]

However, Avudraham (among other liturgical commentators), rejects this interpretation as it is not proper to attach the appellate "great" to an incomplete Name, "שמה רבה" rather means "His great Name".[252]

בעלמא די הוא עתיד לאתחדתא

In the World that He will renovate in the future

This line is a reference to the Messianic Era as stated, "Then saviors (the Mashiach and righteous judges) will ascend Mount Zion to judge Esav, and the kingdom shall be the Eternal's,"[253] and, "Then the Eternal will be King over all the world. On that Day the Eternal will be One and His Name will be One."[254] At that time the Eternal's Name will be complete and the world will be perfected in preparation for its termination at the expiration of six thousand years of existence to make way for a new world that will be created at that juncture.[255]

ולאחיאה מתיא ולאסקא יתהון לחיי עלמא.

So that He may resurrect the dead and elevate them to Eternal Life,

In the transformed world of the Messianic Era, God will bring the dead back to life so that every worthy individual who ever walked upon the face of the earth will be resurrected with their former infirmities and only subsequently be cured by God so that they may first recognize their old selves before being perfected. During this time, they will also live as they did in their lifetimes as it is hence customary for some Jews to stipulate in their wills that their heirs may not sell their homes so that the deceased will have a place to live when he is brought back to life. This life, however, is not the eternal Hereafter; all such individuals will still need to submit to death before they are ultimately granted immortality in the new world.

---

[251] Tehillim 9:7 – 8, Ibid.
[252] Dovair Shalom, Iyun Tefillah
[253] Ovadyah 1:21
[254] Zechariah 14:9
[255] Rosh Hashana 31a, Sanhedrin 97a

THE HADRAN ALACH

ולמבנא קרתא די ירושלם

And to rebuild the city of Yerushalayim

This phrase is based upon, "The Eternal is the builder of Yerushalayim; He will gather together the outcasts of Israel,"[256] *i.e.*, He will rebuild Yerushalayim in the Messianic Era and bring all Jewry to this Holy City at that time even though they are scattered across the entire globe.[257]

ולשכללא היכלה בגוה,

And establish His Temple within its precincts,

The sanctity of Yerushalayim is the Temple. Therefore, Jewry prays not only for a rebuilt Yerushalayim but for the Third Temple, as well.

ולמעקר פולחנא נוכראה מן ארעה

And to uproot alien worship from the earth

This phrase is based upon, "It shall come to pass on that day, says the Eternal of hosts, that I will excise the names of the idols from the earth so that they will no longer be recalled and even the false prophets and the Evil Inclination shall be removed from the land,"[258] *i.e.*, in the newly formed world of truth, all will recognize the falsehood of idolatry and the necessity to perform God's will as there will no longer be a contaminating spirit called the Evil Inclination to befuddle man, mislead him, and bring him to sin.[259]

ולאתבא פולחנא די שמיא לאתרה.

And return Divine Service to its place.

Once all People perceive the truth, they will automatically strive to fulfill God's will and by so doing, His Name will become exalted and sanctified in the minds of all humanity.

---

[256] Tehillim 147:2
[257] Rashi: Tehillim 147:2
[258] Zechariah 13:2
[259] Metzudas David: Tehillim 147:2

KADDISH

וימליך קודשא בריך הוא במלכותה ויקרה

Then the Holy One, may He be blessed, will reign in sovereignty and splendor

When all humanity pays homage to Him and the entire Universe reveres Him, His full sovereignty and splendor will be felt throughout the cosmos. He is called, "the Holy One," because His holiness is absolute; man can attain only a minimal finite level of sanctity.

He is to be blessed by mortal man even though He lacks nothing so that man may feel that he is giving something of himself to God because it is human nature to give as well as to take from a benefactor lest he come to despise the latter individual because of his inability to reciprocate favor to any degree. In fact, by helping others, one comes to like them and by "giving" something to God he is drawn closer to Him and his love of Him is nurtured.

בחייכון וביומיכון ובחיי דכל בית ישראל, בעגלא ובזמן קריב.

During your lifetime and during your days and during the lifetime of the entire House of Jewry, quickly and soon.

This phrase is an allusion to the Scriptural verse, "Repent defiant children," says the Eternal, "I have taken you to Myself and I will take you one out of a city and two from a family and bring you to Yerushalayim,"[260] which speaks of the surviving remnant of Jewry after the war of Gog and Magog who will live to see the advent of the Messianic Era in all its glory. One is therefore duty bound to pray that each member of Jewry lives through this tumultuous era to take part in the Redemption.[261]

Moreover, since there is a rule that one dynasty may not overlap the next, and the King David Dynasty of the Messianic Era represents the establishment of a new set of world leaders and therefore implies the demise of the previous set, Jewry is to beseech the Lord to nonetheless permit all the Sages and *Tzaddikim* to remain alive.[262]

Finally, Jewry is to pray that these events will transpire quickly *i.e.*, the transformation leading to the new World Order should take place

---

[260] Yirmiyahu 3:14
[261] Aitz Yosef, Dovair Shalom
[262] Aitz Yosef

without any appreciable passage of time, and that these events should occur in the immediate future.[263]

ואמרו "אמן"!

Therefore, respond, "Amen!"

All those who hear this *Kaddish* must respond "Amen" to signify their concurrence with the aforementioned request. In fact, the word "Amen" (אמן) is an acronym for

"אֵ-ל מֶלֶךְ נֶאֱמָן"

"God is a trustworthy King."[264]

This phrase, moreover, may be understood in two possible fashions (both of which may be simultaneously correct in a given instance):
1) The listener agrees with the statement
2) The desired favor will be granted[265]

In Kabbalah, the letters of the Amen represent two of the holy Names of HaShem intermingled. The א-ד-נ-י and י-ה-ו-ה. This is because numerically, אמן is 91; the two names of HaShem above, when added together also equals 91.

יהא שמה רבא מברך לעלם ולעלמי עלמיא.
May His great Name be blessed forever and throughout eternity.

Volumes could and have been written about this phrase alone. However, this is not the venue for such expansion and extrapolation. I would like to make just a few points that will enhance the material herein.

Even though the superior taste of food was removed from the crops and the dew lost its vitiating powers after the destruction of the Temple, and even though the curse gets worse from day to day, somehow the world continues to survive. Why? Because of the merit of saying,

---

263 Dovair Shalom
264 Shabbos 119b
265 Mishnah Berura 124:25

"May His great Name be blessed forever and throughout eternity," said in the *Kaddish* recited after learning.[266]

Moreover, whoever enunciates this phrase with complete devotion, concentration, and strength is guaranteed that the gates of Paradise will open wide for him for these words embody the essence of Judaism, our faith in HaShem, and His Torah.[267]

The Zohar[268] states that the textual formula is so powerful that it can destroy the forces of evil that prevent man from receiving the blessings meant for him.

When saying this response, the following are the Kabbalistic intents one should have in mind. Since understanding what this means is beyond most people's understanding (especially my own), just looking at this chart will benefit your soul.

Table 8 יהא שמה רבא

עלמיא	ולעלמי	לעלם	מברך	רבא	שמה	יהא
דגדות	דיניקה	דעיבור	גבורות	חסדים	בינה	חכמה

The expression, "May His great Name be blessed," may be interpreted as explained earlier in this essay, namely, that man wishes to confer his blessing upon God – a personification of Rabbi Yishmael *ben* Elisha's (the High Priest) blessing to God uttered one Yom Kippur in the Holy of Holies to inform all mankind that the blessing of a mortal should not be treated lightly as even God sought the blessing of Rabbi Yishmael (a mortal).[269]

It may likewise be rendered as a statement of fact, "May His great Name be blessed in the eyes of Jewry through their recognition of the fact that He is the Source of all blessings," the fount from which all goodness springs forth.[270]

In any event, the phrase is also a prayer that the Temple be rebuilt for when Jewry recites these words, God bemoans His Sanctuary which lies in ruins as a consequence of man's sins.[271]

Others state that instead of "שמה רבא" the text should say "שם י-ה רבא" (May the Name Yud-Hay be enlarged) *i.e.*, may this abbreviated

---

[266] Sotah 48a, 49a

[267] Shabbos 119b

[268] Parshas Terumah

[269] Berachos 7a

[270] See Avudraham

[271] Dovair Shalom, Berachos 3a

Name expand to its full four letters when iniquity ceases to exist with the advent of the Messianic era. According to this version, the continuation is…

ומברך לעלם ולעלמי עלמיא

And may it (this Name of God – the Eternal) be blessed forever and throughout eternity".[272]

The first version cited contained twenty-eight letters, which numerically in Hebrew is equal to the word – כח (strength), which is also twenty-eight – an allusion to the fact that it must be recited with all our energy, or as some say all our concentration.[273] Moreover, it is the numerical value of ידיד (friend) for he who says this phrase properly is a friend of God entitled to entrance into Gan Eden. Machzor Vitri's text contains thirty letters (an extra י and ו) and hence is rejected by many commentators.

יתברך וישתבח ויתפאר ויתרומם ויתנשא ויתהדר ויתעלה ויתהלל שמה דקדשא
בריך הוא

May the Name of the Holy One, which is blessed, be blessed, lauded, glorified, exalted, upraised, honored, elevated and praised

These eight words of description of God (the first eight words in the above line) and the first two words of *Kaddish* constitute ten expressions corresponding to the ten classifications of Tehillim uttered by King David, viz.:

a)   אישור (verification)
b)   ניצוח (glory)
c)   ניגון (melody)
d)   שיר (song)
e)   מזמור (psalm)
f)   השכל (wisdom)
g)   רנה (rejoice)
h)   תודה (thanks)
i)   תפילה (prayer)

---

[272] See Machzor Vitri
[273] Avodas Yisrael

j)   ברכה (blessing)[274]

Again, the number of ten shows up, indicating its significance in relation to the *Hadran*. It is also an allusion to the Ten Utterances with which the world was created:

a)   In the beginning, God created the Heavens and the earth.[275]

b)   God said, "Let there be light"; and there was light. God saw that the light was good, and God separated the light from the darkness.[276]

c)   God said, "Let there be an expanse in the midst of the water, that it may separate water from water."[277]

d)   God said, "Let the water below the sky be gathered into one area, that the dry land may appear." And it was so."[278]

e)   And God said, "Let the earth sprout vegetation, seed-bearing plants, fruit trees of every kind on earth that bear fruit with the seed in it." And it was so."[279]

f)   God said, "Let there be lights in the expanse of the sky to separate the day from the night; they shall serve as signs for the set times — the days and the years.[280]

g)   God said, "Let the waters bring forth swarms of living creatures and birds that fly above the earth across the expanse of the sky.'[281]

h)   The Almighty said, "Let the earth bring forth living creatures after their kind – animals, reptiles, and wild beasts after their king," and it was so.[282]

i)   And God said, "Let us make humankind in our image, after our likeness. They shall rule the fish of the sea, the birds of the sky, the cattle, the whole earth, and all the creeping things that creep on earth."[283]

---

[274] Anaf Yosef
[275] Beraishis 1:1
[276] Ibid. 1:3
[277] Ibid. 1:6 – 7
[278] Ibid. 1:9
[279] Ibid. 1:11
[280] Ibid. 1:14 – 15
[281] Ibid. 1:20
[282] Ibid. 1:24
[283] Ibid. 1:26

j)   God said, "See, I give you every seed-bearing plant that is upon all the earth, and every tree that has seed-bearing fruit; they shall be yours for food.[284]

Finally, they refer to the Decalogue, of which the first two commands were given by God directly to Jewry, while the remaining eight were given through Moshe – the separation of the first two words of *Kaddish* from the other eight is reminiscent of the comparison of the Decalogue to the *Kaddish*.[285]

The ten classifications of Tehillim, the ten statements through which the world was created, the Decalogue, and the ten expressions of adulation recited in *Kaddish* are closely intertwined with one another.

a)   "אישור" (verification) symbolizes the fact that God exists. "אנכי ה' אלקיך" (I am the Eternal, Your Almighty[286]) that He created the world out of nothing (the Almighty created the Heaven and the earth[287]); and that He continues to guide destiny (I … brought you up out of the land of Egypt).[288]

A person must therefore seek to make the Almighty renowned through his conscious realization of God's existence through conducting himself with the thought that God is viewing his every action and monitoring his every thought.

b)   " ניצוח" (glory) stands for the fact that no Jew shall worship any gods; he shall cling only to the Almighty and revere Him alone. This is the great "light" of Creation, the glory of the Universe – for he who is cognizant of this fact is now able to know right from wrong and can thereby steer clear of iniquity. He can thus sanctify God through his behavior.

c)   "ניגון" (melody) represents the truth that one must sing a beautiful melody to God by the motif of doing only those acts that please God and bring honor to His Name. He must hence be extremely careful to never take His Name in vain or perform any action that desecrates His Holiness. The "upper waters" must thus be

---

[284] Ibid. 1:29 – 30. Avos 5:1, Tiferes. Yisrael: on Avos 5:1; Aitz Yosef
[285] Makos 24a, Aitz Yosef
[286] Shemos 20:2
[287] Beraishis 1:1
[288] Shemos 20:2

separated from the "lower waters", *i.e.* a person must overcome his baser instincts and subjugate his Yetzer Hara to wholeheartedly serve God. He thus blesses God by reciprocating with good for the favors he has received.

d) "שיר" (song) refers to *Shabbos* day during which a person must sing his praises to God who has given him a day of rest to reflect upon his behavior of the past week and rejuvenate his faith. It is an eternal symbol of all *Mitzvos* between man and God which can elevate a person to an honored place in the World of Truth. Creation is symbolized by the formation of dry land versus seas: this world is a great ocean from which ships (humans) sail in search of profit (*Mitzvos*) to bring to port (Olam Haba). It is the temporary abode of mortal life that awaits eternal bliss in the permanent home of dry land (the World-to-Come). It is the primary way of lauding God.

e) "מזמור" (psalm) symbolizes the first precept between man and his fellow human being – honoring his parents. Just as a person must constantly show his appreciation to God for all that he has done for him, so too must he constantly voice his psalms of praise for his parents who brought him into this world nurtured him, and taught him how to faithfully serve God. Honor and respect of one's parents are the "fruit" of Creation – the delicious delicacy which enhances the world and gives it meaning. It is the glorification of God on this earth as he who treats his parents properly thereby glorifying God who is also his Father.

f) "השכל" (wisdom) is personified through a person's conduct. He may not commit murder neither in its most literal sense nor even in a less obvious fashion, such as slandering his fellowman and causing him to lose his livelihood or suffer business reversals. He is not to defame him and cause him to be ostracized by society.

Creation's symbol of this wisdom is the ability to distinguish between day and night (right and wrong) by the light (Torah) emanating from the Heavens (God) so that he can act within the framework of society through the guidelines spelled out in the holy Torah.

Through acting harmoniously toward fellow human beings, man exalts God as he proclaims to all mankind that he can pleasingly conduct his affairs and yet be prosperous in all his undertakings.

g) "רננה" (rejoice) through chastity. By so doing, the fish in the deepest oceans (beings on earth) and the birds in the Heavens (beings in the upper spiritual realms) will be upraised and made holier through the actions of man, thus upraising, so to speak, God Himself.

h) "תודה" (thanks). Give thanks through honesty, do not steal! Do not rob a person of life by wasting his time with idle meaningless chatter. Do not usurp his sleep with night-time racket. Do not cheat him with weights and measures, price-gouging, harsh words about his past, or force your will upon him because of the latter's exploitable status. Instead, let the earth teem with life – animals, reptiles, and wild beasts who live in peace with one another, *i.e.* conquer lusts and passions symbolized by animals and wild beasts – barbarism – and use speech represented by reptiles (*e.g.*, the snake of the Tree of Knowledge) to promote goodwill and serenity. In this manner, God's Name will be honored, for by treating humans with respect, one dignifies the Almighty.

i) "תפילה" (prayer) is represented by the Torah's command not to bear false testimony. Inevitably, such conduct is the result of a person's attempt to guarantee himself wealth, honor, or glory – items that will elude the man who pursues them in such a fashion. By placing one's trust in God and praying to Him for his needs, he will duplicate the behavior of God and become his true image as God too prays that man overcome his evil tendencies and attain lofty spiritual heights. God's Name will hence be elevated when it is used as the means of securing spiritual plenitude.

j) "ברכה" (blessing) is symbolized by God's injunction against coveting. Since everything is dependent upon God and all that exists comes from Him, it is pointless to crave the belongings of another individual. The Lord gave man the world and everything in it to fulfill his every possible need so that he could use all this to praise God through his judicious use of these items.

The text of this section of the *Kaddish* is based on Scriptural verses. In fact, each of the eight terms herein enumerated portends a view of the future in the Messianic Era when God will be both recognized and extolled by all mankind.[289]

1. The term "יתברך" (blessed) is founded upon, "So that he who blesses himself on the earth shall bless himself by the Almighty of truth; and he who swears on the earth shall take an oath in (the

---

[289] Tzelusa D'Avraham

Name of) the Almighty of truth, because the previous tribulations are forgotten and because they are hidden from my eyes.[290]

The first step toward Utopia will occur in the Messianic Era when the wicked are exterminated and no one will remain on earth who is not a firm believer in God; all humanity will have given up all forms of idolatry and revere only the Almighty. Consequently, they will seek their blessings from the Blessed One and will pay homage only to Him. Therefore, even oaths will be taken only in His name as all will recognize Him as truth. In such circumstances, blessings will permeate the world and bring true lasting peace to the globe to such an extent that the concept of war will be forgotten as an unsavory relic of the distant past. In this fashion, the world will be blessed through God.[291]

2. "ישתבך" (lauded) figures prominently in, "Proclaim: 'Save us, Almighty of our salvation and gather us (together) by rescuing us from the nations so that we may offer thanks to Your holy Name – to laud (You) with Your praises.'"[292]

A Jew is to laud God by daily beseeching Him to bring about the Messianic Era knowing that only He can bring about the final redemption of our People.[293]

3. "יתפאר" (glorified) traces its origins to, "He said to me, 'You, Jewry, are my servant through whom I will be glorified.'"[294]

Jewry, both as a community and individually, is like faithful servants, ever ready to fulfill their Master's bidding. Therefore, the Lord is glorified through their behavior just as a parent whose child listens to him reflects positively on that parent.[295]

The verse employs the word "ישראל" for "Jewry" as a symbolic representation of the fact that Jewry encompasses all the exemplary traits of the Patriarchs and Matriarchs because the letters of the word "ישראל" stand for them as in the following chart:

---

[290] Isiah 65:16, Avudraham

[291] Radak: Isiah 65:16

[292] I Divrei Hayamim 16:35, Avudraham

[293] Radak: Yeshayahu 65:16

[294] Yeshayahu 49:3; Avudraham

[295] Radak: Isiah 65:16

Table 9 Yisrael

י	יצחק	Yitzchak
	יעקוב	Yaakov
ש	שרה	Sarah
ר	רבקה	Rivkah
	רחל	Rachel
א	אברהם	Avraham
ל	לאה	Leah

4. "יתרומם" (exalted) is taken from, "Now I will arise," says the Eternal. "Now I will be exalted. Now I will be upraised."[296]

After Jewry has suffered century after century, millennia after millennia, under the yoke, oppression, and torture of those who seek to destroy her, and she has therefore been chastised for her past sins and motivated to complete repentance, these very enemies shall now be purged so that the survivors may witness the true greatness of God who will then restore Jewry to its rightful place at the head of the nations of the world. In this manner, God will be exalted because all humanity will recognize Him and pay homage to Him.

5. "יתנשא" (upraised) is built upon, "You, Eternal, are the personification of greatness, power, glory, victory and majesty for everything that is in Heaven or on the earth is Yours. Eternal, the kingdom is Yours with You upraised as head above all else."[297]

When a person amasses large sums of money with which to perform *Mitzvos* such as King David's building of the Temple, and he conquers an enemy that far outnumbers him in troops, equipment, and superior firepower and he is therefore glorified for his victory and elevated to majesty, he must always realize that none of this was his doing; it was all accomplished through the Will of God because everything that occurs is but a manifestation of His Desire. He alone is upraised above all else and only He will bring about the building of the Third Temple in the Messianic Era.[298]

---

[296] Yeshayahu 33:10, Avudraham
[297] I Dirvrei HaYamim 29:11, Avudraham
[298] Radak: I Dirvrei HaYamim 29:11

6. "יתהדר" (honored) comes from, "Now, I, Nevuchadnezzer, praise, extol and honor the King of Heaven for all His works are truth and His ways are just, and He is able to humble the haughty."[299]

The greatest honor accorded to God is the admission by iniquitous dignitaries like Nevuchadnezzer that God is the true ruler of the Universe – a just God who can humble the proudest of men and teach him who is really in charge of things.

7. "יתעלה" (elevated) is based upon, "For You, Eternal, are superior to anything in the world; You are far more elevated than other (so-called) gods."[300]

At the end of days, mankind will realize that all the gods they worshipped were but vanities and only the Almighty is Supreme and to be worshipped.

8. "יתהלל" (praised) is founded upon, "To see the good (meted out) to Your chosen ones, to rejoice in the gladness of Your Nation, to be praised with Your Inheritance."[301]

Jewry will rejoice with the final reckoning of the Nations and become ecstatic by being praised as the chosen ones of God, His faithful servants.

Throughout *Kaddish*, it is the Name of God that is praised, rather than God Himself for mortals cannot grasp the essence of God Himself. Therefore, the text reads, "May the Name of the Holy One…" Moreover, the very name of God is a unique agent because the world was created with His Name. The holiness of a *sefer* Torah is not its contents, but rather the letters as can be amply demonstrated by the following problem: who wrote the last eight lines of the Torah? Moshe could not have written them because they contain the phrase, "Moshe the servant of the Eternal died there,"[302] (no one knows when or where they are going to die) and Moshe left thirteen complete *Sifrei* Torah to Jewry on the final day of his life. And if a person is to state that Yehoshua wrote these lines after Moshe's death,

---

[299] Daniel 4:34, Avudraham
[300] Tehillim 97:9, Avudraham
[301] Tehillim 105:6, Avudraham
[302] Devarim 34:5

then the Torah is missing a section and hence unfit for use (not complete).[303] The Vilna Ga'on resolves the difficulty by explaining that Moshe indeed wrote the last eight lines of the Torah - "בדמע" – in jumbled up order; Yehoshuah unscrambled the letters after Moshe died to write the concluding verses as they now appear. This proves that the sanctity of the Torah rests in the letters themselves, and not necessarily the order and it also underscores the reason why the Torah is called "שמות" (Names): all of it is but names of God portraying His guiding Hand in the affairs of mankind.

Finally, the text reads, "May the Name of the Holy One, which is blessed, be blessed…"; the very Name is a source of blessing and he who is well-versed in the myriad intricacies of the Kabbalah knows how to use these names for the benefit of Jewry.

לעלא (בעשי"ת לעלא ולעלא מכל) מן כל **ברכתא ושירתא תשבחתא ונחמתא** דאמירן בעלמא.

*Beyond all **blessings**, **songs**, **praises**, and **consolations** that are uttered in the world.*

These four words above that I bolded – blessings, songs, praises, and consolations – symbolize the four letters that formed the tetragram.[304]

The Eternal begins His Name with the letter *Yud* ('י). This letter is different from all others in three ways:

1. It is the smallest
2. It is the only letter that hangs suspended in the air and does not reach the line
3. It is the basic component of all letters and cannot be further broken down to become parts of other letters.

The smallness of this letter is an allusion to the fact that one cannot truly cling to God until he develops humility and recognizes more and more clearly how great the Lord is and how puny and insignificant he is.

The miraculous suspension of the *yud* in mid-air symbolizes the truth that everything occurring in the world is a miracle dependent upon the Will of God. A person must therefore develop complete faith in Him

---

[303] See Bava Basra 15a
[304] Aitz Yosef

and not worry about finances or other matters as it is God who gives him what he has and needs.

The fact that this letter cannot be broken down is meant to convey the message that a person can surmount all life's difficulties and conquer his Yetzer Hara.

This three-pronged gift is the blessing contained in the Name of the Eternal that will help guarantee a man's success in this world.

The letter *hay* (ה') contains a large opening at its bottom and a small aperture in its upper left-hand corner. The former is there to inform man that it is easy to fall into the pit of Gehinnom. If a man is not constantly improving himself, he automatically degenerates. The latter opening symbolizes the struggle and climb necessary to achieve greatness of spirit.

The *hay* is also the final letter of the word "תשובה" (repentance) *i.e.*, "תשוב ה" (return to God). Since there are two levels of repentance, the Eternal's Name contains two letter *hays*. The first type of repentance is the ability to abstain from repeating sin even though the desire to sin is still present. The second level is achieved when the person kills this desire, as well.

When attaining the basic level, a person may sing with joy and happiness that he has finally stopped sinning. When he reaches the top level of *teshuva*, however, and is truly heartbroken over his past actions to such a degree that he has effectively killed his *Yetzer Hara*, the Merciful One consols him with the knowledge that true repentance miraculously transforms a person's iniquities into *Mitzvos* so that he may attain an exalted status in Gan Eden.

The *Vav* (ו') stands straight. It is the symbol of truth. He who lives by truth is surely praised.

This prayer thus informs humanity that since the Name of the Eternal contains blessings, songs, praises, and consolations – all humanity can benefit therefrom by cloaking themselves with these qualities. However, they can only do so to a limited degree; but the Eternal's possession of these attributes is absolute, without limit.

Some state that these four items are portrayed in all the Prophetic Writings as a divinely inspired description of the Eternal. Nevertheless, they cannot do truth to Him who is indescribable.[305]

---

[305] Shibolay Haleket

THE HADRAN ALACH

Avudraham states that the four adulatory phrases mentioned in the text refer to human kings and that this phrase intends to indicate that all the great songs and praises composed over the centuries to laud men do not amount to a fraction of the respect and honor due to God because of His accomplishments.

ואמרו "אמן"!

Therefore, respond, "Amen!"

It should be noted that the numerical value (*gematria*) of Amen is ninety-one. This is the same value of the two names of HaShem added together. These names are י-ה-ו-ה (twenty-six) and א-ד-נ-י (sixty-five). These mean The Eternal Lord and Divine Mercy. By uttering "Amen" a person affirms his belief that the Eternal Lord judges the universe with Mercy and Compassion.

The letters that spell "אמן" (Amen) are also unique in that they point out the unchangeability of the fact that God is a faithful King. The letter 'א looks the same from top to bottom as it does from bottom to top *i.e.*, the upside down 'א looks just the same as the regular 'א, a datum untruc of any other letter of the printed Hebrew alphabet. The letters מ"ם and נו"ן (when spelled out fully) are unique in their spelling as they are unchangeable being read both forward or backward the same way – they are palindromes. The only other letter that has this distinction is the letter וי"ו. It is for this reason that one often finds in the liturgy the expression "אמן ואמן" when the וי"ו has been added to include it among the unchangeable.

על ישראל, ועל רבנן, ועל תלמידיהון, ועל כל תלמידי תלמידיהון, ועל כל מאן דעסקין באוריתא די באתרא (בא"י: קדישא) הדין ודי בכל אתר ואתר - יהא להון ולכון שלמא רבא; חנא וחסדא ורחמין; וחיין אריכין, ומזוני רויחי, ופרקנא מן קדם אבוהון די בשמיא, (וארעא)

Concerning Jewry, the teachers, the students, and all their student's disciples, and all those who engage in the study of Torah who are in this community or anywhere else – may they and you be granted abundant gratification; grace, kindness, and mercy; longevity, prosperity, and salvation from their Father who is in Heaven.

KADDISH

In this prayer, Jewry refers to those who support the Torah rather than those who toil to learn it, as the latter individuals are specifically mentioned in the following phrases.

Those who support the Torah are mentioned first for a variety of reasons. When Moshe blessed the tribes of Yissachar and Zevulun, he blessed the latter first because they enabled the former to study the Torah undisturbed by financial worries.[306] The Talmud also cites he who supports Torah before mentioning the scholar.[307] Furthermore, the number of potential underwriters of Torah personnel far outnumber those who spend their days and nights pouring over the pages of the Talmud. These individuals, moreover, can often attain a greater portion of Olam Haba than the Torah scholar if their attitudes and motivations are correct, as they receive credit for all the Torah learned because of their support. An individual, for example, who provides ten percent of a *Yeshiva's* yearly budget receives ten percent credit for the Torah study of its students during the time in which he supports the institution.

The teachers and Rabbis who transmit the Oral Law are mentioned next as the world's existence is ultimately dependent upon the study of Torah and the fulfillment of its precepts – a goal that is attainable only if there are qualified and dedicated teachers to infuse the Nation with these values.

Students and all these students' disciples are mentioned to indicate that the teacher must make such an impact upon his students that they too will carry on this tradition and teach others. The ideal goal of any *Yeshiva*, therefore, is to infuse its students with such a love of Torah that these students – even in the guise of businessmen and laborers – will set aside time each day to study Torah, and that they will likewise inculcate their children, friends and associates with these important values.

The blessing finally includes all those who engage in the study of Torah to whatever degree since some individuals are self-taught, living far away from a large Torah center, and others whose sole recourse to Torah is what they gleaned from books on Judaica. The main point underscored here is that anyone in any place who learns any amount of Torah is to be blessed by God, as this very beneficence may lead to an increase in the amount and depth of his Torah study.

This prayer beseeches God to bless, "they and you", *i.e.*, those mentioned specifically in this supplication, and you – the congregation of petitioners who are reciting this *Kaddish*.

---

[306] See Devarim 33:18

[307] See Rashi: Sotah 21a, ד"ה שמעון אחי עזריה - ;ד"ה שמעון אחי עזריה Rashi: Zevachim 2a – ד"ה שמעון אחי עזריה

The term "שלמא רבא" is usually rendered as "abundant peace" and interpreted as a request for complete serenity because no other blessing such as wealth or longevity is worth much in an era of turmoil and war.[308]

Rabbi Avraham Landau rejects this interpretation because the subsequent phrase of the *Kaddish*, "May there be abundant peace from Heaven…", would then be redundant. "שלמא רבא" as employed in the present text, ought to be rendered, "abundant gratification". Its meaning is that a person should be happy and content with the blessings bestowed upon him, for otherwise they have no value since in his eyes he is lacking something.[309]

After beseeching the Lord to make sure that Jewry is satiated with favor, specific boons are now sought.

The first set of these boons is grace, kindness, and mercy. Grace is that wondrous something that makes a person beloved by others. Kindness is a personality trait that causes a person to favor others, even when these individuals have not earned this generosity. Mercy is that most desirable quality by which one withholds punishing a person who has wronged him in the hopes that the latter will repent of his misdeed. Jewry prays that they all develop such a personality.[310]

Grace also represents the uppermost spiritual height by which a person is deserving of favor on his own merit. Kindness is a lesser level where an individual's positive accomplishments are insufficient to earn a person favor from God, and the person is yet granted this boon through God's kindness. Mercy is that attribute by which God awards the non-observant sinner with beneficence. Jewry asks God to bless them on all three levels and help them attain the highest stage of spiritual development.[311]

The petitioner now seeks longevity, prosperity, and salvation – a long life jam-packed with *Mitzvos* which are made possible by prosperity which gives him ample time and money to perform good deeds and salvation from the Evil Inclination so that his years will have meaning.

Finally, all pray that these blessings come from God rather than Satanic powers of evil which can unfortunately sometimes be a source of "blessing" to lead a person astray.

Some texts add, "and on earth" to the phrase, "their father who is in Heaven" but many commentators state that such a gloss is incorrect.[312]

---

[308] Uktzin 3:12
[309] Tzelusa D'Avraham
[310] Siach Yitzchak
[311] Rabbi Yitzchak Luria
[312] Avodas Yisrael

KADDISH

יהא שלמא רבא מן שמיא וחיים עלינו ועל כל ישראל. ואמרו "אמן"!
May there be abundant peace from Heaven and a good life for us and for all Jewry. Therefore, respond "Amen!"

In this blessing, Jewry asks God for peace and tranquility so that the aforementioned blessings will be blessings that can be properly enjoyed and experienced.[313]

Dovair Shalom comments that the term "שלמא רבא" could be misconstrued in the sense of dying peacefully, "You will die in peace."[314] The term, "and good life" thus proves that the peace sought after is in life rather than death.

It is also possible to state that the term "שלמא רבא" in the previous clause refers both to abundant peace and abundant gratification simultaneously and that the present phrase has the same meaning and is yet not redundant. The former phrase refers to this world while the present phrase is a prayer that the "good life" *i.e.,* the Hereafter, be attained through a person's accomplishments in this world. This is with the help of God who aids him to steer clear of sin so that he can ultimately bask in the full radiance of Gan Eden and the serenity to be found there.

עושה שלום (בעשי"ת השלום) במרומיו הוא יעשה שלום עלינו ועל כל ישראל ואמרו "אמן"!
May He who makes peace in His heights, make peace in His mercy, for us and all Jewry. Therefore, respond: "Amen!"

Before uttering this phrase, the one who is reciting *Kaddish* bows and while stooped over, takes three backward steps like a servant taking leave of his master. While reciting the phrase "May He who makes peace in His heights", he curtsies to his left (which is to the right of God's Presence). While announcing, "Make peace, in His mercy, for us", he turns to his right (which is to the left of God's presence). And finally, upon uttering, "and all Jewry. Therefore, respond, 'Amen!'", he bows stage center as he leaves His Master.[315]

The phrase, "May He who makes peace in His heights…" is based upon the Scriptural verse, "Kingship and fear are with Him; He makes

---

[313] Avudraham
[314] Yirmiyahu 34:5
[315] Aitz Yosef, Mishnah Berura

peace in His heights,"[316] *i.e.*, the Heavenly beings whose functions often appear contradictory work harmoniously with one another. Thus, mercy and judgment can combine to form compassion whereby a person receives only partial punishment for his sins. Conflicts are relegated to this world.[317]

The very makeup of the angels underscores this point. Although they are composed of fire and water – opposites – they live peacefully together without any internal battle.[318]

The petitioner begs God to make peace among human beings for if spiritual beings require God's help to create harmony among themselves, then man who contains an Evil Inclination surely needs such assistance to achieve this end.[319]

This peace is sought even if Jewry is undeserving of it – a plea for divine mercy – a yearning that the Third Temple be speedily established in our days with the advent of the Messianic Era.

---

[316] Iyov 25:2
[317] Rashi and Ibn Ezra: Ad. loc.; Rav Yitzchak Luria
[318] Aitz Yosef
[319] Ibid.

OTHER VERSES

SOME AUTHORITIES CONTEND THAT TO ensure that a person learns Torah at every repast, he is to recite the following nine verses just before reciting "Grace after Meals" and that he who does so will never lack food during his entire life. The first three verses are from the Chumash, the second three are from the Prophets, and the final three are from Tehillim. Some will make sure to say these *pesukim* before *birchas hamazon* but after the *seudas Mitzvah* of a *siyum*.

Table 10 Nine Pesukim

HEBREW	ENGLISH
וַיֹּאמֶר יְהֹוָה אֶל־מֹשֶׁה הִנְנִי מַמְטִיר לָכֶם לֶחֶם מִן־הַשָּׁמָיִם וְיָצָא הָעָם וְלָקְטוּ דְּבַר־יוֹם בְּיוֹמוֹ לְמַעַן אֲנַסֶּנּוּ הֲיֵלֵךְ בְּתוֹרָתִי אִם־לֹא:	The Eternal spoke to Moshe, "Behold. I will cause bread to rain from the Heaven for you and the People shall go out and gather a fixed amount daily in order that I may test them to see whether or not they will uphold My command!"[320]
וַעֲבַדְתֶּם אֵת יְהֹוָה אֱלֹהֵיכֶם וּבֵרַךְ אֶת־לַחְמְךָ וְאֶת־	You shall serve the Eternal, your Almighty, and He shall bless your bread

---

[320] Shemos 16:4

מִימֶיךָ וַהֲסִרֹתִי מַחֲלָה מִקִּרְבֶּךָ:	and water: I will uproot sickness from your midst.[321]
וַיְעַנְּךָ וַיַּרְעִבֶךָ וַיַּאֲכִלְךָ אֶת הַמָּן אֲשֶׁר לֹא־יָדַעְתָּ וְלֹא יָדְעוּן אֲבֹתֶיךָ לְמַעַן הוֹדִעֲךָ כִּי לֹא עַל־הַלֶּחֶם לְבַדּוֹ יִחְיֶה הָאָדָם כִּי עַל־כָּל־מוֹצָא פִי־ יְהוָה יִחְיֶה הָאָדָם:	So, He humbled you and afflicted you with starvation and subsequently fed you with manna – a quantum unknown until now to neither you nor your ancestors – in order to demonstrate to you that a man does not live by bread alone; he is rather sustained by every word uttered by the Eternal.[322]
הוּא מְרוֹמִים יִשְׁכֹּן מְצָדוֹת סְלָעִים מִשְׂגַּבּוֹ לַחְמוֹ נִתָּן מֵימָיו נֶאֱמָנִים:	He shall dwell on high. His rock fortress shall be his line of defense. His bread shall be given him, and his water supply assured.[323]
לָמָּה תִשְׁקְלוּ־כֶסֶף בְּלוֹא־ לֶחֶם וִיגִיעֲכֶם בְּלוֹא לְשָׂבְעָה שִׁמְעוּ שָׁמוֹעַ אֵלַי וְאִכְלוּ־ טוֹב וְתִתְעַנַּג בַּדֶּשֶׁן נַפְשְׁכֶם:	Why do you spend money for that which is not bread and toil for that which does not satiate you? Listen carefully to Me and you shall eat well, and your soul shall delight itself in luxury.[324]
הֲלוֹא פָרֹס לָרָעֵב לַחְמֶךָ וַעֲנִיִּים מְרוּדִים תָּבִיא בָיִת כִּי־תִרְאֶה עָרֹם וְכִסִּיתוֹ וּמִבְּשָׂרְךָ לֹא תִתְעַלָּם:	Should you not share your bread with the hungry and bring the destitute and homeless to your house from your own flesh and blood?[325]
וְיַיִן יְשַׂמַּח לְבַב־אֱנוֹשׁ לְהַצְהִיל פָּנִים מִשָּׁמֶן וְלֶחֶם לְבַב־אֱנוֹשׁ יִסְעָד:	And wine which gladdens man's heart, oil to brighten his face, and bread to satiate him.[326]
טֶרֶף נָתַן לִירֵאָיו יִזְכֹּר לְעוֹלָם בְּרִיתוֹ:	He has given food to those who fear Him; He will always keep in mind His covenant.[327]
עֹשֶׂה מִשְׁפָּט לָעֲשׁוּקִים נֹתֵן לֶחֶם לָרְעֵבִים יְהוָה מַתִּיר אֲסוּרִים:	He executes judgment on behalf of the oppressed and gives bread to the starving: it is the Eternal who frees the imprisoned.[328]

---

[321] Ibid. 23:25
[322] Devarim 8:3
[323] Yeshayahu 33:16
[324] Ibid. 55:2
[325] Ibid. 58:7
[326] Tehillim 104:15
[327] Ibid. 111:5
[328] Ibid. 146:7

The above nine verses whose recital guarantees a person his food are occasionally said at the conclusion of a *siyum*.[329] However, I have rarely seen them being recited.

---

[329] Ta'amay Haminhagim: Birchas Hamazon #183

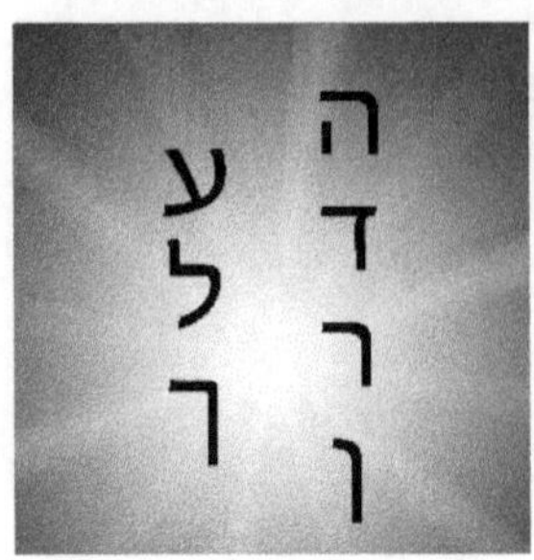

MISHNAH TAMID 7:4

AT THIS POINT IN THE *Hadran*, in honor of the completion of a *seder* of Mishnayos, it is customary to recite the final Mishnah of Tractate Tamid which speaks of the Tehillim which the Levites used to chant in the morning and evening at the time the Libation-Offering was poured upon the Altar in the Temple.[330] See Appendix Two[331] for the entire Mishnah in Tamid with its translation, while here, I will expand it and expound on it.

Instead of disputes between sages, heaps of logic, and laws, we get an intricate description of the Temple service. Indeed, although the language is rabbinic Hebrew, its descriptive style is more characteristic of the Torah than of rabbinic literature. It is likely that these descriptions, or at least parts thereof, come from Temple times. They were preserved because the rabbis fervently hoped the Temple would be rebuilt during their lifetimes. Part of the prayers we say at a siyum, express the hopes that the Holy Temple will be built speedily in our day. Even though it was performed every day, twice every day, they do not seem to have lost their sense of wonder at the intimate connection that they received with God through the sacrificial process.

These verses were probably added in place of the ten sons of Rav Papa – as it was hardly considered proper to mention Amoraim after completing a *seder* of *Mishnayos* whose authors were all Tannaim. But

---

[330] Tiferes Yisrael: Ad. loc.
[331] See Page 212

just as the names of Rav Papa and his ten sons were mentioned to recall Creation – a Creation devoted to Torah – so too, do these verses remind Jewry of the seven days of the beginning and encourage the masses to devote their time to learning Torah. As mentioned above, the last Mishnah of Tamid (without all the extras I included below) is said before the *Kaddish HaGadol*.

THE TEMPLE TEHILLIM

השיר שהיו הלוים אומרים במקדש,

The song that the Levites were accustomed to chant in the Temple

These Tehillim, alluded to by their opening line in this Mishnah, were recited in their entirety on their respective day in honor of God.[332]

SUNDAY

ביום הראשון היו אומרים: "לה' הארץ ומלואה, תבל וישבי בה".

On Sundays, they used to recite, "The Earth and all its contents, the inhabited world and those who dwell in it, belong to the Eternal."[333]

They chanted the entire Tehillim 24.[334]

Table 11 Temple Tehillim for Sunday

HEBREW		ENGLISH
לְדָוִד מִזְמוֹר לַיהוָה הָאָרֶץ וּמְלוֹאָהּ תֵּבֵל וְיֹשְׁבֵי בָהּ:	1	A psalm of David: The Earth and its contents, the inhabited world, and those who dwell in it, belong to the Eternal.

---

332 Tiferes Yisrael: Tamid 7:4
333 Tehillim 24:1
334 Tiferes Yisrael

Hebrew	#	English
כִּי־הוּא עַל־יַמִּים יְסָדָהּ וְעַל־נְהָרוֹת יְכוֹנְנֶהָ׃	2	For He founded it upon the oceans and established it upon the rivers.
מִי־יַעֲלֶה בְהַר־יְהֹוָה וּמִי־יָקוּם בִּמְקוֹם קָדְשׁוֹ׃	3	Who may ascend the mountain of the Eternal (Mount Moriah – the site of the Temple) and who may stand in the place (the Temple Court) of his holiness?
נְקִי כַפַּיִם וּבַר־לֵבָב אֲשֶׁר לֹא־נָשָׂא לַשָּׁוְא נַפְשִׁי וְלֹא נִשְׁבַּע לְמִרְמָה׃	4	He whose hands are clean (from sin) and whose heart is pure (and free of the thought of committing a transgression): one whose piety is genuine, a person who will not take an oath (with God's Name) to deceive others.
יִשָּׂא בְרָכָה מֵאֵת יְהֹוָה וּצְדָקָה מֵאֱלֹהֵי יִשְׁעוֹ׃	5	Such an individual will receive the Eternal's blessings, and righteousness from the Almighty for his salvation.
זֶה דּוֹר דרשו [דֹּרְשָׁיו] מְבַקְשֵׁי פָנֶיךָ יַעֲקֹב סֶלָה׃	6	This is the generation of those who seek Him; those who beseech the (God of) Yaakov (to reveal His) Presence forever.
שְׂאוּ שְׁעָרִים רָאשֵׁיכֶם וְהִנָּשְׂאוּ פִּתְחֵי עוֹלָם וְיָבוֹא מֶלֶךְ הַכָּבוֹד׃	7	Lift up your heads, ye gates, and be lifted up (your) portals to eternity, so that the King of Glory may enter.
מִי זֶה מֶלֶךְ הַכָּבוֹד יְהֹוָה עִזּוּז וְגִבּוֹר יְהֹוָה גִּבּוֹר מִלְחָמָה׃	8	Who is this King of Glory? The Eternal, strong and mighty; the Eternal, the Mighty One in battle.
שְׂאוּ שְׁעָרִים רָאשֵׁיכֶם וּשְׂאוּ פִּתְחֵי עוֹלָם וְיָבֹא מֶלֶךְ הַכָּבוֹד׃	9	Lift up your heads, ye gates, and lift up (you) portals to Eternity, so that the King of Glory may enter.
מִי הוּא זֶה מֶלֶךְ הַכָּבוֹד יְהֹוָה צְבָאוֹת הוּא מֶלֶךְ הַכָּבוֹד סֶלָה׃	10	Who, then, is this King of Glory? The Eternal of Hosts. He is the King of Glory forever.

The reason this psalm was chosen for the first day of the week was that it is reminiscent of the first day of Creation when God took possession of His newly formed universe for Himself to give it to mankind for their benefit while remaining its sole Master.[335]

For this reason, the psalmist reiterates that the world belongs to God and is given to man only on the condition that he sanctify himself by purging his body and soul of all iniquity so that he may enter God's House in righteousness as a worthy recipient of the Almighty's blessings and a proper vessel to glorify God's Name.

MONDAY

בשני היו אומרים: "גדול ה' ומהלל מאד בעיר אלקינו הר קדשו".
On Mondays, they said, "The Eternal is great and should be highly praised in the city of the A-mighty, the mountain of His sanctity."[336]

Psalm #48 is among the eleven Tehillim composed by the righteous sons of Korach, namely Psalms #42 – 49, #84 – 85, and #87 – 88. The entirety of each of these Tehillim was chanted by the Levites.[337]

Table 12 Temple Tehillim for Monday

HEBREW		ENGLISH
שִׁיר מִזְמוֹר לִבְנֵי־קֹרַח:	1	A song, a psalm by the sons of Korach:
גָּדוֹל יְהוָה וּמְהֻלָּל מְאֹד בְּעִיר אֱלֹהֵינוּ הַר־קָדְשׁוֹ:	2	The Lord is great and much acclaimed in the city of our God, His holy mountain
יְפֵה נוֹף מְשׂוֹשׂ כָּל־הָאָרֶץ הַר־צִיּוֹן יַרְכְּתֵי צָפוֹן קִרְיַת מֶלֶךְ רָב:	3	The fair-crested, joy of all the earth, Mount Zion, summit of Tzaphon, city of the great king.
אֱלֹהִים בְּאַרְמְנוֹתֶיהָ נוֹדַע לְמִשְׂגָּב:	4	Through its citadels, God has made Himself known as a haven.
כִּי־הִנֵּה הַמְּלָכִים נוֹעֲדוּ עָבְרוּ יַחְדָּו:	5	Because the kings were assembled (for an assault upon Yerushalayim) and they joined forces (in the attack),
הֵמָּה רָאוּ כֵּן תָּמָהוּ נִבְהֲלוּ נֶחְפָּזוּ:	6	But as soon as they beheld (the magnificent sight of the city), they

---

[335] Rosh Hashanah 31a
[336] Tehillim 48:2
[337] Tiferes Yisrael: Tamid 7:4

Hebrew	#	English
		became confused and frightened, and they fled.
רְעָדָה אֲחָזָתַם שָׁם חִיל כַּיּוֹלֵדָה:	7	Terror clawed at them, and pain like a woman in labor.
בְּרוּחַ קָדִים תְּשַׁבֵּר אֳנִיּוֹת תַּרְשִׁישׁ:	8	With an East Wind, you shattered the ships of Tarshish.
כַּאֲשֶׁר שָׁמַעְנוּ כֵּן רָאִינוּ בְּעִיר־יְהֹוָה צְבָאוֹת בְּעִיר אֱלֹהֵינוּ אֱלֹהִים יְכוֹנְנֶהָ עַד־עוֹלָם סֶלָה:	9	As we heard, so did we see in the city of the Eternal of hosts, in the metropolis of our Almighty – may the Almighty establish it forever and ever.
דִּמִּינוּ אֱלֹהִים חַסְדֶּךָ בְּקֶרֶב הֵיכָלֶךָ:	10	We contemplated your lovingkindness, Almighty, within Your Temple.
כְּשִׁמְךָ אֱלֹהִים כֵּן תְּהִלָּתְךָ עַל־קַצְוֵי־אֶרֶץ צֶדֶק מָלְאָה יְמִינֶךָ:	11	As Your Name, Almighty, so is Your praise to the ends of the earth (as Your wondrous deeds certainly match the prophetic descriptions of Your might). Your right hand is full of righteousness.
יִשְׂמַח הַר־צִיּוֹן תָּגֵלְנָה בְּנוֹת יְהוּדָה לְמַעַן מִשְׁפָּטֶיךָ:	12	Let Mount Zion rejoice, the cities of Judea exult, on account of Your judgments.
סֹבּוּ צִיּוֹן וְהַקִּיפוּהָ סִפְרוּ מִגְדָּלֶיהָ:	13	Surround Zion and encircle her. Count her towers,
שִׁיתוּ לִבְּכֶם לְחֵילָה פַּסְּגוּ אַרְמְנוֹתֶיהָ לְמַעַן תְּסַפְּרוּ לְדוֹר אַחֲרוֹן:	14	Consider well her ramparts, and think about her palaces so that you may tell of it to further generations,
כִּי זֶה אֱלֹהִים אֱלֹהֵינוּ עוֹלָם וָעֶד הוּא יְנַהֲגֵנוּ עַל־מוּת:	15	For this is the Almighty, our Almighty for all time. He will lead us beyond death.

This song was chanted in honor of the second day of Creation when the Lord separated the Heavenly and earthly parts of the Universe, and even though He ascended to Heaven, as it were, He still guides the destiny of the world; the Universe was not simply created and then abandoned to its fate. For this reason, this psalm is devoted to demonstrating the fact that the Lord always protects Jewry against her enemies and keeps her alive in the face of impossible odds in anticipation of the day when the Temple will be rebuilt, and Yerushalayim's former beauty restored.[338]

TUESDAY

בשלישי היו אומרים "אלקים נצב בעדת קל בקרב אלקים ישפט".

On Tuesdays, they proclaimed, "The Almighty stands in the congregation of God; He judges in the midst of the judges."[339]

Tehillim #82 is one of the twelve psalms written by Assaf. He composed chapters #50 and #73 – 83 and was one of the ten men who contributed his expertise to the creation of the book of Tehillim.

Table 13 Temple Tehillim for Tuesday

HEBREW		ENGLISH
מִזְמוֹר לְאָסָף אֱלֹהִים נִצָּב בַּעֲדַת־אֵל בְּקֶרֶב אֱלֹהִים יִשְׁפֹּט:	1	A psalm of Asaph. God stands in the divine assembly; among the divine beings, He pronounces judgment.
עַד־מָתַי תִּשְׁפְּטוּ־עָוֶל וּפְנֵי רְשָׁעִים תִּשְׂאוּ־סֶלָה:	2	How long will you judge perversely, showing favor to the wicked? *Selah.*
שִׁפְטוּ־דַל וְיָתוֹם עָנִי וָרָשׁ הַצְדִּיקוּ:	3	Judge the wretched and the orphan, vindicate the lowly and the poor,
פַּלְּטוּ־דַל וְאֶבְיוֹן מִיַּד רְשָׁעִים הַצִּילוּ:	4	Rescue the wretched and the needy; save them from the hand of the wicked.
לֹא יָדְעוּ וְלֹא יָבִינוּ בַּחֲשֵׁכָה יִתְהַלָּכוּ יִמּוֹטוּ כָּל־מוֹסְדֵי אָרֶץ:	5	They neither know nor understand, they go about in darkness; all the foundations of the earth totter.
אֲנִי־אָמַרְתִּי אֱלֹהִים אַתֶּם וּבְנֵי עֶלְיוֹן כֻּלְּכֶם:	6	I had taken you for divine beings, sons of the Most High, all of you;
אָכֵן כְּאָדָם תְּמוּתוּן וּכְאַחַד הַשָּׂרִים תִּפֹּלוּ:	7	But you shall die as men do, fall like any prince.
קוּמָה אֱלֹהִים שָׁפְטָה הָאָרֶץ כִּי־אַתָּה תִנְחַל בְּכָל־הַגּוֹיִם:	8	Arise, O' God, judge the earth, for all the nations are Your possession.

---

[338] Rosh HaShanah 31a; Tiferes Yisrael 7:4
[339] Tehillim 82:1

On the Third Day of Creation, God set aside boundaries to the oceans and thereby created land masses – a locale for humans to populate with a law-abiding society that is judged with justice.[340]

WEDNESDAY

ברביעי היו אומרים "קל נקמות ה', קל נקמות הופיע וגו'."
On Wednesdays, they declared, "The Almighty is a God of vengeance. God of vengeance – Reveal yourself!"[341]

The entire chapter of 94 was recited in the Temple on Wednesdays.[342]

Table 14 Temple Tehillim for Wednesday

HEBREW		ENGLISH
אֵל־נְקָמוֹת יְהֹוָה אֵל נְקָמוֹת הוֹפִיעַ:	1	God of retribution, Lord, God of retribution, appear!
הִנָּשֵׂא שֹׁפֵט הָאָרֶץ הָשֵׁב גְּמוּל עַל־גֵּאִים:	2	Rise up, judge of the earth, give the arrogant their deserts!
עַד־מָתַי רְשָׁעִים יְהֹוָה עַד־מָתַי רְשָׁעִים יַעֲלֹזוּ:	3	How long shall the wicked, O' Lord, how long shall the wicked exult,
יַבִּיעוּ יְדַבְּרוּ עָתָק יִתְאַמְּרוּ כָּל־פֹּעֲלֵי אָוֶן:	4	Shall they utter insolent speech, shall all evildoers vaunt themselves?
עַמְּךָ יְהֹוָה יְדַכְּאוּ וְנַחֲלָתְךָ יְעַנּוּ:	5	They crush Your people, O' Lord, they afflict Your very own;
אַלְמָנָה וְגֵר יַהֲרֹגוּ וִיתוֹמִים יְרַצֵּחוּ:	6	They kill the widow and the stranger; they murder the fatherless,
וַיֹּאמְרוּ לֹא יִרְאֶה־יָּהּ וְלֹא־יָבִין אֱלֹהֵי יַעֲקֹב:	7	Thinking, "The Lord does not see it, the God of Yaakob does not pay heed."
בִּינוּ בֹּעֲרִים בָּעָם וּכְסִילִים מָתַי תַּשְׂכִּילוּ:	8	Take heed, you most brutish people; fools, when will you get wisdom?

---

[340] Rosh Hashanah 31a; Tiferes Yisrael and Tosefos Yom Tov: Tamid 7:4
[341] Tehillim 94:1
[342] Tiferes Yisrael: Tamid 7:4

Hebrew	#	English
הֲנֹטַע אֹזֶן הֲלֹא יִשְׁמָע אִם־יֹצֵר עַיִן הֲלֹא יַבִּיט:	9	Shall He who implants the ear not hear, He who forms the eye not see?
הֲיֹסֵר גּוֹיִם הֲלֹא יוֹכִיחַ הַמְלַמֵּד אָדָם דָּעַת:	10	Shall He who disciplines nations not punish, He who instructs men in knowledge?
יְהוָה יֹדֵעַ מַחְשְׁבוֹת אָדָם כִּי־הֵמָּה הָבֶל:	11	The Lord knows the designs of men to be futile.
אַשְׁרֵי הַגֶּבֶר אֲשֶׁר־תְּיַסְּרֶנּוּ יָּהּ וּמִתּוֹרָתְךָ תְלַמְּדֶנּוּ:	12	Happy is the man whom You discipline, O' Lord, the man You instruct in Your teaching,
לְהַשְׁקִיט לוֹ מִימֵי רָע עַד יִכָּרֶה לָרָשָׁע שָׁחַת:	13	To give him tranquility in times of misfortune, until a pit be dug for the wicked.
כִּי לֹא־יִטֹּשׁ יְהוָה עַמּוֹ וְנַחֲלָתוֹ לֹא יַעֲזֹב:	14	For the Lord will not forsake His people; He will not abandon His very own.
כִּי־עַד־צֶדֶק יָשׁוּב מִשְׁפָּט וְאַחֲרָיו כָּל־יִשְׁרֵי־לֵב:	15	Judgment shall again accord with justice and all the upright shall rally to it.
מִי־יָקוּם לִי עִם־מְרֵעִים מִי־יִתְיַצֵּב לִי עִם־פֹּעֲלֵי אָוֶן:	16	Who will take my part against evil men? Who will stand up for me against wrongdoers?
לוּלֵי יְהוָה עֶזְרָתָה לִּי כִּמְעַט שָׁכְנָה דוּמָה נַפְשִׁי:	17	Were not the Lord my help, I should soon dwell in silence.
אִם־אָמַרְתִּי מָטָה רַגְלִי חַסְדְּךָ יְהוָה יִסְעָדֵנִי:	18	When I think my foot has given way, Your faithfulness, O' Lord, supports me.
בְּרֹב שַׂרְעַפַּי בְּקִרְבִּי תַּנְחוּמֶיךָ יְשַׁעַשְׁעוּ נַפְשִׁי:	19	When I am filled with cares, Your assurance soothes my soul.
הַיְחָבְרְךָ כִּסֵּא הַוּוֹת יֹצֵר עָמָל עֲלֵי־חֹק:	20	Shall the seat of injustice be Your partner, that frames mischief by statute?
יָגוֹדּוּ עַל־נֶפֶשׁ צַדִּיק וְדָם נָקִי יַרְשִׁיעוּ:	21	They band together to do away with the righteous; they condemn the innocent to death.
וַיְהִי יְהוָה לִי לְמִשְׂגָּב וֵאלֹהַי לְצוּר מַחְסִי:	22	But the Lord is my haven; my God is my sheltering rock.
וַיָּשֶׁב עֲלֵיהֶם אֶת־אוֹנָם וּבְרָעָתָם יַצְמִיתֵם יַצְמִיתֵם יְהוָה אֱלֹהֵינוּ:	23	He will make their evil recoil upon them, annihilate them through their own wickedness; the Lord our God will annihilate them.

The sun, moon, and stars were made on the Fourth day of Creation. Those who worshipped these celestial beings were destined to be destroyed for their insolence.[343]

This chapter thus declares that the Lord is a God of vengeance who will enact retribution from the iniquitous, for idolatry in one form or another, has been the catalyst that has led people astray. Judges have been corrupted by the god of money, and businessmen cheat their customers to pay homage to gold and silver coins. And although the wicked seem to lead triumphant lives while they may stomp the weak underfoot, oppress the poor, and exploit the needy, they will eventually be forced to account for their actions. The meek, shall indeed one day inherit the earth when the righteous are granted their reward for their faithful attachment to God and Torah.

THURSDAY

בחמישי היו אומרים: "הרנינו לאלקים עוזנו, הריעו לאלקי יעקב."
On Thursdays, they chant, "Joyously sing to the Almighty, our strength. Sounds (trumpets) to the Almighty of Yaakov."[344]

Tehillim #81 is one of the twelve written by Assaf and sung to the accompaniment of a musical instrument manufactured in the township of Gat called appropriately enough a *Gittis*.[345]

Table 15 Temple Tehillim for Thursday

HEBREW		ENGLISH
לַמְנַצֵּחַ עַל־הַגִּתִּית לְאָסָף׃	1	For the leader; on the *Gittis*. Of Asaph.
הַרְנִינוּ לֵאלֹהִים עוּזֵּנוּ הָרִיעוּ לֵאלֹהֵי יַעֲקֹב׃	2	Sing joyously to God, our strength; raise a shout for the God of Yaakov.
שְׂאוּ־זִמְרָה וּתְנוּ־תֹף כִּנּוֹר נָעִים עִם־נָבֶל׃	3	Take up the song, sound the timbrel, the melodious lyre and harp.
תִּקְעוּ בַחֹדֶשׁ שׁוֹפָר בַּכֶּסֶה לְיוֹם חַגֵּנוּ׃	4	Blow the horn on the new moon, on the full moon for our feast day.

---

[343] Rambam: Tamid 7 – 4; Rosh HaShanah 31a
[344] Tehillim 81:2
[345] Rashi: Tehillim 81:2

Hebrew	#	English
כִּי חֹק לְיִשְׂרָאֵל הוּא מִשְׁפָּט לֵאלֹהֵי יַעֲקֹב:	5	For it is a law for Israel, a ruling of the God of Yaakov;
עֵדוּת בִּיהוֹסֵף שָׂמוֹ בְּצֵאתוֹ עַל־אֶרֶץ מִצְרָיִם שְׂפַת לֹא־יָדַעְתִּי אֶשְׁמָע:	6	He imposed it as a decree upon Joseph when he went forth from the land of Egypt; I heard a language that I knew not.
הֲסִירוֹתִי מִסֵּבֶל שִׁכְמוֹ כַּפָּיו מִדּוּד תַּעֲבֹרְנָה:	7	I relieved his shoulder of the burden; his hands were freed from the basket.
בַּצָּרָה קָרָאתָ וָאֲחַלְּצֶךָּ אֶעֶנְךָ בְּסֵתֶר רַעַם אֶבְחָנְךָ עַל־מֵי מְרִיבָה סֶלָה:	8	In distress, you called, and I rescued you; I answered you from the secret place of thunder I tested you at the waters of Merivah. *Selah.*
שְׁמַע עַמִּי וְאָעִידָה בָּךְ יִשְׂרָאֵל אִם־תִּשְׁמַע־לִי:	9	Hear, My people, and I will admonish you; Israel, if you would but listen to Me!
לֹא־יִהְיֶה בְךָ אֵל זָר וְלֹא תִשְׁתַּחֲוֶה לְאֵל נֵכָר:	10	You shall have no foreign god, you shall not bow to an alien god.
אָנֹכִי יְהוָה אֱלֹהֶיךָ הַמַּעַלְךָ מֵאֶרֶץ מִצְרָיִם הַרְחֶב־פִּיךָ וַאֲמַלְאֵהוּ:	11	I the Lord am your God who brought you out of the land of Egypt; open your mouth wide and I will fill it.
וְלֹא־שָׁמַע עַמִּי לְקוֹלִי וְיִשְׂרָאֵל לֹא־אָבָה לִי:	12	But My people would not listen to Me, Israel would not obey Me.
וָאֲשַׁלְּחֵהוּ בִּשְׁרִירוּת לִבָּם יֵלְכוּ בְּמוֹעֲצוֹתֵיהֶם:	13	So I let them go after their willful heart that they might follow their own devices.
לוּ עַמִּי שֹׁמֵעַ לִי יִשְׂרָאֵל בִּדְרָכַי יְהַלֵּכוּ:	14	If only My people would listen to Me, if Israel would follow My paths,
כִּמְעַט אוֹיְבֵיהֶם אַכְנִיעַ וְעַל צָרֵיהֶם אָשִׁיב יָדִי:	15	Then would I subdue their enemies at once, strike their foes again and again.
מְשַׂנְאֵי יְהוָה יְכַחֲשׁוּ־לוֹ וִיהִי עִתָּם לְעוֹלָם:	16	Those who hate the Lord shall cower before Him; their doom shall be eternal.
וַיַּאֲכִילֵהוּ מֵחֵלֶב חִטָּה וּמִצּוּר דְּבַשׁ אַשְׂבִּיעֶךָ:	17	He fed them the finest wheat; I sated you with honey from the rock.

On the Fifth Day of Creation, God made birds and fish. When humanity views the myriad species of flyers and swimmers, they become awed by the miracle of Creation and spontaneously give thanks to God and praise Him endlessly.[346]

---

[346] Rosh Hashanah 31a; Tiferes Yisrael: Tamid 7:4

Not only must one praise the Lord with song and dance; but he must also recall the good that God has wrought throughout history just as this psalm proclaims.

FRIDAY

בששי היו אומרים: "ה' מלך גאות לבש וגו'".

On Fridays, they would say, "The Eternal reigns. He has clothed Himself with majesty, etc."

The entire Psalm 93 was recited:[347]

Table 16 Temple Tehillim for Friday

HEBREW		ENGLISH
יְהֹוָה מָלָךְ גֵּאוּת לָבֵשׁ לָבֵשׁ יְהֹוָה עֹז הִתְאַזָּר אַף־תִּכּוֹן תֵּבֵל בַּל־תִּמּוֹט:	1	The Lord is king, He is robed in grandeur; the Lord is robed, He is girded with strength. The world stands firm; it cannot be shaken.
נָכוֹן כִּסְאֲךָ מֵאָז מֵעוֹלָם אָתָּה:	2	Your throne stands firm from of old; from eternity You have existed.
נָשְׂאוּ נְהָרוֹת יְהֹוָה נָשְׂאוּ נְהָרוֹת קוֹלָם יִשְׂאוּ נְהָרוֹת דָּכְיָם:	3	The ocean sounds, O' Lord, the ocean sounds its thunder, the ocean sounds its pounding.
מִקֹּלוֹת מַיִם רַבִּים אַדִּירִים מִשְׁבְּרֵי־יָם אַדִּיר בַּמָּרוֹם יְהֹוָה:	4	Above the thunder of the mighty waters, more majestic than the breakers of the sea is the Lord, majestic on high.
עֵדֹתֶיךָ נֶאֶמְנוּ מְאֹד לְבֵיתְךָ נַאֲוָה־קֹדֶשׁ יְהֹוָה לְאֹרֶךְ יָמִים:	5	Your decrees are indeed enduring; holiness befits Your house, O' Lord, for all times.

On the Sixth Day of Creation, man was formed. With his keen intelligence. he was able to appreciate what God had done and perceive the magnificence of the Universe – the subject matter of this psalm.[348]

---

[347] Tiferes Yisrael: Tamid 7:4

[348] Rosh Hashana 31a; Rambam: Tamid 7:4

SHABBOS

בשבת היו אומרים: "מזמור שיר ליום השבת. מזמור שיר לעתיד לבא, ליום שכלו
שבת מנוחה לחיי העולמים:"

On Shabbos *they proclaim: "A psalm, a song for the Day of* Shabbos*".*[349]
A psalm, a song for the future – for the time that is one continuous Shabbos
of rest for all Creation.

Table 17 Temple Tehillim for Shabbos

HEBREW		**ENGLISH**
מִזְמוֹר שִׁיר לְיוֹם הַשַּׁבָּת:	1	A psalm. A song; for the *Shabbos* day.
טוֹב לְהֹדוֹת לַיהוָה וּלְזַמֵּר לְשִׁמְךָ עֶלְיוֹן:	2	It is good to praise the Lord, to sing hymns to Your name, O' Most High,
לְהַגִּיד בַּבֹּקֶר חַסְדֶּךָ וֶאֱמוּנָתְךָ בַּלֵּילוֹת:	3	To proclaim Your steadfast love at daybreak, Your faithfulness each night
עֲלֵי־עָשׂוֹר וַעֲלֵי־נָבֶל עֲלֵי הִגָּיוֹן בְּכִנּוֹר:	4	With a ten-stringed harp, with voice and lyre together.
כִּי שִׂמַּחְתַּנִי יְהוָה בְּפָעֳלֶךָ בְּמַעֲשֵׂי יָדֶיךָ אֲרַנֵּן:	5	You have gladdened me by Your deeds, O' Lord; I shout for joy at Your handiwork.
מַה־גָּדְלוּ מַעֲשֶׂיךָ יְהוָה מְאֹד עָמְקוּ מַחְשְׁבֹתֶיךָ:	6	How great are Your works, O' Lord, how very subtle Your designs!
אִישׁ־בַּעַר לֹא יֵדָע וּכְסִיל לֹא־יָבִין אֶת־זֹאת:	7	A brutish man cannot know, a fool cannot understand this:
בִּפְרֹחַ רְשָׁעִים כְּמוֹ עֵשֶׂב וַיָּצִיצוּ כָּל־פֹּעֲלֵי אָוֶן לְהִשָּׁמְדָם עֲדֵי־עַד:	8	Though the wicked sprout like grass, though all evildoers blossom, it is only that they may be destroyed forever.
וְאַתָּה מָרוֹם לְעֹלָם יְהוָה:	9	But You are exalted, O' Lord, for all time.
כִּי הִנֵּה אֹיְבֶיךָ יְהוָה כִּי־הִנֵּה אֹיְבֶיךָ יֹאבֵדוּ יִתְפָּרְדוּ כָּל־פֹּעֲלֵי אָוֶן:	10	Surely, Your enemies, O' Lord, surely, Your enemies perish; all evildoers are scattered.

---

[349] Tehillim 92:1

וַתָּרֶם כִּרְאֵים קַרְנִי בַּלֹּתִי בְּשֶׁמֶן רַעֲנָן׃	11	You raise my horn high like that of a wild ox; I am soaked in freshening oil.
וַתַּבֵּט עֵינִי בְּשׁוּרָי בַּקָּמִים עָלַי מְרֵעִים תִּשְׁמַעְנָה אָזְנָי׃	12	I shall see the defeat of my watchful foes, hear of the downfall of the wicked who beset me.
צַדִּיק כַּתָּמָר יִפְרָח כְּאֶרֶז בַּלְּבָנוֹן יִשְׂגֶּה׃	13	The righteous bloom like a date palm; they thrive like a cedar in Lebanon;
שְׁתוּלִים בְּבֵית יְהוָה בְּחַצְרוֹת אֱלֹהֵינוּ יַפְרִיחוּ׃	14	Planted in the house of the Lord, they flourish in the courts of our God.
עוֹד יְנוּבוּן בְּשֵׂיבָה דְּשֵׁנִים וְרַעֲנַנִּים יִהְיוּ׃	15	In old age they still produce fruit; they are full of sap and freshness,
לְהַגִּיד כִּי־יָשָׁר יְהוָה צוּרִי וְלֹא־עֹלָתה [עַוְלָתָה] בּוֹ׃	16	Attesting that the Lord is upright, my rock, in whom there is no wrong.

On *Shabbos* mornings, the Levites sang the entire Psalm #92. At the *Musaf* Services, they chanted selections from *Parshas Haazinu*, and at *Mincha* time, they sang a portion from the "Song upon the Red Sea" (as shall be explained later in this commentary).[350]

This phrase, "A psalm, a song for the future – for the time that is one continuous *Shabbos* of rest for all Creation" was not chanted by the Levites. This segment of the *Mishnah* is but an allusion to the reason why this psalm was recited on *Shabbos*, even though it does not mention a word about *Shabbos* Day itself. The Tanna explains that this psalm – in contradistinction to those recited on Sunday through Friday – speaks of the future rather than the past. This psalm speaks of three types of futures:

1. The future (מזמור שיר לעתיד לבא) – a psalm, a song for the future
2. The Hereafter, (ליום שכלו שבת) – a song for the time that is one continuous *Shabbos*
3. Gan Eden after the termination of this world – a place where all beings will rest for at least a thousand years until the Lord creates a new world, (מנוחה לחיי העולמים) – of rest for all Creation.[351]

We will now demonstrate how each section of the psalm alludes to one of these three futures.

---

[350] Tiferes Yisrael: Tamid 7:4
[351] Ibid.

(1) מזמור שיר ליום השבת.

1) A psalm, a song for the day of Shabbos.

Shabbos is a fine day to sing and play musical instruments in the Temple (in honor of God).[352] Nowadays, we do not play musical instruments on *Shabbos*, but they were permitted in the Holy Temple.

(2) טוב להודות לה' ולזמר לשמך עליון;

2) It is proper to give thanks to the Eternal and to sing (praises) to Your Name, (O God, the) Supreme.

On this day, when a person is free of the mundane worries of the workweek, he has ample time for introspection, and he can thank the Lord for the past good that He has bestowed upon him.[353]

Even if the person has suffered terribly in this lifetime, he should nonetheless rejuvenate his soul with song on *Shabbos* as this will strengthen his belief in God and bolster his faith regarding the future. Although the individual may not comprehend why tragedy or calamity is ultimately for his benefit, he will recognize that God is great and certainly knows how to do what is best for a person's welfare.[354]

(3) להגיד בבקר חסדך ואמונתך בלילות

3) To relate Your lovingkindness in the morning and Your faithfulness in the evening

When a person beholds the good that God has showered upon him, he must be cognizant that all this is from God, and that these benefits will increase exponentially in the future just as the morning brightens towards its noon zenith.[355]

If pain, anguish, and oppression cast a person into the deep blackness of the night, he too must have faith that these difficulties are analogous to a father disciplining his son and that all is ultimately for his benefit, even though these things are hidden from his view.[356]

---

[352] Ibid.

[353] Ibid.

[354] Ibid.

[355] Ibid.

[356] Ibid.

(4) עלי־עשור ועלי־נבל עלי הגיון בכנור

4) Upon (a musical instrument of) ten (strings) and upon the harp to the melody of the lyre

A person must serve the Lord in deed, word, and thought as symbolized by the playing of the instrument itself (action) the singing of this psalm (word), and the composition of the melody (thought). With all these powers, an individual is to permeate himself with the truth that all that God does is good.[357]

(5) כי שמחתני ה' בפעלך במעשי ידיך ארנן.

5) Because You have made me happy through Your actions. I will rejoice in the works of Your Hands.

When a person takes a good look at the world in general, he will note that it consists of contrasting elements; opposites such as day and night, winter and summer, and life and death. Yet all these things are good and benefit mankind in general and can be readily understood by all. For these things, a person should surely be happy.[358]

However, the Lord does not just guide the world in a general fashion; He takes care of each person on an individual basis providing him with what is best for his welfare. That realization should not just make a person happy; it should make him ecstatic![359]

(6) מה־גדלו מעשיך ה' מאד עמקו מחשבתיך.

6) How great are your works, Eternal; Your thoughts are so profound.

One can certainly appreciate the greatness of God in this world where He turns apparent darkness into light, the supposedly bitter into sweets, and the so-called bad into good. A person's mind, however, is incapable of grasping the profundities of God's treatment of individuals in

---

[357] Ibid.

[358] Ibid.

[359] Ibid.

the Hereafter when a person's body and soul are separated from one another.[360]

The psalm, having completed its discussion of life in this world, now elaborates upon the situation after a person dies and is taken before the Heavenly Court to account for his actions in this life, pending his judgment for life or death in the Hereafter.[361]

(7) אִישׁ־בַּעַר לֹא יֵדָע וּכְסִיל לֹא־יָבִין אֶת־זֹאת.

7) A barbarian cannot know, nor can a fool comprehend this.

The barbarian who is a slave to his animal instincts and constantly sins to satisfy his lusts and passions as well as the fool who intentionally discards the Torah in the erroneous belief that his life thoughts are the correct ones both miss the main point of existence and the purpose of life – to learn Torah and faithfully serve the Lord – a Lord who will reward those who hearken to His word and punish those who flaunt Him, as the next verse elucidates.[362]

(8) בִּפְרֹחַ רְשָׁעִים כְּמוֹ־עֵשֶׂב וַיָּצִיצוּ כָּל־פֹּעֲלֵי אָוֶן לְהִשָּׁמְדָם עֲדֵי־עַד.

8) When the wicked sprout up like grass and the iniquitous flourish, it is in order that they may be utterly destroyed forever.

The wicked "barbarian" and the iniquitous "fool" think that their success in this world is a result of their cunning and astuteness. They do not comprehend that the very prosperity is a sign of their permanent loss of Gan Eden and their ultimate destruction in Hell (as they are being paid now for their few good deeds so that they may be annihilated at a later stage.) These individuals, however, do not choose to investigate the matter and verify this truth.[363]

(9) וְאַתָּה מָרוֹם לְעֹלָם ה'.

9) And You, Eternal, are supreme forever.

---

[360] Ibid.

[361] Ibid.

[362] Ibid.

[363] Ibid.

The "barbarian" and "fool" think that their opulence is due to their efforts. However, their financial success is never assured as it is dependent upon the will of God Who may snatch it from them at any moment.[364]

(10) כי הנה איביך ה' כי־הנה אויביך יאבדו; יתפרדו כל־פעלי און.

10) But eventually Your enemies – Eternal – but eventually Your enemies will be annihilated; the iniquitous shall be scattered.

These sinners are not capable of winning their battle against God. Ultimately, they will die and be scattered *i.e.*, they will lose both this world and the next.[365]

(11) ותרם כראים קרני בלתי בשמן רענן.

11) On the other hand, You shall exalt my horn like that of a wild ox and anoint me with fragrant oil.

The term "קרן" (horn) also means "principle". The faithful servant of God who has not received the principle due him shall receive it in the World-to-Come and he will be strengthened in other ways as well. Moreover, death shall make him more beautiful in the Hereafter like the olive tree which lives a long time, always remains green, and continuously produces luscious fruit.[366]

(12) ותבט עיני בשורי בקמים עלי מרעים תשמענה אזני.

12) My eye has witnessed the downfall of my adversaries and my ears have heard the fate of the wicked who rise up against me.

Although many have tried to demonstrate the correctness of their path in life by showing off their visible wealth and others have tried to prove through philosophical argumentation the rightness of their lifestyles, the person who seeks to live after this world ceases to be is not fooled by any of this. He knows on faith that the Torah view is the only guarantee of true life.[367]

---

[364] Ibid.

[365] Ibid.

[366] Ibid.

[367] Ibid.

(13) ‫צדיק כתמר יפרח כארז בלבנון ישגה.‬
13) The righteous man will blossom like the Palm Tree; he will grow like a Cedar of Lebanon.

Just as the palm tree produces late in life, so too will the righteous ultimately receive their just reward in the Hereafter. And should one think that just as a palm tree that is cut down cannot be regenerated through grafting onto a young sapling, so too will the righteous be destroyed when the world ceases to exist after its final one thousand years, he is told that this is not the case. The righteous are like the cedar of Lebanon which may be given new life through grafting; when replanted in Gan Eden, they will live eternally with increased vigor and strength in the new world which the Lord will create.[368]

The remainder of the psalm now summarizes the three types of future that have just been defined and elaborated upon.[369]

(14) ‫שתולים בבית ה' בחצרות אלקינו יפריחו.‬
14) Those who are transplanted to the House of the Eternal shall flourish in the courtyard of the Almighty.

The righteous will be transplanted from this world and given new life in the Hereafter.[370]

(15) ‫עוד ינובון בשיבה דשנים ורעננים יהיו.‬
15) They still bear fruit in their old age, and they shall be well and robust

The righteous shall receive constant reward and continue to live in bliss for eternity.[371]

---

[368] Ibid.
[369] Ibid.
[370] Ibid.
[371] Ibid.

(16) ‫להגיד כי־ישר ה' צורי ולא־עולתה בו.‬

16) In order to declare that the Eternal is upright; He is my Rock and there is no fault in Him.

A person must never, Heaven forbid, deny that the righteous will not be compensated for their difficult lives; ultimately, they shall receive rewards that are beyond description.[372]

MUSAF SONGS OF SHABBOS DAY

IN THE TIMES OF THE Beis Hamikdash, the *musaf* Tehillim changed on a week-to-week basis for a total of six weeks and was then again repeated indefinitely. These six sections were taken from *Parshas Haazinu*. The first four selections contained six verses apiece, while the final two contained eight.[373]

According to the numbering system in today's texts, *Parshas Haazinu* contains forty-three verses rather than the forty implied by Rashi. Consequently, these three verses change the weekly numbers so that they are six, six, six, eight, nine, and eight respectively.[374]

WEEK ONE

Devarim 32:1 – 6

---

[372] Ibid.

[373] Rashi: Rosh HaShanah 31a - ‫ד"ה הזי"ו ל"ד‬; Tosefos: Ibid. - ‫ד"ה הזי"ו ל"ד‬, Tiferes Yisrael: Tamid 7:4

[374] The numbering of the *pesukim* of the Torah as we know them today was introduced in the thirteenth century by non-Jewish scholars. They did this to facilitate them remembering the verses for theological debates with Jewish rabbis.

MISHNAH TAMID 7:4

Table 18 Musaf of Week One

HEBREW		ENGLISH
הַאֲזִינוּ הַשָּׁמַיִם וַאֲדַבֵּרָה וְתִשְׁמַע הָאָרֶץ אִמְרֵי־פִי:	1	Listen, Heavens, and I will speak; pay heed, earth, to the words of My mouth.
יַעֲרֹף כַּמָּטָר לִקְחִי תִּזַּל כַּטַּל אִמְרָתִי כִּשְׂעִירִם עֲלֵי־דֶשֶׁא וְכִרְבִיבִים עֲלֵי־עֵשֶׂב:	2	My Torah shall saturate (you) as rain (does to the earth); My word shall invigorate like the dew – like gentle showers upon the vegetation, and strong rains upon the grass (and trees).
כִּי שֵׁם יְהֹוָה אֶקְרָא הָבוּ גֹדֶל לֵאלֹהֵינוּ:	3	When I mention the Name of the Eternal, you shall laud the greatness of our Almighty.
הַצּוּר תָּמִים פָּעֳלוֹ כִּי כָל־דְּרָכָיו מִשְׁפָּט אֵל אֱמוּנָה וְאֵין עָוֶל צַדִּיק וְיָשָׁר הוּא:	4	He is the Rock. His work is perfect, for all His ways are justice. He is the God of truth, free of iniquity; He is just and righteous.
שִׁחֵת לוֹ לֹא בָּנָיו מוּמָם דּוֹר עִקֵּשׁ וּפְתַלְתֹּל:	5	Corruption is not from Him, but rather the blemish of his children. They are a perverse and dishonest generation.
הֲ־לַיְהֹוָה תִּגְמְלוּ־זֹאת עַם נָבָל וְלֹא חָכָם הֲלוֹא־הוּא אָבִיךָ קָּנֶךָ הוּא עָשְׂךָ וַיְכֹנְנֶךָ:	6	Do you think the Eternal is the cause of this (state of affairs) you Nation of fools and imbeciles? Is He not your Father, to whom you owe gratitude; He made you and established you.

WEEK TWO

Devarim 32:7 – 12

Table 19 Musaf of Week Two

HEBREW		ENGLISH
זְכֹר יְמוֹת עוֹלָם בִּינוּ שְׁנוֹת דּוֹר־וָדוֹר שְׁאַל אָבִיךָ וְיַגֵּדְךָ זְקֵנֶיךָ וְיֹאמְרוּ לָךְ:	7	Remember the days of old. Contemplate the years of countless generations. Ask your father, and he will explain it to you; your elders, and they will tell you.

Hebrew		English
בְּהַנְחֵל עֶלְיוֹן גּוֹיִם בְּהַפְרִידוֹ בְּנֵי אָדָם יַצֵּב גְּבֻלֹת עַמִּים לְמִסְפַּר בְּנֵי יִשְׂרָאֵל:	8	When the Supreme gave the Gentiles an inheritance and He separated the sons of Adam, He established a limit to the nations in accordance with the population of Jewry.
כִּי חֵלֶק יְהֹוָה עַמּוֹ יַעֲקֹב חֶבֶל נַחֲלָתוֹ:	9	The Eternal's portion is His People; Yaakov is the lot of His inheritance.
יִמְצָאֵהוּ בְּאֶרֶץ מִדְבָּר וּבְתֹהוּ יְלֵל יְשִׁמֹן יְסֹבְבֶנְהוּ יְבוֹנְנֵהוּ יִצְּרֶנְהוּ כְּאִישׁוֹן עֵינוֹ:	10	He found him in a desert land, in the waste of a howling wilderness. He led him about and He instructed him; He watched over him like the apple of His eye.
כְּנֶשֶׁר יָעִיר קִנּוֹ עַל־גּוֹזָלָיו יְרַחֵף יִפְרֹשׂ כְּנָפָיו יִקָּחֵהוּ יִשָּׂאֵהוּ עַל־אֶבְרָתוֹ:	11	As an eagle stirs up her nest, broods over her young, spreads abroad her wings, takes them and carries them aloft on her wings.
יְהֹוָה בָּדָד יַנְחֶנּוּ וְאֵין עִמּוֹ אֵל נֵכָר:	12	So too did the Eternal alone guide him. There is no strange god with him.

WEEK THREE

Devarim 32:13 – 18

Table 20 Musaf of Week Three

HEBREW		**ENGLISH**
יַרְכִּבֵהוּ עַל־במותי (בָּמֳתֵי) אֶרֶץ וַיֹּאכַל תְּנוּבֹת שָׂדָי וַיֵּנִקֵהוּ דְבַשׁ מִסֶּלַע וְשֶׁמֶן מֵחַלְמִישׁ צוּר:	13	He made him ride on the high places of the earth, and he ate the produce of the fields. He made him suck honey out of rocks and oil from flinty stones.
חֶמְאַת בָּקָר וַחֲלֵב צֹאן עִם־חֵלֶב כָּרִים וְאֵילִים בְּנֵי־בָשָׁן וְעַתּוּדִים עִם־חֵלֶב כִּלְיוֹת חִטָּה וְדַם־עֵנָב תִּשְׁתֶּה־חָמֶר:	14	Cattle butter and sheep's milk together with the fat of lambs, Bashan rams, and goats, with the fat of wheat kidneys – and you drank red wine of the vine.
וַיִּשְׁמַן יְשֻׁרוּן וַיִּבְעָט שָׁמַנְתָּ עָבִיתָ כָּשִׂיתָ וַיִּטֹּשׁ אֱלוֹהַּ עָשָׂהוּ וַיְנַבֵּל צוּר יְשֻׁעָתוֹ:	15	But Yeshurun (Jewry) grew fat and kicked. You have become corpulent, thick, and blubbery; He forsook his

HEBREW		ENGLISH
		Almighty who made him and treated with scorn the Rock of his salvation.
יַקְנִאֻהוּ בְּזָרִים בְּתוֹעֵבֹת יַכְעִיסֻהוּ:	16	They antagonized Him with strange gods and angered Him with abominations.
יִזְבְּחוּ לַשֵּׁדִים לֹא אֱלֹהַּ אֱלֹהִים לֹא יְדָעוּם חֲדָשִׁים מִקָּרֹב בָּאוּ לֹא שְׂעָרוּם אֲבֹתֵיכֶם:	17	They sacrificed to powerless spirits, to foreign gods – to new idols recently created whom your ancestors did not revere.
צוּר יְלָדְךָ תֶּשִׁי וַתִּשְׁכַּח אֵל מְחֹלְלֶךָ:	18	You do not consider the Rock that made you, and you have forgotten that God who formed you.

WEEK FOUR

Devarim 32:19 – 26

Table 21 Musaf of Week Four

HEBREW		ENGLISH
וַיַּרְא יְהֹוָה וַיִּנְאָץ מִכַּעַס בָּנָיו וּבְנֹתָיו:	19	The Eternal saw this and He was angered by the provocations of his sons and daughters.
וַיֹּאמֶר אַסְתִּירָה פָנַי מֵהֶם אֶרְאֶה מָה אַחֲרִיתָם כִּי דוֹר תַּהְפֻּכֹת הֵמָּה בָּנִים לֹא־אֵמֻן בָּם:	20	He said: "I will conceal My face from them. I will see what their End shall be for they are a topsy-turvey Nation – children utterly lacking in piety.
הֵם קִנְאוּנִי בְלֹא־אֵל כִּעֲסוּנִי בְּהַבְלֵיהֶם וַאֲנִי אַקְנִיאֵם בְּלֹא־עָם בְּגוֹי נָבָל אַכְעִיסֵם:	21	They have aroused my vengeance with false gods and angered Me with their vanities. I will therefore upset them with a vile People, and I will anger them with a perverse Nation.
כִּי־אֵשׁ קָדְחָה בְאַפִּי וַתִּיקַד עַד־שְׁאוֹל תַּחְתִּית וַתֹּאכַל אֶרֶץ וִיבֻלָהּ וַתְּלַהֵט מוֹסְדֵי הָרִים:	22	For fire shall rage in My anger and sear to the deepest parts of the earth, and consume the land with its produce, and set on fire the foundations of the mountains.

אַסְפֶּה עָלֵימוֹ רָעוֹת חִצַּי אֲכַלֶּה־בָּם:	23	I will heap tragedies upon them. My arrows shall finish them off.
מְזֵי רָעָב וּלְחֻמֵי רֶשֶׁף וְקֶטֶב מְרִירִי וְשֶׁן־בְּהֵמוֹת אֲשַׁלַּח־בָּם עִם־חֲמַת זֹחֲלֵי עָפָר:	24	They shall be sucked dry by hunger and devoured with blistering heat and terrible afflictions. I will also dispatch the teeth of beasts against them together with the venom of things that crawl in the dust.
מִחוּץ תְּשַׁכֶּל־חֶרֶב וּמֵחֲדָרִים אֵימָה גַּם־בָּחוּר גַּם־בְּתוּלָה יוֹנֵק עִם־אִישׁ שֵׂיבָה:	25	The sword without, and terror within, shall destroy both the youngster and the virgin, the nursing infant and the aged.
אָמַרְתִּי אַפְאֵיהֶם אַשְׁבִּיתָה מֵאֱנוֹשׁ זִכְרָם:	26	I said that I would disperse them (throughout the world) and cause men to forget them".

WEEK FIVE

Devarim 32:27 – 35

Table 22 Musaf of Week Five

HEBREW		**ENGLISH**
לוּלֵי כַּעַס אוֹיֵב אָגוּר פֶּן־יְנַכְּרוּ צָרֵימוֹ פֶּן־יֹאמְרוּ יָדֵינוּ רָמָה וְלֹא יְהֹוָה פָּעַל כָּל־זֹאת:	27	(I would have done all the aforementioned) if not for the heaped-up wrath of the enemy lest these adversaries discount (God) and claim: "Our land is mighty, and it is not the Eternal who has done this."
כִּי־גוֹי אֹבַד עֵצוֹת הֵמָּה וְאֵין בָּהֶם תְּבוּנָה:	28	For they are a nation devoid of counsel and lacking in perception.
לוּ חָכְמוּ יַשְׂכִּילוּ זֹאת יָבִינוּ לְאַחֲרִיתָם:	29	If they are wise, they would understand this; they would consider their fate.
אֵיכָה יִרְדֹּף אֶחָד אֶלֶף וּשְׁנַיִם יָנִיסוּ רְבָבָה אִם־לֹא כִּי־צוּרָם מְכָרָם וַיהֹוָה הִסְגִּירָם:	30	How is it possible for one (man) to rout a thousand or two to panic ten thousand if the Rock had not abandoned them, or the Eternal not locked them up?
כִּי לֹא כְצוּרֵנוּ צוּרָם וְאֹיְבֵינוּ פְּלִילִים:	31	Our Rock is not like theirs, as even our enemies are (our) magistrates.

Hebrew		English
כִּי־מִגֶּפֶן סְדֹם גַּפְנָם וּמִשַּׁדְמֹת עֲמֹרָה עֲנָבֵמוֹ עִנְּבֵי־רוֹשׁ אַשְׁכְּלֹת מְרֹרֹת לָמוֹ:	32	Their vine is of the vine of Sodom and of the fields of Amorah. Their grapes are full of sores, and their clusters are bitter.
חֲמַת תַּנִּינִם יֵינָם וְרֹאשׁ פְּתָנִים אַכְזָר:	33	Their wine is as fierce as sea monsters, and the poison of wasps.
הֲלֹא־הוּא כָּמֻס עִמָּדִי חָתֻם בְּאוֹצְרֹתָי:	34	Is this not in My storage, and sealed up among My treasures?
לִי נָקָם וְשִׁלֵּם לְעֵת תָּמוּט רַגְלָם כִּי קָרוֹב יוֹם אֵידָם וְחָשׁ עֲתִדֹת לָמוֹ:	35	To me belong vengeance and recompense, when their foot slips, as their final reckoning is at hand, and their fate is imminent.

WEEK SIX

Devarim 32:36 – 43

Table 23 Musaf of Week Six

HEBREW		ENGLISH
כִּי־יָדִין יְהֹוָה עַמּוֹ וְעַל־עֲבָדָיו יִתְנֶחָם כִּי יִרְאֶה כִּי־אָזְלַת יָד וְאֶפֶס עָצוּר וְעָזוּב:	36	For the Eternal shall judge His People and avenge Himself for his servants when he sees that their energy has dissipated, and nothing is left over in the reserve.
וְאָמַר אֵי אֱלֹהֵימוֹ צוּר חָסָיוּ בוֹ:	37	And He shall ask where their gods are, their rock in whom they placed their faith.
אֲשֶׁר חֵלֶב זְבָחֵימוֹ יֹאכֵלוּ יִשְׁתּוּ יֵין נְסִיכָם יָקוּמוּ וְיַעְזְרֻכֶם יְהִי עֲלֵיכֶם סִתְרָה:	38	Let those who ate the fat of their sacrifices and drank their Libation-Offerings rise up and help you and be your protection.
רְאוּ עַתָּה כִּי אֲנִי אֲנִי הוּא וְאֵין אֱלֹהִים עִמָּדִי אֲנִי אָמִית וַאֲחַיֶּה מָחַצְתִּי וַאֲנִי אֶרְפָּא וְאֵין מִיָּדִי מַצִּיל:	39	Behold that I, just I, am He and there is no god beside Me. I (alone) cause death and grant life, I wound, and I cure, and no one can flee My clutches.

כִּי־אֶשָּׂא אֶל־שָׁמַיִם יָדִי וְאָמַרְתִּי חַי אָנֹכִי לְעֹלָם:	40	For I lift up My hand to the Heaven and proclaim: "I live forever."
אִם־שַׁנּוֹתִי בָּרַק חַרְבִּי וְתֹאחֵז בְּמִשְׁפָּט יָדִי אָשִׁיב נָקָם לְצָרָי וְלִמְשַׂנְאַי אֲשַׁלֵּם:	41	If I whet My glittering sword and court judgment, I will take out My vengeance against My enemies and enact payment from those who hate Me.
אַשְׁכִּיר חִצַּי מִדָּם וְחַרְבִּי תֹּאכַל בָּשָׂר מִדַּם חָלָל וְשִׁבְיָה מֵרֹאשׁ פַּרְעוֹת אוֹיֵב:	42	I will make My arrows drunk with blood, and My sword shall eat flesh through the blood of the slain and of the captives and the heads of marauding enemy terrorists.
הַרְנִינוּ גוֹיִם עַמּוֹ כִּי דַם־עֲבָדָיו יִקּוֹם וְנָקָם יָשִׁיב לְצָרָיו וְכִפֶּר אַדְמָתוֹ עַמּוֹ:	43	Rejoice Nations with His People, for He will avenge the blood of His servants and take vengeance against His enemies, and He will forgive His Land and His People.

It is probable that since the *Shabbos* morning psalm spoke of three types of future, the *Musaf* psalm alluded to the past and summarized six Days of Creation, which led to the Seventh Day – a Day of Rest.

1.   If so, the first *Shabbos* alludes to the first Day upon which God created the Heavens and earth for the sake of the Torah so that humans would be able to listen to His Word and obey His every command.

2.   *Shabbos* two hints to the second day of Creation when the upper Heavens were separated from the lower and yet this lower water was to be uplifted and sanctified upon the Altar as a Libation-Offering on *Sukkos*. Similarly, a Jew is to remember the days of old and the miracles that the Lord has wrought throughout the ages and realize that these events are designed to mold a Jew and show him how to mend his faults and elevate himself to the utmost heights of spirituality.

3.   The third *Shabbos* represents the Creation of vegetation – food for man so that he might be healthy and strong to serve His Creator rather than let this bounty go to his head and consequently claim that he is the source of this blessing.

4.   The fourth *Shabbos* signifies the sun, moon, and stars which were created on day four, and worshipped as idols – false deities that will ultimately lead to their worshipper's annihilation.

5.   The fifth *Shabbos* illuminates the lesson that although Jewry is often deserving of chastisement because of her iniquities, the Lord often withholds these punishments to prevent the non-Jewish nations from

claiming that they are not bound by God's decrees and can do as they choose with impudence. And so, God created the birds above and the fish below to fill the air and the water, but not animals – an allusion that there are occasions when Jewry are not deserving of bounty and yet receive it.
6.	The Final Day of Creation when animals were formed, and man was created to rule with intelligence over the universe represents the role of man in this world. If he upholds this trust, his enemies shall ultimately be destroyed in this world and inherit Gehinnom in the next while he will bask in the radiance of the Hereafter.

MINCHA SONGS OF SHABBOS DAY

IN THE MINCHA SERVICES, THERE are three readings over each three-week period.[375]

WEEK ONE

Shemos 15:1 – 10

Table 24 Mincha Songs of Week One

HEBREW		ENGLISH
אָז יָשִׁיר־מֹשֶׁה וּבְנֵי יִשְׂרָאֵל אֶת־הַשִּׁירָה הַזֹּאת לַיהוָה וַיֹּאמְרוּ לֵאמֹר אָשִׁירָה לַיהוָה כִּי־גָאֹה גָּאָה סוּס וְרֹכְבוֹ רָמָה בַיָּם:	1	Then Moshe and Jewry sang this song to the Eternal saying, I will sing to the Eternal because He is so Superior; He threw the horse with its rider into the seas.
עָזִּי וְזִמְרָת יָהּ וַיְהִי־לִי לִישׁוּעָה זֶה אֵלִי וְאַנְוֵהוּ אֱלֹהֵי אָבִי וַאֲרֹמְמֶנְהוּ:	2	The strength and retribution of the Lord led to my deliverance; This is my God, and I will glorify Him, the Almighty of my father and I will extol Him.

---

375 Rashi: Rosh Hashana 31a – ד"ה אז ישיר; Tiferes Yisrael: Tamid 7:4

HEBREW		ENGLISH
יְהֹוָה אִישׁ מִלְחָמָה יְהֹוָה שְׁמוֹ:	3	The Eternal is a man of war; the Eternal is His Name.
מַרְכְּבֹת פַּרְעֹה וְחֵילוֹ יָרָה בַיָּם וּמִבְחַר שָׁלִשָׁיו טֻבְּעוּ בְיַם־סוּף:	4	He tossed Pharaoh's chariots and troops into the sea, and his elite officers were drowned in the Sea of Reeds.
תְּהֹמֹת יְכַסְיֻמוּ יָרְדוּ בִמְצוֹלֹת כְּמוֹ־אָבֶן:	5	The depths have covered them; they plummeted to the bottom like stones.
יְמִינְךָ יְהֹוָה נֶאְדָּרִי בַּכֹּחַ יְמִינְךָ יְהֹוָה תִּרְעַץ אוֹיֵב:	6	Your right hand, Eternal is adorned with power; Your right hand, Eternal, pulverizes the enemy.
וּבְרֹב גְּאוֹנְךָ תַּהֲרֹס קָמֶיךָ תְּשַׁלַּח חֲרֹנְךָ יֹאכְלֵמוֹ כַּקַּשׁ:	7	In Your abundant glory, You have destroyed those who rose up against You; You sent forth Your fury which consumed them like straw.
וּבְרוּחַ אַפֶּיךָ נֶעֶרְמוּ מַיִם נִצְּבוּ כְמוֹ־נֵד נֹזְלִים קָפְאוּ תְהֹמֹת בְּלֶב־יָם:	8	And from the wind in Your nostrils, the waters were piled up; flowing water stood upright like a wall – the deep waters congealed (and became hard like rock) in the heart of the sea (so that God might smash the Egyptians against it like one shattering glass)."
אָמַר אוֹיֵב אֶרְדֹּף אַשִּׂיג אֲחַלֵּק שָׁלָל תִּמְלָאֵמוֹ נַפְשִׁי אָרִיק חַרְבִּי תּוֹרִישֵׁמוֹ יָדִי:	9	The enemy (Pharaoh) exclaimed: "I will pursue (the Jews) I will overtake (them). I will divide the spoils. I will satiate myself. I will unsheathe my sword; my hand shall destroy them."
נָשַׁפְתָּ בְרוּחֲךָ כִּסָּמוֹ יָם צָלֲלוּ כַּעוֹפֶרֶת בְּמַיִם אַדִּירִים:	10	You blew with Your wind; the sea covered them. The mighty sank like lead in the waters.

WEEK TWO

Shemos 15:11 – 19

Table 25 Mincha Songs of Week Two

HEBREW		**ENGLISH**

Hebrew	#	English
מִי־כָמֹכָה בָּאֵלִם יְהֹוָה מִי כָּמֹכָה נֶאְדָּר בַּקֹּדֶשׁ נוֹרָא תְהִלֹּת עֹשֵׂה פֶלֶא:	11	Who is like You among the gods, Eternal, and who is like You – glorious in holiness, awesome in praise, performing wonders?
נָטִיתָ יְמִינְךָ תִּבְלָעֵמוֹ אָרֶץ:	12	You extended Your right hand; the earth swallowed them.
נָחִיתָ בְחַסְדְּךָ עַם־זוּ גָּאָלְתָּ נֵהַלְתָּ בְעָזְּךָ אֶל־נְוֵה קָדְשֶׁךָ:	13	In Your kindness, You guided this People whom you redeemed; with Your might, You led them to Your holy abode.
שָׁמְעוּ עַמִּים יִרְגָּזוּן חִיל אָחַז יֹשְׁבֵי פְּלָשֶׁת:	14	Nations heard and trembled; terrors seized the inhabitants of Peleshes.
אָז נִבְהֲלוּ אַלּוּפֵי אֱדוֹם אֵילֵי מוֹאָב יֹאחֲזֵמוֹ רָעַד נָמֹגוּ כֹּל יֹשְׁבֵי כְנָעַן:	15	Then the commanders of the Edomites panicked; the warriors of Mo'av were seized with trembling; all the inhabitants of Canaan melted away.
תִּפֹּל עֲלֵיהֶם אֵימָתָה וָפַחַד בִּגְדֹל זְרוֹעֲךָ יִדְּמוּ כָּאָבֶן עַד־יַעֲבֹר עַמְּךָ יְהֹוָה עַד־יַעֲבֹר עַם־זוּ קָנִיתָ:	16	Fear and dread shall fall upon them; because of the greatness of Your arm, they were as silent as stone; until Your Nation crosses over, Eternal, until the People You have acquired have crossed over.
תְּבִאֵמוֹ וְתִטָּעֵמוֹ בְּהַר נַחֲלָתְךָ מָכוֹן לְשִׁבְתְּךָ פָּעַלְתָּ יְהֹוָה מִקְּדָשׁ אֲדֹנָי כּוֹנְנוּ יָדֶיךָ:	17	You shall bring them (to Eretz Yisrael) and plant them on the mountain of Your inheritance, the place of Your habitation which You, Eternal, have made; the Temple, Lord, which Your hands have Established.
יְהֹוָה יִמְלֹךְ לְעֹלָם וָעֶד:	18	The Eternal shall reign forever and ever.
כִּי בָא סוּס פַּרְעֹה בְּרִכְבּוֹ וּבְפָרָשָׁיו בַּיָּם וַיָּשֶׁב יְהֹוָה עֲלֵהֶם אֶת־מֵי הַיָּם וּבְנֵי יִשְׂרָאֵל הָלְכוּ בַיַּבָּשָׁה בְּתוֹךְ הַיָּם:	19	Because Pharoah's horses, chariots, and riders went into the sea and the Eternal turned the waters of the sea back upon while Jewry walked on dry land in the midst of the sea.

WEEK THREE

Bamidbar 21:17 – 20

Table 26 Mincha Songs of Week Three

HEBREW		ENGLISH
אָז יָשִׁיר יִשְׂרָאֵל אֶת־הַשִּׁירָה הַזֹּאת עֲלִי בְאֵר עֱנוּ־לָהּ:	17	Then Jewry sang this song: "Rise up, o well; sing to it
בְּאֵר חֲפָרוּהָ שָׂרִים כָּרוּהָ נְדִיבֵי הָעָם בִּמְחֹקֵק בְּמִשְׁעֲנֹתָם וּמִמִּדְבָּר מַתָּנָה:	18	The well that the princes dug, that the nobles of the People scraped out with scepters and canes; (the well of life-giving water which accompanied Jewry) in the desert to Mattana,
וּמִמַּתָּנָה נַחֲלִיאֵל וּמִנַּחֲלִיאֵל בָּמוֹת:	19	And from Mattana to Nachliel and from Nachliel to Bamos
וּמִבָּמוֹת הַגַּיְא אֲשֶׁר בִּשְׂדֵה מוֹאָב רֹאשׁ הַפִּסְגָּה וְנִשְׁקָפָה עַל־פְּנֵי הַיְשִׁימֹן:	20	And from Bamos to the valley that is in the territory of Mo'av to the top of Pisga which overlooks the desert."

Since the Temple was created to prolong the existence of the world, it is logical that the *Shabbos* Mincha Tehillim should allude to this truth – the datum that the world is founded upon three pillars – Torah, Divine Service, and Acts of Lovingkindness.[376] The triple song of praise hints at these verifiable facts.

The first section of the Song of the Red Sea symbolizes lovingkindness: The Lord, in His Mercy, destroyed the enemy to bring Jewry out of slavery. He likewise proved to the world that He does exist, and people cannot do as they please without considering the consequences of their actions: Egypt tried to destroy Jewry through torturous bondage; they were instead wiped off the face of the earth.

The second part of this Song represents Divine Service – the recognition that God not only exists but that He guides the world both in general and in particular. He did not merely set the world into motion and forget about it. Therefore, when the nations witnessed the miracle of Exodus and the fate of Egypt, they were compelled to realize that God's guiding Hand rules the universe and that they must pay homage to Him.

The well of Miryam which sustained Jewry in her forty-year trek across the Desert is the symbol of Torah as Torah is the water that quenches the spiritual thirst of Jews and assures them of plenitude in their

---

[376] Avos 1:2

various journeys in this world and the next. God demonstrated that not only does He guide the World, but there is also a reward-punishment system through which the good receive Gan Eden and the wicked, Gehinnom.

In summary, this six-week cycle is portrayed in the following chart:

Table 27 Musaf Songs Review

	MUSAF SERVICES	**MINCHA SERVICES**
WEEK 1	Devarim 32:1 – 6	Shemos 15:1 – 10
WEEK 2	Devarim 32:7 – 12	Shemos 15:11 – 19
WEEK 3	Devarim 32:13 – 18	Bamidbar 21:17 – 20
WEEK 4	Devarim 32:19 – 26	Shemos 15:1 – 10
WEEK 5	Devarim 32:27 – 35	Shemos 15:11 – 19
WEEK 6	Devarim 32:36 - 43	Bamidbar 21:17 – 20

Table 28 Other Pesukim

HEBREW	**ENGLISH**
לְהוֹדוֹת לְהַלֵּל לְשַׁבֵּחַ לְפָאֵר לְרוֹמֵם לְהַדֵּר לְבָרֵךְ לְעַלֵּה וּלְקַלֵּס. עַל כָּל דִּבְרֵי שִׁירוֹת וְתִשְׁבָּחוֹת דָּוִד בֶּן יִשַׁי עַבְדְּךָ מְשִׁיחֶךָ:	(It is the obligation of all Creation) to offer thanks (to You) and to laud (You); to praise, glorify, and exalt (You); to extol (You) and make (You) illustrious even more than all the word of the songs and adulations of David, the son of Yishai, Your anointed servant.
בַּעֲצָתְךָ תַנְחֵנִי וְאַחַר כָּבוֹד תִּקָּחֵנִי:	"You have guided me with your counsel so that I should consequently be honored."[377]
וְהוּא רַחוּם יְכַפֵּר עָוֹן וְלֹא־יַשְׁחִית וְהִרְבָּה לְהָשִׁיב אַפּוֹ וְלֹא־יָעִיר כָּל־חֲמָתוֹ:	"He is compassionate, forgiving iniquity. Consequently, he did not annihilate (them). He, instead, often subdues His anger and keeps the majority of His wrath dormant."[378]

---

[377] Tehillim 73:24
[378] Ibid. 78:38

אַשְׁרֵי הַגֶּבֶר אֲשֶׁר־תְּיַסְּרֶנּוּ יָּהּ וּמִתּוֹרָתְךָ תְלַמְּדֶנּוּ:	"Fortunate is the man who is admonished by You, the Eternal, and whom You teach out of your Torah."[379]
וַאֲנִי בְּחַסְדְּךָ בָטַחְתִּי יָגֵל לִבִּי בִּישׁוּעָתֶךָ אָשִׁירָה לַיהוָה כִּי גָמַל עָלָי:	"But I have placed my complete trust in Your mercy. My heart shall (therefore) rejoice in Your salvation. I will sing to the Eternal, because he has showered me with His favor."[380]
שׂוֹשׂ אָשִׂישׂ בַּיהוָה תָּגֵל נַפְשִׁי בֵּאלֹהַי כִּי הִלְבִּישַׁנִי בִּגְדֵי־יֶשַׁע מְעִיל צְדָקָה יְעָטָנִי כֶּחָתָן יְכַהֵן פְּאֵר וְכַכַּלָּה תַּעְדֶּה כֵלֶיהָ:	"I will greatly rejoice in the Eternal (and) my soul will be ecstatic in my Almighty because He has clothed me with the garments of salvation, and wrapped me in the cloak of righteousness just as a bridegroom beautifies himself with splendor, and a bride adorns herself with her jewelry."[381]
וְיִבְטְחוּ בְךָ יוֹדְעֵי שְׁמֶךָ כִּי לֹא־עָזַבְתָּ דֹרְשֶׁיךָ יְהוָה:	"Therefore, those who are cognizant of Your Name shall place their trust in You because You, Eternal, have never forsaken those who seek You."[382]
שִׂמְחוּ בַיהוָה וְגִילוּ צַדִּיקִים וְהַרְנִינוּ כָּל־יִשְׁרֵי־לֵב:	"Let the righteous be glad with the Eternal, and rejoice; and let the upright in heart shout for joy."[383]
נֵר־לְרַגְלִי דְבָרֶךָ וְאוֹר לִנְתִיבָתִי:	"Your word is a lamp to my feet, and a light to my path."[384]
אוֹדְךָ כִּי עֲנִיתָנִי וַתְּהִי־לִי לִישׁוּעָה:	"I will give You thanks, because You have answered me, and become my salvation."[385]

---

[379] Ibid. 94.12

[380] Ibid.13:6

[381] Yeshayahu 61:10

[382] Tehillim 9:11

[383] Ibid. 32:11

[384] Ibid.119:105

[385] Ibid. 118:21

The song that the Levites were accustomed to chant in the Temple:

- On Sundays they used to recite, "The earth, and all its contents, the inhabited world, and those who dwell in it, belong to the Eternal."[386]
- On Mondays they said, "The Eternal is great and should be highly praised in the city of our Almighty, the mountain of His Sanctity."[387]
- On Tuesdays, they proclaimed, "The Almighty stands in the congregation of God; He judges in the midst of judges."[388]
- On Wednesdays they declared, "The Almighty is a God of vengeance. God of vengeance – Reveal Yourself."[389]
- On Thursdays they chant, "Joyously sing to the Almighty, our strength. Sound (trumpets) to the Almighty of Yaakov."[390]
- On Fridays they would say, "The Eternal reigns. He has clothed Himself with majesty."[391]
- On *Shabbos* they proclaimed, "A psalm, a song for the Day of *Shabbos*."[392] A psalm, a song for the future – for the time that is one continuous *Shabbos* of rest for all Creation.

---

[386] Ibid. 24:1
[387] Ibid. 48:2
[388] Ibid. 82:1
[389] Ibid. 94:1
[390] Ibid. 81:2
[391] Ibid. 93:1
[392] Ibid. 92:1

SECTION THREE

THE HADRAN ALACH

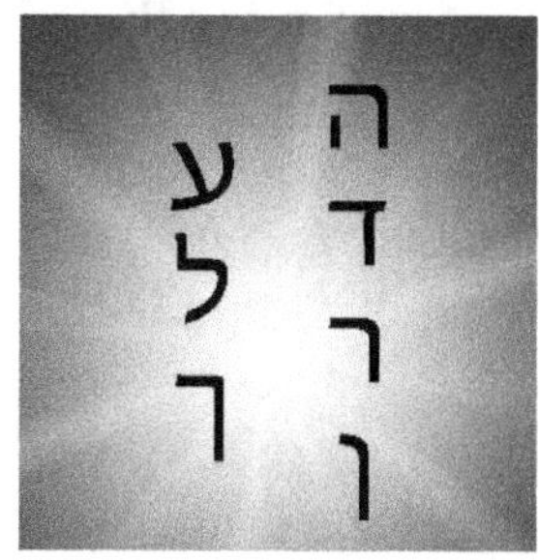

THE HADRAN FOR A SEDER OF MISHNAYOS

THIS CHAPTER, IN ITS ENTIRETY, is recited after the completion of a *seder* of Mishnayos or the complete Six Orders of Mishnayos. Afterward, the Great *Kaddish* is recited which can be found on Page 185.

Table 29 Hadran for Mishnayos

HEBREW	ENGLISH
הֲדְרָן עֲלָךְ סדר **(יאמר שם הסדר)** וְהַדְרָךְ עֲלָן. דַּעְתָּן עֲלָךְ סדר **(יאמר שם הסדר)** וְדַעְתָּךְ עֲלָן. לָא נִתְנַשֵׁי מִינָךְ סדר **(יאמר שם הסדר)** וְלֹא תִתְנְשֵׁי מִינָן, לָא בְּעָלְמָא הָדֵין וְלֹא בְּעָלְמָא דְאָתֵי: **(This is said thrice)**	We will return to you, *seder* ____ **(fill in the name of the Order)**, and you will return to us; our mind is on you, *seder* ____, and your mind is on us; we will not forget you, *seder* ____, and you will not forget us – not in this world and not in the next world. **(This is said thrice)**

If one is making a *siyum* on the entire Six Orders of Mishnayos, he substitutes the following paragraph for the one above

הַדְרָן עֲלָךְ שִׁשָּׁה סִדְרֵי מִשְׁנָה וְהַדְרָךְ עֲלָן. דַּעְתָּן עֲלָךְ שִׁשָּׁה סִדְרֵי מִשְׁנָה וְדַעְתָּךְ עֲלָן. לָא נִתְנְשֵׁי מִינָךְ סֵדֶר שִׁשָּׁה סִדְרֵי מִשְׁנָה וְלֹא תִתְנְשֵׁי מִינָן, לָא בְּעָלְמָא הָדֵין וְלֹא בְּעָלְמָא דְאָתֵי: **(This is said thrice)**	We will return to you, the Six Orders of Mishnayos, and you will return to us; our mind is on you, the Six Orders of Mishnayos, and your mind is on us; we will not forget you, the Six Orders of Mishnayos, and you will not forget us – not in this world and not in the next world. **(This is said thrice)**

For both a *siyum* on a *seder* of Mishnayos or the entire Six Orders of Mishnayos, continue below

הַעֲרֶב נָא יְיָ אֱלֹהֵינוּ, אֶת דִּבְרֵי תוֹרָתְךָ בְּפִינוּ וּבְפִיפִיּוֹת עַמְּךָ בֵּית יִשְׂרָאֵל, וְנִהְיֶה כּוּלָנוּ אֲנַחְנוּ וְצֶאֱצָאֵינוּ וְצֶאֱצָאֵי עַמְּךָ בֵּית יִשְׂרָאֵל, כּוּלָנוּ יוֹדְעֵי שְׁמֶךָ וְלוֹמְדֵי תוֹרָתֶךָ. מֵאֹיְבַי תְּחַכְּמֵנִי מִצְוֺתֶךָ כִּי לְעוֹלָם הִיא לִי. יְהִי לִבִּי תָמִים בְּחֻקֶּיךָ לְמַעַן לֹא אֵבוֹשׁ. לְעוֹלָם לֹא אֶשְׁכַּח פִּקּוּדֶיךָ כִּי בָם חִיִּיתָנִי. בָּרוּךְ אַתָּה יְיָ לַמְּדֵנִי חֻקֶּיךָ. אָמֵן אָמֵן אָמֵן סֶלָה וָעֶד:	Please make it sweet, God our God, the words of Your Torah. In our mouths, and the mouths of your nation the House of Israel. And it should be that we, all of us, our children and the children of your nation the House of Israel, that we should all know Your name and learn Your Torah. "Your commandment makes me wiser than my enemies, for it is ever with me."[1] "Let my heart be complete in Your statutes, in order that I may not be put to shame."[2] "I will never forget Your precepts; for with them You have quickened me."[3] "Blessed are You O' God, teach

---

[1] Tehillim 119:98

[2] Ibid.: 119:80

[3] Ibid.: 119:93

	me Your statutes."[4] Amen, Amen, Amen, and forever Sela.
מוֹדִים אֲנַחְנוּ לְפָנֶיךָ יְיָ אֱלֹהֵינוּ וֵאלֹהֵי אֲבוֹתֵינוּ שֶׁשַּׂמְתָּ חֶלְקֵנוּ מִיוֹשְׁבֵי בֵּית הַמִּדְרָשׁ, וְלֹא שַׂמְתָּ חֶלְקֵנוּ מִיוֹשְׁבֵי קְרָנוֹת. שֶׁאָנוּ מַשְׁכִּימִים וְהֵם מַשְׁכִּימִים. אָנוּ מַשְׁכִּימִים לְדִבְרֵי תוֹרָה וְהֵם מַשְׁכִּימִים לִדְבָרִים בְּטֵלִים. אָנוּ עֲמֵלִים וְהֵם עֲמֵלִים. אָנוּ עֲמֵלִים וּמְקַבְּלִים שָׂכָר וְהֵם עֲמֵלִים וְאֵינָם מְקַבְּלִים שָׂכָר. אָנוּ רָצִים וְהֵם רָצִים. אָנוּ רָצִים לְחַיֵּי הָעוֹלָם הַבָּא, וְהֵם רָצִים לִבְאֵר שַׁחַת. שֶׁנֶּאֱמַר: וְאַתָּה אֱלֹהִים תּוֹרִדֵם לִבְאֵר שַׁחַת אַנְשֵׁי דָמִים וּמִרְמָה לֹא יֶחֱצוּ יְמֵיהֶם וַאֲנִי אֶבְטַח בָּךְ:	We give thanks before You, Lord, our God and God of our fathers, for You gave us a share among those who sit in the study hall, and not among those who sit on street corners. For we arise early, and they arise early; we arise for words of Torah, and they arise for words of emptiness. We work, and they work; we work and receive a reward, and they work and do not receive a reward. We run, and they run; we run towards eternal life, and they run to a pit of desolation. As it says, "And You, O' Lord, bring them down into a pit of desolation, people of blood and deceit will not live out half of their days; and I, I will trust in You."[5]
יְהִי רָצוֹן מִלְפָנֶיךָ יְיָ אֱלֹהַי, כְּשֵׁם שֶׁעֲזַרְתַּנִי לְסַיֵּם סֵדֶר (**יאמר שם הסדר**),	May it be your will, Lord my God, just as You have helped me to complete the Order of _____,

If one is making a *siyum* on the entire Six Orders of Mishnayos, he substitutes the following paragraph for the one above

יְהִי רָצוֹן מִלְפָנֶיךָ יְיָ אֱלֹהַי, כְּשֵׁם שֶׁעֲזַרְתַּנִי לְסַיֵּם שִׁשָּׁה סִדְרֵי מִשְׁנָה	May it be your will, Lord, my God, just as You have helped me to complete the Six Orders of Mishnayos

For both a *siyum* on a *seder* of Mishnayos or the entire Six Orders of Mishnayos, continue below

---

[4] Ibid.: 119:12
[5] Ibid.: 55:24

כֵּן תְּעַזְּרֵנִי לְהַתְחִיל מַסֶּכְתּוֹת וּסְפָרִים אֲחֵרִים וּלְסַיְּמָם, לִלְמֹד וּלְלַמֵּד, לִשְׁמֹר וְלַעֲשׂוֹת וּלְקַיֵּם אֶת כָּל דִּבְרֵי תַלְמוּד תּוֹרָתֶךָ בְּאַהֲבָה, וּזְכוּת כָּל הַתַּנָּאִים וַאֲמוֹרָאִים וְתַלְמִידֵי חֲכָמִים יַעֲמוֹד לִי וּלְזַרְעִי שֶׁלֹּא תָמוּשׁ הַתּוֹרָה מִפִּי וּמִפִּי זַרְעִי עַד עוֹלָם. וְיִתְקַיֵּם בִּי: בְּהִתְהַלֶּכְךָ תַּנְחֶה אֹתָךָ בְּשָׁכְבְּךָ תִּשְׁמֹר עָלֶיךָ וַהֲקִיצוֹתָ הִיא תְשִׂיחֶךָ. כִּי בִי יִרְבּוּ יָמֶיךָ וְיוֹסִיפוּ לְךָ שְׁנוֹת חַיִּים. אֹרֶךְ יָמִים בִּימִינָהּ בִּשְׂמֹאולָהּ עֹשֶׁר וְכָבוֹד. יְיָ עֹז לְעַמּוֹ יִתֵּן יְיָ יְבָרֵךְ אֶת עַמּוֹ בַשָּׁלוֹם:

So too may you help me to start other tractates and books, and to complete them, to learn and to teach, to observe and to enact and to fulfill all the words of the teaching of your Torah with love. And may the merit of all the Tannaim and Amoraim and Torah scholars be present for me and for my descendants, to ensure that the Torah does not depart from my mouth and from the mouths of my descendants for all eternity. And may the following be fulfilled for me, "When you walk, it will lead you, when you lie down, it will watch over you. When you awake, it will speak with you."[6] "For through me your days will be multiplied, and the years of your life will be increased."[7] "Length of days is in her right hand; in her left, riches and honor."[8] "God will give strength to his nation, God will bless his nation with peace."[9]

The custom is to say the following verses at this point in the *Hadran*. They hold deep mystical significance for whoever says them after learning and concluding Mishnayos. Some skip to the *Kaddish* at this point, while most will say the rest of this chapter here (or privately after the *Kaddish)*.

---

[6] Mishlei 6:22

[7] Ibid.: 9:11

[8] Ibid. 3:16

[9] Tehillim 29:11

THE HADRAN FOR A SEDER OF MISHNAYOS

Table 30 Additional Pesukim for Mishnayos

HEBREW	ENGLISH
לְהוֹדוֹת לְהַלֵּל לְשַׁבֵּחַ לְפָאֵר לְרוֹמֵם לְהַדֵּר לְבָרֵךְ לְעַלֵּה וּלְקַלֵּס. עַל כָּל דִּבְרֵי שִׁירוֹת וְתִשְׁבָּחוֹת דָּוִד בֶּן יִשַׁי עַבְדְּךָ מְשִׁיחֶךָ:	(It is the obligation of all Creation) to offer thanks (to You) and to laud (You); to praise, glorify, and exalt (You); to extol (You) and make (You) illustrious even more than all the word of the songs and adulations of David, the son of Yishai, Your anointed servant.
בַּעֲצָתְךָ תַנְחֵנִי וְאַחַר כָּבוֹד תִּקָּחֵנִי:	You have guided me with Your counsel so that I could consequently be honored.
וְהוּא רַחוּם יְכַפֵּר עָוֹן וְלֹא־יַשְׁחִית וְהִרְבָּה לְהָשִׁיב אַפּוֹ וְלֹא־יָעִיר כָּל־חֲמָתוֹ:	He is compassionate, forgiving iniquity. Consequently, He did not annihilate (them). He, instead, often subdues His anger and keeps the majority of His wrath dormant.
אַשְׁרֵי הַגֶּבֶר אֲשֶׁר־תְּיַסְּרֶנּוּ יָּהּ וּמִתּוֹרָתְךָ תְלַמְּדֶנּוּ:	Fortunate is the man who is admonished by You, the Eternal, and whom You teach Your Torah.
וַאֲנִי בְּחַסְדְּךָ בָטַחְתִּי יָגֵל לִבִּי בִּישׁוּעָתֶךָ אָשִׁירָה לַיהֹוָה כִּי גָמַל עָלָי:	But I have placed complete trust in Your mercy. My heart shall (therefore) rejoice in Your salvation. I will sing to the Eternal because he has showered me with His favor.
שׂוֹשׂ אָשִׂישׂ בַּיהֹוָה תָּגֵל נַפְשִׁי בֵּאלֹהַי כִּי הִלְבִּישַׁנִי בִּגְדֵי־יֶשַׁע מְעִיל צְדָקָה יְעָטָנִי כֶּחָתָן יְכַהֵן פְּאֵר וְכַכַּלָּה תַּעְדֶּה כֵלֶיהָ:	I will greatly rejoice in the Eternal (and) my soul will be ecstatic in my Almighty because He has clothed me with the garment of salvation and wrapped me in the cloak of righteousness just as a bridegroom beautifies himself with the splendor and a bride adorns herself with her jewelry.
וְיִבְטְחוּ בְךָ יוֹדְעֵי שְׁמֶךָ כִּי לֹא־עָזַבְתָּ דֹרְשֶׁיךָ יְהֹוָה:	Therefore, those who are cognizant of Your Name shall place their trust in You because You, Eternal, have never forsaken those who seek You.

שִׂמְחוּ בַיהוָה וְגִילוּ צַדִּיקִים וְהַרְנִינוּ כָּל־יִשְׁרֵי־לֵב:	Let the righteous be glad with the Eternal and rejoice, and let the upright in heart shout for joy.
נֵר־לְרַגְלִי דְבָרֶךָ וְאוֹר לִנְתִיבָתִי:	Your word is a lamp to my feet and a light to my path.
אוֹדְךָ כִּי עֲנִיתָנִי וַתְּהִי־לִי לִישׁוּעָה:	I will give You thanks because You have answered me and become my salvation.

The last Mishnah of *Maseches* Tamid is recited at this point.

Table 31 Last Mishnah of Tamid

HEBREW	**ENGLISH**
הַשִּׁיר שֶׁהָיוּ הַלְוִיִּם אוֹמְרִים בַּמִּקְדָּשׁ,	(The following is a list of each daily) the psalm that the Levites would recite in the Temple.
בַּיּוֹם הָרִאשׁוֹן הָיוּ אוֹמְרִים לַיָי הָאָרֶץ וּמְלוֹאָהּ תֵּבֵל וְיֹשְׁבֵי בָהּ.	On the first day (of the week) they would recite (the psalm beginning: "A psalm of David.) The earth is the Lord's and all it contains, the world and all who live in it."[10]
בַּשֵּׁנִי הָיוּ אוֹמְרִים, גָּדוֹל יְהוָה וּמְהֻלָּל מְאֹד בְּעִיר אֱלֹהֵינוּ הַר קָדְשׁוֹ.	On the second (day) they would recite (the psalm beginning: "A song; a psalm of the sons of Korach.) Great is the Lord and highly to be praised in the city of God, on His sacred mountain."[11]
בַּשְּׁלִישִׁי הָיוּ אוֹמְרִים, אֱלֹהִים נִצָּב בַּעֲדַת אֵל בְּקֶרֶב אֱלֹהִים יִשְׁפֹּט.	On the third (day) they would recite (the psalm beginning: "A psalm of Asaph.) God stands in the divine assembly; among the judges He delivers judgment."[12]

---

[10] Tehillim: 24
[11] Ibid.: 48
[12] Ibid.: 82

בָּרְבִיעִי הָיוּ אוֹמְרִים, אֵל נְקָמוֹת יְהֹוָה אֵל נְקָמוֹת הוֹפִיעַ.	On the fourth (day) they would recite (the psalm beginning:) "O Lord God, to Whom vengeance belongs, God to Whom vengeance belongs, shine forth."[13]
בַּחֲמִישִׁי הָיוּ אוֹמְרִים, הַרְנִינוּ לֵאלֹהִים עוּזֵּנוּ, הָרִיעוּ לֵאלֹהֵי יַעֲקֹב.	On the fifth (day) they would recite (the psalm beginning: "For the leader; upon the *Gittis*, a psalm of Asaph.) Sing for joy to God, our strength; shout aloud to the God of Yaakov."[14]
בַּשִּׁשִּׁי הָיוּ אוֹמְרִים, יְהֹוָה מָלָךְ גֵּאוּת לָבֵשׁ וְגו'.	On the sixth (day) they would recite (the psalm beginning:) "The Lord reigns: He is robed in majesty; the Lord is robed, (girded with strength)."[15]
בְּשַׁבָּת הָיוּ אוֹמְרִים , מִזְמוֹר שִׁיר לְיוֹם הַשַּׁבָּת, מִזְמוֹר שִׁיר לֶעָתִיד לָבֹא, לְיוֹם שֶׁכֻּלּוֹ שַׁבָּת מְנוּחָה לְחַיֵּי הָעוֹלָמִים:	On *Shabbos* they would recite (the psalm beginning), "A psalm, a song for *Shabbos* day." (This is interpreted as) a psalm, a song for the future, for the day that will be entirely *Shabbos* and rest for everlasting life.[16]

It is at this point that the *Kaddish HaGadol* which can be found on page 185 is recited.

---

[13] Ibid.: 94

[14] Ibid.: 81

[15] Ibid.: 93

[16] Ibid.: 92

THE HADRAN ALACH

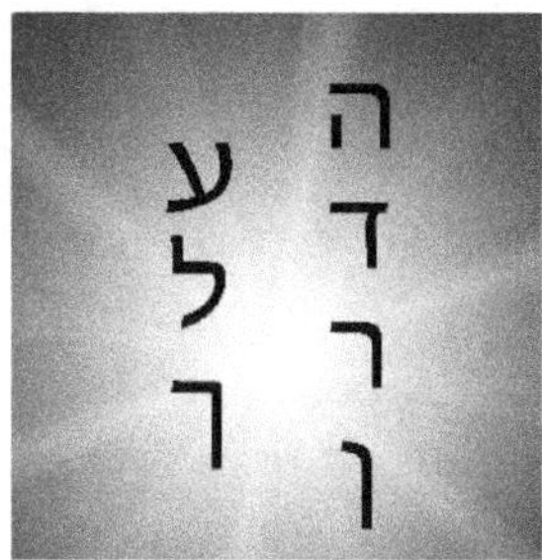

THE HADRAN FOR A TRACTATE OF THE TALMUD

THIS CHAPTER, IN ITS ENTIRETY, is recited after the completion of a Tractate of Gemara. Afterward, the Great *Kaddish* is recited which can be found on Page 185.

Table 32 Hadran for Gemara

HEBREW	ENGLISH
הַדְרָן עֲלָךְ מַסֶּכֶת (**יאמר שם המסכת**) וְהַדְרָךְ עֲלָן. דַּעְתָּן עֲלָךְ מַסֶּכֶת (**יאמר שם המסכת**) וְדַעְתָּךְ עֲלָן. לָא נִתְנְשֵׁי מִינָךְ מַסֶּכֶת (**יאמר שם המסכת**) וְלֹא תִתְנְשֵׁי מִינָן, לָא בְּעָלְמָא הָדֵין וְלֹא בְּעָלְמָא דְאָתֵי: (**This is said thrice**)	We will return to you, Tractate ____ (**fill in the name of the tractate**), and you will return to us; our mind is on you, Tractate ____, and your mind is on us; we will not forget you, Tractate ____, and you will not forget us – not in this world and not in the next world. (**This is said thrice**)

יְהִי רָצוֹן מִלְפָנֶיךָ יְיָ אֱלֹהֵינוּ וֵאלֹהֵי אֲבוֹתֵינוּ שֶׁתְּהֵא תוֹרָתְךָ אֻמָּנוּתֵנוּ בָּעוֹלָם הַזֶּה וּתְהֵא עִמָּנוּ לָעוֹלָם הַבָּא. חֲנִינָא בַּר פָּפָּא, רָמִי בַּר פָּפָּא, נַחְמָן בַּר פָּפָּא, אַחַאי בַּר פָּפָּא, אַבָּא מָרִי בַּר פָּפָּא, רִפְרָם בַּר פָּפָּא, רָכִישׁ בַּר פָּפָּא, סוּרְחָב בַּר פָּפָּא, אַדָּא בַּר פָּפָּא, דָרוּ בַּר פָּפָּא:

May it be Your will, our God, and the God of our fathers, that we should be loyal to Your Torah in this world, and it should be with us in the next world. Chaninah *bar* Pappa, Rami *bar* Pappa, Nachman *bar* Pappa, Achai *bar* Pappa, Aba Mari *bar* Pappa, Rafram *bar* Pappa, Rachish *bar* Pappa, Sorchav *bar* Pappa, Ada *bar* Pappa, Daro *bar* Pappa.

הַעֲרֶב נָא יְיָ אֱלֹהֵינוּ, אֶת דִּבְרֵי תוֹרָתְךָ בְּפִינוּ וּבְפִיּוֹת עַמְּךָ בֵּית יִשְׂרָאֵל, וְנִהְיֶה כֻּולָּנוּ אֲנַחְנוּ וְצֶאֱצָאֵינוּ וְצֶאֱצָאֵי עַמְּךָ בֵּית יִשְׂרָאֵל, כֻּולָנוּ יוֹדְעֵי שְׁמֶךָ וְלוֹמְדֵי תוֹרָתֶךָ. מֵאֹיְבַי תְּחַכְּמֵנִי מִצְוֹתֶךָ כִּי לְעוֹלָם הִיא לִי. יְהִי לִבִּי תָמִים בְּחֻקֶּיךָ לְמַעַן לֹא אֵבוֹשׁ. לְעוֹלָם לֹא אֶשְׁכַּח פִּקּוּדֶיךָ כִּי בָם חִיִּיתָנִי. בָּרוּךְ אַתָּה יְיָ לַמְּדֵנִי חֻקֶּיךָ. אָמֵן אָמֵן אָמֵן סֶלָה וָעֶד:

Please make it sweet, God our God, the words of Your Torah. In our mouths, and the mouths of your nation the House of Israel. And it should be that we, all of us, our children and the children of your nation the House of Israel, that we should all know Your name and learn Your Torah. "Your commandment makes me wiser than my enemies, for it is ever with me." [17] "Let my heart be complete in Your statutes, in order that I may not be put to shame." [18] "I will never forget Your precepts; for with them You have quickened me." [19] "Blessed are You O' God, teach me Your statutes."[20] Amen, Amen, Amen, and forever Sela.

מוֹדִים אֲנַחְנוּ לְפָנֶיךָ יְיָ אֱלֹהֵינוּ וֵאלֹהֵי אֲבוֹתֵינוּ שֶׁשַּׂמְתָּ חֶלְקֵנוּ מִיּוֹשְׁבֵי בֵית

We give thanks before You, Lord, our God and God of our fathers, for you gave us a share among those who sit in the study hall, and not

---

[17] Tehillim 119:98
[18] Ibid.: 119:80
[19] Ibid.: 119:93
[20] Ibid.: 119:12

THE HADRAN FOR A TRACTATE OF THE TALMUD

הַמִּדְרָשׁ, וְלֹא שַׂמְתָּ חֶלְקֵנוּ מִיּוֹשְׁבֵי קְרָנוֹת. שֶׁאָנוּ מַשְׁכִּימִים וְהֵם מַשְׁכִּימִים. אָנוּ מַשְׁכִּימִים לְדִבְרֵי תוֹרָה וְהֵם מַשְׁכִּימִים לִדְבָרִים בְּטֵלִים. אָנוּ עֲמֵלִים וְהֵם עֲמֵלִים. אָנוּ עֲמֵלִים וּמְקַבְּלִים שָׂכָר וְהֵם עֲמֵלִים וְאֵינָם מְקַבְּלִים שָׂכָר. אָנוּ רָצִים וְהֵם רָצִים. אָנוּ רָצִים לְחַיֵּי הָעוֹלָם הַבָּא, וְהֵם רָצִים לִבְאֵר שַׁחַת. שֶׁנֶּאֱמַר: וְאַתָּה אֱלֹהִים תּוֹרִדֵם לִבְאֵר שַׁחַת אַנְשֵׁי דָמִים וּמִרְמָה לֹא יֶחֱצוּ יְמֵיהֶם וַאֲנִי אֶבְטַח בָּךְ:

among those who sit on street corners. For we arise early, and they arise early; we arise for words of Torah, and they arise for words of emptiness. We work, and they work; we work and receive a reward, and they work and do not receive a reward. We run, and they run; we run towards eternal life, and they run to a pit of desolation. As it says, "And You, O' Lord, bring them down into a pit of desolation, people of blood and deceit will not live out half of their days; and I, I will trust in You."[21]

יְהִי רָצוֹן מִלְפָנֶיךָ יְיָ אֱלֹהַי, כְּשֵׁם שֶׁעֲזַרְתַּנִי לְסַיֵּם מַסֶּכֶת **(יֹאמַר שֵׁם הַמַּסֶּכֶת)**, כֵּן תַּעֲזְרֵנִי לְהַתְחִיל מַסֶּכְתּוֹת וּסְפָרִים אֲחֵרִים וּלְסַיְּמָם, לִלְמֹד וּלְלַמֵּד, לִשְׁמֹר וְלַעֲשׂוֹת וּלְקַיֵּם אֶת כָּל דִּבְרֵי תַלְמוּד תּוֹרָתֶךָ בְּאַהֲבָה, וּזְכוּת כָּל הַתַּנָּאִים וַאֲמוֹרָאִים וְתַלְמִידֵי חֲכָמִים יַעֲמֹד לִי וּלְזַרְעִי שֶׁלֹּא תָמוּשׁ הַתּוֹרָה מִפִּי וּמִפִּי זַרְעִי עַד עוֹלָם. וְיִתְקַיֵּם בִּי: בְּהִתְהַלֶּכְךָ תַּנְחֶה אֹתָךְ בְּשָׁכְבְּךָ תִּשְׁמֹר עָלֶיךָ וַהֲקִיצוֹתָ הִיא תְשִׂיחֶךָ. כִּי בִי יִרְבּוּ יָמֶיךָ וְיוֹסִיפוּ לְךָ

May it be your will, Lord, my God, just as You have helped me to complete tractate ______, so too may you help me to start other tractates and books, and to complete them, to learn and to teach, to observe and to enact and to fulfill all the words of the teaching of your Torah with love. And may the merit of all the Tannaim and Amoraim and Torah scholars be present for me and for my descendants, to ensure that the Torah does not depart from my mouth and from the mouths of my descendants for all eternity. And may the following be fulfilled for me, "When you walk, it will lead you, when you lie down, it will watch over you. When you awake, it

---

[21] Tehillim 55:24

שְׁנוֹת חַיִּים. אֹרֶךְ יָמִים בִּימִינָהּ בִּשְׂמֹאולָהּ עֹשֶׁר וְכָבוֹד. יְיָ עֹז לְעַמּוֹ יִתֵּן יְיָ יְבָרֵךְ אֶת עַמּוֹ בַשָּׁלוֹם:	will speak with you."[22] "For through me your days will be multiplied, and the years of your life will be increased."[23] "Length of days is in her right hand; in her left, riches and honor."[24] "God will give strength to his nation, God will bless his nation with peace."[25]

It is at this point that the *Kaddish HaGadol* which can be found on page 185 is recited.

---

[22] Mishlei 6:22
[23] Ibid.: 9:11
[24] Misheli 3:16
[25] Tehillim 29:11

THE HADRAN FOR TANACH

THE 21ST-CENTURY VERSION OF the Hadran is meant to be recited upon completion of the study of the twenty-four books of TaNaCH. I found this on Sefaria by Rabbi Yona Reiss, Shlita. It would be followed by the Great *Kaddish* found on Page 185.

Table 33 Hadran for TaNaCH

הדרן עלך עשרים וארבעה ספרי התנ"ך דעתן עלך ודעתך עלן עשרים וארבעה ספרי התנ"ך. לא נתנשא מנך ולא תתנשא מנן לא בעלמא הדן ולא בעלמא דאתי.	We will return to you, the twenty-four books of TaNaCH, and you will return to us; our mind is on you, the twenty-four books of TaNaCH, and your mind is on us; we will not forget you, the twenty-four books of TaNaCH, and you will not forget us – not in this world and not in the next world.
וִיהִי רָצוֹן מִלְּפָנֶיךָ יְיָ אֱלֹהֵינוּ וֵאלֹהֵי אֲבוֹתֵינוּ אֲשֶׁר בָּחַר בִּנְבִיאִים טוֹבִים וְרָצָה בְדִבְרֵיהֶם הַנֶּאֱמָרִים בֶּאֱמֶת	And may the Lord our God and the God of our forefathers please You, who chose good prophets and favored their spoken words with truth that in the merit of the books

שבזכות ספרי התנ"ך
ממקראי קודש ובזכות
פסוקיהם ותיבותיהם
ואותיותיהם ונקודותיהם
וטעמיהם ושמות הקדושים
היוצאים מהם, ובזכות נביאי
האמת, שופטי ישראל,
וצדיקי הדורות המוזכרים
בספרי התנ"ך נזכה להיות
נועם ה' אלוקינו עלינו
ומעשה ידינו כוננה עלינו
ומעשה ידינו כוננהו, להיות
זוכים היום ביום חתונתנו
וביום שמחת לבנו. לעורר
אם הבנים שמחה וליחד סוד
תורה שבכתב עם סוד תורה
שבעל פה ביחודא שלים
באהבה ואחוה ורעות. האל
הנאמן בכל דבריו ימשיך
עלינו שפע אור החיים לנפש,
רוח ונשמה, להאריך ימינו
בטוב ובייראת יְיָ כל הימים.

of TaNaCH, the holy scriptures, and in the merit of the verses, the words, the letters, the vowels, the crowns, the holy names that emanate from them, and in the merit of the true prophets, the judges of Israel, the righteous of the generations who are mentioned in TaNaCH, may we be meritorious to be pleasant for HaShem our God, and May the favor of the Lord, our God, be upon us; let the work of our hands prosper, O prosper the work of our hands! May we merit today on the day of our wedding (to the Torah) and the day of the joy of our heart; to awaken the children to the joy of divining foundations of the written Torah along with the secrets of the Oral traditions; with love, brotherhood, and friendship. God who is trustworthy in all his words, He will draw over us an abundance of the light for the soul, and the light for the spirit to lengthen our days with good and fear of HaShem for all our days.

וְהַעֲרֶב נָא יְיָ אֱלֹהֵינוּ, אֶת
דִּבְרֵי תוֹרָתְךָ בְּפִינוּ וּבְפִיפִיּוֹת
עַמְּךָ בֵּית יִשְׂרָאֵל, וְנִהְיֶה
כֻּלָּנוּ אֲנַחְנוּ וְצֶאֱצָאֵינוּ
וְצֶאֱצָאֵי עַמְּךָ בֵּית יִשְׂרָאֵל,
כֻּלָּנוּ יוֹדְעֵי שְׁמֶךָ וְלוֹמְדֵי
תוֹרָתֶךָ. ונשמח ונעלוז בדברי
תלמוד תורתך ובמצותיך
ובחוקותיך לעולם ועד. כִּי

And please make it sweet, God our God, the words of Your Torah. In our mouths, and in the mouths of your nation the House of Israel. And it should be that we, all of us, our children and the children of your nation the House of Israel, that we should all know Your name and learn Your Torah for its sake. We should be happy and rejoice in the words of Torah, *Mitzvos*, and Your laws forever. Because they are our

הֵם חַיֵּינוּ וְאֹרֶךְ יָמֵינוּ וּבָהֶם נֶהְגֶּה יוֹמָם וָלָיְלָה.	lives and the length of our days, and we shall dwell in them day and night.
יהי יְיָ אלוקינו עמנו כאשר היה עם אבותינו, אל יעזבנו ואל יטשנו להיטיב לבבנו אליו, ללכת בכל דרכיו ולשמור מצותיו וחוקותיו ומשפטיו אשר צוה את אבותינו	May HaShem our God be with us as He was with our ancestors, do not leave us and do not abandon us for the benefit of our children so that we will go in all Your ways, to keep the *Mitzvos* and laws and judgments which you commanded to our fathers.
וִיהִי רָצוֹן מִלְּפָנֶיךָ יְיָ אֱלֹהַי, כְּשֵׁם שֶׁעֲזַרְתַּנִי לְסַיֵּים עֶשְׂרִים וְאַרְבָּעָה סִפְרֵי הַתַּנַ"ךְ מִמִּקְרָאֵי קוֹדֶשׁ כֵּן תַּעְזְרֵנוּ לְהַמְשִׁיךְ לִלְמוֹד סְפָרִים מִתוֹרָה שֶׁבִּכְתָב וּמִתוֹרָה שֶׁבְּעַל פֶּה וּלְסַיְּימָם, לִלְמֹד וּלְלַמֵּד. לִשְׁמֹר וְלַעֲשׂוֹת וּלְקַיֵּים אֶת כָּל דִּבְרֵי תַלְמוּד תּוֹרָתֶךָ בְּאַהֲבָה.	May it be your will, Lord, my God, just as You have helped me to complete the twenty-four books of TaNach of holy scriptures, so too may You help me to start other books of the written Torah and the oral Torah, and to complete them, to learn and to teach, to observe and to enact and to fulfill all the words of the teaching of your Torah with love.
ותפתח לבבנו הערל בסודות תורתך הקדושה, ותאציל עלינו אור מקור נשמותינו בכל בחינותינו, ושיתנוצצו ניצוצי אבינו רועה משה רבנו ע"ה אשר על ידו גלית עמקי סודי תורתך.	And open our hearts and reveal to us the secrets of Your holy Torah, and delegate on us the light from the Source of our soul with all our actions, and our sparks and the sparks of our father, Your shepherd Moshe Rabaynu, of blessed memory, by whose hand You revealed the secrets of Your Torah.
וזכותו וזכות כל נביאי ישראל הקדושים וספריהם וקדושתם יעמדו לנו שלא נכשל לעולם ועד, מתט אשורינו מתורתך הקדושה ח"ו, ולהיות דבריהם נאמנים	In his merit and the merit of all the holy prophets of Israel, their writings and holiness should stand for us that we shall never make any mistakes, or errors in Your holy Torah, Heaven forefend, and their words shall be true and dear,

ונחמדים, חיים וקיימים לעד ולעולמי עולמים עלינו ועל בנינו ועל דורותינו ועל כל דורות זרע ישראל עבדיך, על הראשונים ועל האחרונים דבר טוב וקיים באמת ובאמונה, חוק ולא יעבור .	existing and established forever and ever on us, our children and for all our generations and the generations of the seed of Yisrael. On our predecessors and those who come after us for the good, be established for truth and faith, a statue that shall not turn away from us.
ונזכה ונחיה ונראה ונירש טובה וברכה לחיי העולם הבא. ובזכות התורה הקדושה שבכתב ושבע"פ הושיענו ה' אלוקינו וקבצנו מן הגוים, ומלוך על כל העולם כולו בכבודך והנשא על כל הארץ ביקרך. והשפיע עלינו אור ישועה ורחמים ממעייני הישועה . אמן כן יהי רצון . יהיו לרצון אמרי פי והגיון לבי לפניך יְיָ צורי וגואלי	And we shall be meritorious and live and see and inherit good and blessing for life in the World-to-Come. In the merit of the Holy written Torah and the oral Torah, HaShem our God will save us and gather us from amongst the nations, and rule over us with His glory. And may You be honored throughout the land. And pour over us the light of salvation and mercy from the wellsprings of salvation. Amen. May it be so. May the words of my mouth be acceptable and the thoughts of my heart — before You HaShem, my Rock and my Redeemer.

It is at this point that the *Kaddish HaGadol* which can be found on page 185 would be recited.

THE KADDISH

KADDISH MAY BE THE BEST-known prayer, but it is the least understood. It may be recited only if ten adult men are present at the *siyum*.

The Great *Kaddish* (*Kaddish Hagadol*) is recited on two special occasions: when making a *siyum* upon the completion of a Tractate of Talmud or an order of Mishnah, and at a funeral. These two occasions are radically different, but there is something in common. The theme of this *Kaddish* is that, in the merit of Torah study, the world will be renewed, including the eventual revival of the dead. Therefore, it is appropriate for both a *siyum* (recognizing as it does the rewards of Torah study) and a funeral (as it contains within it the consolation that those who have passed on will someday return to us).

Table 34 Kaddish HaGadol

ARAMAIC	ENGLISH
יִתְגַּדַּל וְיִתְקַדַּשׁ שְׁמֵהּ רַבָּא.	Exalted and hallowed be His great Name.
Respondents say, "Amen"	
בְּעָלְמָא דִּי הוּא עָתִיד לְאִתְחַדְּתָא. וּלְאַחֲיָאה מֵתַיָּא. וּלְאַסָּקָא יַתְהוֹן לְחַיֵּי עָלְמָא.	In the world which He will create anew, where He will revive the dead, construct His temple,

וּלְמִבְנָא קַרְתָּא דִּי יְרוּשְׁלֵם. וּלְשַׁכְלְלָא הֵיכָלֵהּ בְּגַוַּהּ. וּלְמֶעְקַר פּוּלְחָנָא נוּכְרָאָה מִן אַרְעָהּ. וּלְאָתָבָא פּוּלְחָנָא דִּי שְׁמַיָּא לְאַתְרֵהּ. וְיַמְלִיךְ קוּדְשָׁא בְּרִיךְ הוּא בְּמַלְכוּתֵהּ וִיקָרֵהּ.	deliver life, and rebuild the city of Yerushalayim, and uproot foreign idol worship from His land, and restore the holy service of Heaven to its place, along with His radiance, splendor, and *Shechinah,*

Some add the following

וְיַצְמַח פֻּרְקָנֵהּ וִיקָרֵב (קיץ) מְשִׁיחֵהּ	And may His salvation blossom and His anointed be near

When adding the above, the respondents say, "Amen"

בְּחַיֵּיכוֹן וּבְיוֹמֵיכוֹן וּבְחַיֵּי דְכָל בֵּית יִשְׂרָאֵל, בַּעֲגָלָא וּבִזְמַן קָרִיב. וְאִמְרוּ אָמֵן.	In your lifetime and in your days and in the lifetime of the entire House of Israel, sword, famine, and death shall cease from us and from the entire Jewish nation, speedily and soon, and say, Amen.

Respondents say, "Amen" and the following line, and repeated by the one saying the Kaddish

יְהֵא שְׁמֵהּ רַבָּא מְבָרַךְ לְעָלַם וּלְעָלְמֵי עָלְמַיָּא.	May His great Name be blessed forever and to all eternity.
יִתְבָּרַךְ וְיִשְׁתַּבַּח וְיִתְפָּאַר וְיִתְרוֹמַם וְיִתְנַשֵּׂא וְיִתְהַדָּר וְיִתְעַלֶּה וְיִתְהַלָּל שְׁמֵהּ דְּקֻדְשָׁא. בְּרִיךְ הוּא.	Blessed and praised, glorified, exalted and extolled, honored, adored and lauded be the Name of the Holy One, blessed be He.

Respondents say, "Berich Hu"

לְעֵלָּא (בעשי"ת לְעֵלָּא לְעֵלָּא מִכָּל) מִן כָּל בִּרְכָתָא וְשִׁירָתָא תֻּשְׁבְּחָתָא וְנֶחֱמָתָא דַּאֲמִירָן בְּעָלְמָא. וְאִמְרוּ אָמֵן	Beyond all the blessings, hymns, praises, and consolations that are uttered in the world; and say, Amen.

Respondents say, "Amen"

עַל יִשְׂרָאֵל וְעַל רַבָּנָן. וְעַל תַּלְמִידֵיהוֹן וְעַל כָּל תַּלְמִידֵי תַלְמִידֵיהוֹן. וְעַל כָּל מַאן דְּעָסְקִין בְּאוֹרַיְתָא. דִּי בְאַתְרָא	Upon Israel, and upon our sages, and upon their disciples, and upon all the disciples of their disciples, and upon all those who occupy themselves with the Torah, here or

186

קַדִּישָׁא הָדֵין וְדִי בְכָל אֲתַר וַאֲתַר. יְהֵא לְהוֹן וּלְכוֹן שְׁלָמָא רַבָּא חִנָּא וְחִסְדָּא וְרַחֲמִין וְחַיִּין אֲרִיכִין וּמְזוֹנֵי רְוִיחֵי וּפֻרְקָנָא מִן קֳדָם אֲבוּהוֹן דְּבִשְׁמַיָּא וְאִמְרוּ אָמֵן.	in any other place, upon them and upon you, may there be abundant peace, grace, kindness, compassion, long life, ample sustenance, and deliverance, from their Father in Heaven; and say, Amen.

Respondents say, "Amen"

יְהֵא שְׁלָמָא רַבָּא מִן שְׁמַיָּא וְחַיִּים עָלֵינוּ וְעַל כָּל יִשְׂרָאֵל. וְאִמְרוּ אָמֵן:	May there be abundant peace from Heaven, and life, upon us and upon all Israel; and say, Amen.

Respondents say, "Amen"

עוֹשֶׂה שָׁלוֹם (בעשי״ת הַשָּׁלוֹם) בִּמְרוֹמָיו הוּא יַעֲשֶׂה שָׁלוֹם עָלֵינוּ וְעַל כָּל יִשְׂרָאֵל וְאִמְרוּ אָמֵן:	He Who makes peace (Between *Rosh Hashana* and *Yom Kippur* substitute: "the peace") in His Heavens, may He make peace for us and for all Israel; and say, Amen

Respondents say, "Amen"

KADDISH TRANSLITERATED

Yisgadal v'yiskadash sh'mei raba

B'olmo d'hu osid lischadta ulachyo'oh maysayo ulshachl'loh haych'lay, ul'mifrak chayo, ulmivnay karto dirushlaym, ule'me'ekar pulchono nuchro'oh mayaray, v'la'asovo pulchano kadisho dishmayo l'asray, v'zivay vikoray ush'chintay.

B'chayeichon uvyomeichon uvchayei d'chol beis Yisrael, ba'agala uvizman kariv, v'im'ru: "amen."

Y'hei sh'mei raba m'varach l'alam ul'almei almaya.

Yisbarach v'yishtabach, v'yispa'ar v'yisromam v'yisnaseh, v'yis'hadar v'yis'aleh v'yis'halal sh'mei d'kud'sha, b'rich hu,

L'eila min-kol-birchasa v'shirasa, tushb'chasa v'nechemasa da'amiran b'alma, v'im'ru: "amen."

Al yisra-eil v'al rabanan, v'al talmideihon v'al kol talmidei salmideihon, v'al kol man d'as'kin b'oraysa, di v'asra hadein v'di v'chol asar va-asar. Y'hei l'hon ul'chon sh'lama raba, china v'chisda v'rachamin, v'chayin arichin, um'zonei r'vichei, ufurkana, min kodam avuhon di vishmaya (vara), v'imru amen.

Y'hei shlama raba min-sh'maya v'chayim aleinu v'al-kol-Yisrael, v'im'ru: "amen."

Oseh shalom bimromav, hu ya'aseh shalom aleinu v'al kol-yisrael, v'imru: "amen."

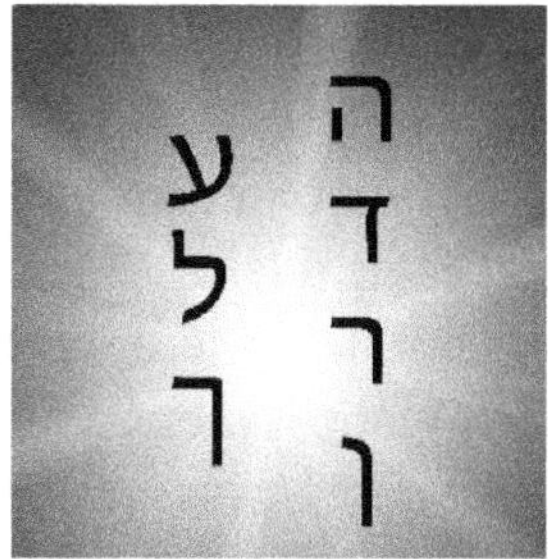

BIRCHAS HAMAZON

FOR YOUR CONVENIENCE, WE HAVE included the *birchas hamazon,* which is said at the conclusion of the festive meal when eaten with bread. *Birchas Hamazon,* known in English as the "Grace After Meals," is the series of four blessings recited after a meal in which one has eaten bread. While all other blessings are commanded by the rabbis, proclaiming thanks to God after a meal is a commandment from the Torah.[26]

For your convenience, we have **bolded** the instructions and gray-highlighted paragraphs that are only said on special occasions.

It is customary for the person making the *siyum* to make a *bracha* on a cup of wine (or grape juice). However, if there is a Kohen present, he takes precedence in leading the *birchas hamazon.* I have included the appropriate *brachos* and instructions. There are several kabbalistic reasons behind using wine at the conclusion of a *siyum* for *birchas hamazon.* It should be noted that anytime there are ten men at a meal, the *birchas hamazon* should be said over a cup of wine.

---

[26] Devarim 8:10

Table 35 Introduction to Birchas Hamazon

בחול קודם ברכת המזון אומרים:	Psalm 137 is recited before *Birchas Hamazon* on weekdays in memory of the destruction of the Beis HaMikdash:
עַל־נַהֲרוֹת בָּבֶל שָׁם יָשַׁבְנוּ גַּם־בָּכִינוּ בְּזָכְרֵנוּ אֶת־צִיּוֹן: עַל־עֲרָבִים בְּתוֹכָהּ תָּלִינוּ כִּנֹּרוֹתֵינוּ: כִּי שָׁם שְׁאֵלוּנוּ שׁוֹבֵינוּ דִּבְרֵי־שִׁיר וְתוֹלָלֵינוּ שִׂמְחָה שִׁירוּ לָנוּ מִשִּׁיר צִיּוֹן: אֵיךְ נָשִׁיר אֶת־שִׁיר־יְהוָה עַל אַדְמַת נֵכָר: אִם־אֶשְׁכָּחֵךְ יְרוּשָׁלָםִ תִּשְׁכַּח יְמִינִי: תִּדְבַּק לְשׁוֹנִי לְחִכִּי אִם־לֹא אֶזְכְּרֵכִי אִם־לֹא אַעֲלֶה אֶת־יְרוּשָׁלַםִ עַל רֹאשׁ שִׂמְחָתִי: זְכֹר יְהוָה לִבְנֵי אֱדוֹם אֵת יוֹם יְרוּשָׁלָםִ הָאֹמְרִים עָרוּ עָרוּ עַד הַיְסוֹד בָּהּ: בַּת־בָּבֶל הַשְּׁדוּדָה אַשְׁרֵי שֶׁיְּשַׁלֶּם־לָךְ אֶת־גְּמוּלֵךְ שֶׁגָּמַלְתְּ לָנוּ: אַשְׁרֵי שֶׁיֹּאחֵז וְנִפֵּץ אֶת־עֹלָלַיִךְ אֶל־הַסָּלַע:	By the rivers of Babylon, there we sat and we also wept, when we remembered Zion. Upon the willows in its midst, we hung our harps. For there our captors demanded of us words of song, and our tormentors asked of us (with) mirth; Sing to us from the song(s) of Zion. How shall we sing the song of the Lord on alien soil? If I ever forget you, Yerushalayim, may my right hand forget (its movement). May my tongue cleave to my palate, if I remember you not; if I set not Yerushalayim above my highest joy. Remember, Lord, to the sons of Edom the day of Yerushalayim, (it was they) who said, Raze it, raze it to its very foundation. Daughter of Babylon, you are the annihilated one; fortunate is he who will repay you for all you have done for us. Fortunate is he who will take and dash your little ones against the rock.
בשבת קודם ברכת המזון אומרים:	Psalm 126 is recited on *Shabbos* and *Yom Tov*
שִׁיר הַמַּעֲלוֹת בְּשׁוּב יְהוָה אֶת־שִׁיבַת צִיּוֹן הָיִינוּ כְּחֹלְמִים: אָז יִמָּלֵא שְׂחוֹק פִּינוּ וּלְשׁוֹנֵנוּ רִנָּה, אָז יֹאמְרוּ בַגּוֹיִם הִגְדִּיל יְהוָה	A Song of Ascents. When Lord brings about the return to Zion we

לַעֲשׂוֹת עִם־אֵלֶּה: הִגְדִּיל יְהֹוָה לַעֲשׂוֹת עִמָּנוּ, הָיִינוּ שְׂמֵחִים: שׁוּבָה יְהֹוָה אֶת־שְׁבִיתֵנוּ כַּאֲפִיקִים בַּנֶּגֶב: הַזֹּרְעִים בְּדִמְעָה, בְּרִנָּה יִקְצֹרוּ: הָלוֹךְ יֵלֵךְ וּבָכֹה, נֹשֵׂא מֶשֶׁךְ־הַזָּרַע, בֹּא־יָבֹא בְרִנָּה, נֹשֵׂא אֲלֻמֹּתָיו:	will have been like dreamers.[27] [28]Then will our mouths be filled with laughter,[29] and our tongue with joyous song. Then will they say among the nations: "Lord has done great things for them." Lord had done great things for us; we will (then) rejoice. Lord! bring back our exiles like springs in the desert.[30] Those who sow in tears will reap with joyous song.[31] (Though) he walks along weeping, carrying the bag of seed, he will return with joyous song carrying his sheaves.

Table 36 Invitation to Birchas Hamazon

If using a cup of wine, hold it in your right hand and raise it a few inches. Hold it aloft until noted herein to place it down.	
הַמְזַמֵּן אוֹמֵר:	**The leader begins by saying:**
רַבּוֹתַי נְבָרֵךְ:	Gentlemen, let us say the blessing:
הַמְסוּבִּים עוֹנִים:	**The others respond:**
יְהִי שֵׁם יְהֹוָה מְבֹרָךְ מֵעַתָּה וְעַד־עוֹלָם:	The Name of the Lord will be blessed from now and forever.

---

[27] According to the Radak, this means that upon the Redemption and return to Zion, the harshness of the exile will seem to the Jews like a terrible dream.

[28] The Seforno says, the splendor of the return to Zion will be like the realization of an impossible dream

[29] In the Gemara (Maseches Berachos 31a) Rabbi Shimon *bar* Yochai rules that a Jew is forbidden to fill his mouth with laughter in this world until the time comes when all nations declare, "Lord has done great things for them" — as the *Pasuk* says, "אז ימלא שחוק פינו", then: only then, when God's love for us is universally recognized, may we experience total exultation.

[30] Rashi says, that just as springs of water can transform an arid desert into a fertile oasis, so will we be transformed, and flourish when God delivers us from exile.

[31] According to the Radak, a person who plants in desert-like soil is always fearful that his crops will not grow. If a spring of water should suddenly appear on his land, his joy will know no bounds. So great will our joy be at the ultimate redemption that will follow the oppression of exile.

וחוזר המזמן:	The leader repeats:
יְהִי שֵׁם יְהֹוָה מְבֹרָךְ מֵעַתָּה וְעַד־עוֹלָם : בִּרְשׁוּת מָרָנָן וְרַבָּנָן וְרַבּוֹתַי נְבָרֵךְ (בעשרה אֱלֹהֵינוּ) שֶׁאָכַלְנוּ מִשֶּׁלוֹ:	The Name of the Lord will be blessed from now and forever. With your permission our masters and teachers, let us bless Him (our God[32]), for we have eaten of His bounty.
המסובים עונים:	The others respond accordingly:
בָּרוּךְ (בעשרה אֱלֹהֵינוּ) שֶׁאָכַלְנוּ מִשֶּׁלוֹ וּבְטוּבוֹ חָיִינוּ:	Blessed is He (our God[32]) for we have eaten of His bounty and through His goodness we live.
מי שלא אכל עונה:	One who did not eat, responds:
בָּרוּךְ (בעשרה או יותר אֱלֹהֵינוּ) וּמְבוֹרָךְ שְׁמוֹ תָּמִיד לְעוֹלָם וָעֶד:	Blessed is He (our God[32]), and His Name constantly, forever and ever.
וחוזר המזמן:	The leader repeats:
בָּרוּךְ (בעשרה אֱלֹהֵינוּ) שֶׁאָכַלְנוּ מִשֶּׁלוֹ וּבְטוּבוֹ חָיִינוּ:	Blessed is He (our God[32]) for we have eaten of His bounty and through His goodness we live.

Table 37 Birchas Hamazon

ברכה ראשונה	FIRST *BRACHA*[33]
בָּרוּךְ אַתָּה יְהֹוָה אֱלֹהֵינוּ מֶלֶךְ הָעוֹלָם הַזָּן אֶת־הָעוֹלָם כֻּלּוֹ בְּטוּבוֹ בְּחֵן בְּחֶסֶד וּבְרַחֲמִים הוּא נוֹתֵן לֶחֶם לְכָל־בָּשָׂר כִּי לְעוֹלָם חַסְדּוֹ וּבְטוּבוֹ הַגָּדוֹל תָּמִיד לֹא־חָסַר לָנוּ וְאַל־יֶחְסַר	Blessed are You, Lord our God, King of the Universe, Who nourishes the entire world with His goodness, with favor, with kindness, and with mercy.[34] He

---

[32] "Our God" is inserted when there are ten or more men

[33] The first *bracha* was fixed by Moshe Rabaynu when the manna fell from Heaven. The source for all four *brachos* is from Maseches Berachos 48b.

[34] The righteous find favor in the eyes of God and are nourished because of their merit. Those who are not so worthy and do not find favor, are provided for through God's beneficent kindness, while even the least worthy are recipients of God's mercy. (Maharal in Nesivos Olom)

לָנוּ מָזוֹן לְעוֹלָם וָעֶד בַּעֲבוּר שְׁמוֹ הַגָּדוֹל כִּי הוּא אֵל זָן וּמְפַרְנֵס לַכֹּל וּמֵטִיב לַכֹּל וּמֵכִין מָזוֹן לְכָל־בְּרִיּוֹתָיו אֲשֶׁר בָּרָא: בָּרוּךְ אַתָּה יְהֹוָה הַזָּן אֶת־הַכֹּל:	provides food for all flesh,[35] for His kindness endures forever. And through His great goodness, we have never lacked, and we will not lack food forever and ever, for the sake of His great Name. For He is Almighty Who nourishes[36] and maintains all, does good to all, and prepares nourishment for all His creatures which He has created. Blessed are You, Lord Who nourishes all.
ברכה שניה	**SECOND *BRACHA*[37]**
נוֹדֶה לְךָ יְהֹוָה אֱלֹהֵינוּ עַל שֶׁהִנְחַלְתָּ לַאֲבוֹתֵינוּ אֶרֶץ חֶמְדָּה טוֹבָה וּרְחָבָה וְעַל שֶׁהוֹצֵאתָנוּ יְהֹוָה אֱלֹהֵינוּ מֵאֶרֶץ מִצְרַיִם וּפְדִיתָנוּ מִבֵּית עֲבָדִים וְעַל בְּרִיתְךָ שֶׁחָתַמְתָּ בִּבְשָׂרֵנוּ וְעַל תּוֹרָתְךָ שֶׁלִּמַּדְתָּנוּ וְעַל חֻקֶּיךָ שֶׁהוֹדַעְתָּנוּ וְעַל חַיִּים חֵן וָחֶסֶד שֶׁחוֹנַנְתָּנוּ וְעַל אֲכִילַת מָזוֹן	We thank You, Lord, our God, for Your parceling out as a heritage to our fathers, a land which is desirable,[38] good, and spacious; for Your bringing us out, Lord, our God, from the land of Egypt, and redeeming us from the house of bondage; for Your covenant which You sealed in our flesh; for Your Torah[39] which You taught us; for Your statutes which You

---

[35] This citation from Tehillim 136:25 indicates that God's kindness and compassion are universal, relating to all flesh, including animals. (Avudraham)

[36] "Nourishes" refers to food, "maintains" refers to clothing, and "does good" refers to shelter. These are the basic needs of man, all of which God provides. (Aitz Yosef)

[37] The second *bracha* was established by Yehoshua upon the Jewish people's entrance to Israel

[38] The Land is mentioned even before the Exodus from Egypt because God demonstrated His extraordinary concern for the Jewish people at the very beginning of their history; first by the promise He gave to the Patriarchs concerning the Land of Israel and then, with the fulfillment of that promise, once He redeemed them from Egypt to enter the Land. (Rabbi Samson Raphael Hirsch)

[39] "Torah" refers to laws that are comprehensible to the human intellect; it is therefore taught. "Statutes" (חֻקִּים) are beyond human understanding and are therefore merely made known to man, for man cannot comprehend them. (Iyun Tefillah)

שָׁאַתָּה זָן וּמְפַרְנֵס אוֹתָנוּ תָּמִיד בְּכָל־יוֹם וּבְכָל־עֵת וּבְכָל שָׁעָה:	made known to us; for the life, favor, and kindness which You granted us; and for the provision of food with which You nourish and maintain us constantly, every day, at all times and in every hour.
בחנוכה ופורים אומרים כאן על הניסים. ואם לא אמרו אין מחזירין אותו. ומכל מקום יוכל לאמרו בתוך שאר הרחמן. ויאמר הָרַחֲמָן הוּא יַעֲשֶׂה־לָנוּ נִסִּים וְנִפְלָאוֹת כְּמוֹ שֶׁעָשָׂה לַאֲבוֹתֵינוּ בַּיָּמִים הָהֵם בַּזְּמַן הַזֶּה וכו' בִּימֵי מַתִּתְיָהוּ וכו' אוֹ בִּימֵי מָרְדְּכַי וכו'.	**On regular weekdays, continue, "For everything". On Chanukah and Purim add עַל הַנִּסִּים. If you forgot to say עַל הַנִּסִּים, you may include it when you reach הָרַחֲמָן by saying: הָרַחֲמָן הוּא יַעֲשֶׂה־לָנוּ נִסִּים וְנִפְלָאוֹת כְּמוֹ שֶׁעָשָׂה לַאֲבוֹתֵינוּ בַּיָּמִים הָהֵם בַּזְּמַן הַזֶּה. and then continue on Chanukah with: בִּימֵי מַתִּתְיָהוּ, and on Purim with: בִּימֵי מָרְדְּכַי וְאֶסְתֵּר. If you reminded yourself before concluding the second blessing עַל הָאָרֶץ וְעַל הַמָּזוֹן, you may repeat it at that time and continue with the *Birchas Hamazon*.**
(וְ)עַל הַנִּסִּים וְעַל הַפֻּרְקָן וְעַל הַגְּבוּרוֹת וְעַל הַתְּשׁוּעוֹת וְעַל הַמִּלְחָמוֹת שֶׁעָשִׂיתָ לַאֲבוֹתֵינוּ בַּיָּמִים הָהֵם בַּזְּמַן הַזֶּה:	(We thank You) for the miracles for the redemption, for the mighty deeds, for the deliverances, for the wonders for the consolations, and for the wars that You performed for our fathers in those days at this season.
בחנוכה אומרים:	**On Chanukah:**
בִּימֵי מַתִּתְיָהוּ בֶּן־יוֹחָנָן כֹּהֵן גָּדוֹל חַשְׁמוֹנַאי וּבָנָיו כְּשֶׁעָמְדָה מַלְכוּת יָוָן הָרְשָׁעָה עַל־עַמְּךָ יִשְׂרָאֵל לְהַשְׁכִּיחָם תּוֹרָתֶךָ	In the days of Matisyahu, son of Yochanan the High Priest, the Chashmonai and his sons, when the evil Greek kingdom rose up against Your people Israel to

make them forget Your Torah and to turn them away from the statutes of Your will — You, in Your abundant mercy, stood by them in their time of distress, You defended their cause, You judged their grievances, You avenged them. You delivered the mighty into the hands of the weak, many into the hands of the few, defiled people into the hands of the undefiled, the wicked into the hands of the righteous, and insolent (sinners) into the hands of diligent students of Your Torah. And You made Yourself a great and sanctified name in Your world. And for Your people, Israel, You performed a great deliverance and redemption unto this very day. Afterward, Your sons entered the Holy of Holies of Your Abode, cleaned Your Temple, purified Your Sanctuary, and kindled lights in the Courtyards of Your Sanctuary, and designated these eight days of Chanukah to thank and praise Your great Name.

וּלְהַעֲבִירָם מֵחֻקֵּי רְצוֹנֶךָ: וְאַתָּה בְּרַחֲמֶיךָ הָרַבִּים עָמַדְתָּ לָהֶם בְּעֵת צָרָתָם רַבְתָּ אֶת־רִיבָם דַּנְתָּ אֶת־דִּינָם נָקַמְתָּ אֶת־ נִקְמָתָם מָסַרְתָּ גִבּוֹרִים בְּיַד חַלָּשִׁים וְרַבִּים בְּיַד מְעַטִּים וּטְמֵאִים בְּיַד טְהוֹרִים וּרְשָׁעִים בְּיַד צַדִּיקִים וְזֵדִים בְּיַד עוֹסְקֵי תוֹרָתֶךָ וּלְךָ עָשִׂיתָ שֵׁם גָּדוֹל וְקָדוֹשׁ בְּעוֹלָמֶךָ וּלְעַמְּךָ יִשְׂרָאֵל עָשִׂיתָ תְּשׁוּעָה גְדוֹלָה וּפֻרְקָן כְּהַיּוֹם הַזֶּה וְאַחַר כַּךְ בָּאוּ בָנֶיךָ לִדְבִיר בֵּיתֶךָ וּפִנּוּ אֶת הֵיכָלֶךָ וְטִהֲרוּ אֶת מִקְדָּשֶׁךָ וְהִדְלִיקוּ נֵרוֹת בְּחַצְרוֹת קָדְשֶׁךָ וְקָבְעוּ שְׁמוֹנַת יְמֵי חֲנֻכָּה אֵלּוּ לְהוֹדוֹת וּלְהַלֵּל לְשִׁמְךָ הַגָּדוֹל:

On Purim:	בפורים אומרים:

In the days of Mordechai and Ester in Shushan the Capital (of Persia), when the evil Haman rose up against them, he sought to destroy, to kill, and to annihilate all the Jews, young and old, infants and women, in one day, the thirteenth day of the twelfth

בִּימֵי מָרְדְּכַי וְאֶסְתֵּר בְּשׁוּשַׁן הַבִּירָה כְּשֶׁעָמַד עֲלֵיהֶם הָמָן הָרָשָׁע בִּקֵּשׁ לְהַשְׁמִיד לַהֲרוֹג וּלְאַבֵּד אֶת־כָּל־הַיְּהוּדִים מִנַּעַר וְעַד־זָקֵן טַף וְנָשִׁים בְּיוֹם אֶחָד בִּשְׁלוֹשָׁה עָשָׂר לְחֹדֶשׁ שְׁנֵים־ עָשָׂר הוּא חֹדֶשׁ אֲדָר וּשְׁלָלָם

לָבוֹז: וְאַתָּה בְּרַחֲמֶיךָ הָרַבִּים הֵפַרְתָּ אֶת־עֲצָתוֹ וְקִלְקַלְתָּ אֶת מַחֲשַׁבְתּוֹ וַהֲשֵׁבוֹתָ לּוֹ גְּמוּלוֹ בְּרֹאשׁוֹ וְתָלוּ אוֹתוֹ וְאֶת־בָּנָיו עַל־הָעֵץ:	month, which is the month of Adar, and to plunder their wealth And You, in Your abundant mercy, annulled his counsel, frustrated his intention, and brought his evil plan upon his own head, and they hanged him and his sons upon the gallows.
וְעַל הַכֹּל יְהֹוָה אֱלֹהֵינוּ אֲנַחְנוּ מוֹדִים לָךְ וּמְבָרְכִים אוֹתָךְ יִתְבָּרַךְ שִׁמְךָ בְּפִי כָּל־חַי תָּמִיד לְעוֹלָם וָעֶד כַּכָּתוּב וְאָכַלְתָּ וְשָׂבָעְתָּ וּבֵרַכְתָּ אֶת־יְהֹוָה אֱלֹהֶיךָ עַל־הָאָרֶץ הַטּוֹבָה אֲשֶׁר נָתַן־לָךְ בָּרוּךְ אַתָּה יְהֹוָה עַל־הָאָרֶץ וְעַל־הַמָּזוֹן:	For everything Lord, our God, We thank You and bless You. Blessed be Your Name through the mouth of all the living, constantly, forever, as it is written:[40] When You have eaten and are satisfied, You will bless Lord, your God, for the good land which He has given to you. Blessed are You, Lord, for the land and for the food.
בְּרָכָה שְׁלִישִׁית	**THIRD *BRACHA*[41]**
רַחֵם יְהֹוָה אֱלֹהֵינוּ עַל־יִשְׂרָאֵל עַמֶּךָ וְעַל יְרוּשָׁלַיִם עִירֶךָ וְעַל צִיּוֹן מִשְׁכַּן כְּבוֹדֶךָ וְעַל מַלְכוּת בֵּית דָּוִד מְשִׁיחֶךָ וְעַל־הַבַּיִת הַגָּדוֹל וְהַקָּדוֹשׁ שֶׁנִּקְרָא שִׁמְךָ עָלָיו אֱלֹהֵינוּ אָבִינוּ רְעֵנוּ זוּנֵנוּ פַּרְנְסֵנוּ וְכַלְכְּלֵנוּ וְהַרְוִיחֵנוּ וְהַרְוַח־לָנוּ יְהֹוָה אֱלֹהֵינוּ מְהֵרָה מִכָּל־צָרוֹתֵינוּ וְנָא אַל־תַּצְרִיכֵנוּ	Have compassion, Lord, our God, on Israel, Your people, on Yerushalayim, Your city, on Zion, the dwelling place of Your glory, on the kingship of the house of David, Your anointed; and on the great and holy House upon which Your Name is called. Our God, our Father tend us, nourish us,[42] maintain us, sustain us, relieve us,[43] and grant us relief Lord, our

---

[40] Devarim 8:10

[41] The third *bracha* until "Yerushalayim Your city" was composed by King David and the rest was composed by King Shlomo.

[42] "Tend us" by providing the basic necessities of life such as bread and water; "nourish" us with an enriched diet including foods such as fruits and vegetables. (Aitz Yosef)

[43] "Maintain us" with food and shelter; "sustain us" by providing our needs on a regular basis, not on a feast or famine cycle; and "relieve us" by giving us ample means to live comfortably. (Aitz Yosef)

יְהֹוָה אֱלֹהֵינוּ לֹא לִידֵי מַתְּנַת בָּשָׂר וָדָם וְלֹא לִידֵי הַלְוָאָתָם כִּי אִם לְיָדְךָ הַמְּלֵאָה הַפְּתוּחָה הַקְּדוֹשָׁה וְהָרְחָבָה שֶׁלֹּא נֵבוֹשׁ וְלֹא נִכָּלֵם לְעוֹלָם וָעֶד:	God, speedily from all our troubles. Lord, our God — may we never need the gifts of men nor their loans, but only of Your hand which is full, open, holy, and generous, so that we may not be shamed nor humiliated[44] forever and ever.
בשבת מוסיפים:	**On regular weekdays, continue, "Rebuild". On *Shabbos* add:**
רְצֵה וְהַחֲלִיצֵנוּ יְהֹוָה אֱלֹהֵינוּ בְּמִצְוֹתֶיךָ וּבְמִצְוַת יוֹם הַשְּׁבִיעִי הַשַּׁבָּת הַגָּדוֹל וְהַקָּדוֹשׁ הַזֶּה כִּי יוֹם זֶה גָּדוֹל וְקָדוֹשׁ הוּא לְפָנֶיךָ לִשְׁבָּת בּוֹ וְלָנוּחַ בּוֹ בְּאַהֲבָה כְּמִצְוַת רְצוֹנֶךָ וּבִרְצוֹנְךָ הָנִיחַ לָנוּ יְהֹוָה אֱלֹהֵינוּ שֶׁלֹּא תְהֵא צָרָה וְיָגוֹן וַאֲנָחָה בְּיוֹם מְנוּחָתֵנוּ וְהַרְאֵנוּ יְהֹוָה אֱלֹהֵינוּ בְּנֶחָמַת צִיּוֹן עִירֶךָ וּבְבִנְיַן יְרוּשָׁלַיִם עִיר קָדְשֶׁךָ כִּי אַתָּה הוּא בַּעַל הַיְשׁוּעוֹת וּבַעַל הַנֶּחָמוֹת:	May it please You, to strengthen us Lord, our God, through Your commandments, and through the commandment of the seventh day, this great and holy *Shabbos*. For this day is great and holy before You, to refrain from work on it and to rest on it with love, as ordained by Your will. And by Your will, grant us repose Lord, our God, that there be no distress, sorrow, or sighing on the day of our rest.[45] Show us Lord, our God, the consolation of Zion, Your city, and the rebuilding of Yerushalayim, the city of Your Sanctuary, for You are the Master of deliverance and the Master of consolation.
בראש חודש ובחול המועד אומרים כאן "יעלה ויבא"	**On *Rosh Chodesh* and *Yom Tov* add:**

---

[44] May we not be "ashamed" in this world due to poverty and may we not be "humiliated" in the World-to-Come, because of our transgressions. Poverty often brings shame which in turn might cause a person to lose faith. (Aitz Yosef)

[45] Typically, prayers for personal needs are not recited on *Shabbos*, this prayer does contain such a request because it is so closely interwoven with the commandment to rest on *Shabbos*. Since we are commanded to make *Shabbos* a day of sacred rest, we ask that our repose not be desecrated by distress or misfortune. (Avudraham)

אֱלֹהֵינוּ וֵאלֹהֵי אֲבוֹתֵינוּ יַעֲלֶה וְיָבֹא וְיַגִּיעַ וְיֵרָאֶה וְיֵרָצֶה וְיִשָּׁמַע וְיִפָּקֵד וְיִזָּכֵר זִכְרוֹנֵנוּ וּפִקְדוֹנֵנוּ וְזִכְרוֹן אֲבוֹתֵינוּ וְזִכְרוֹן מָשִׁיחַ בֶּן־דָּוִד עַבְדֶּךָ וְזִכְרוֹן יְרוּשָׁלַיִם עִיר קָדְשֶׁךָ וְזִכְרוֹן כָּל־עַמְּךָ בֵּית יִשְׂרָאֵל לְפָנֶיךָ, לִפְלֵיטָה לְטוֹבָה לְחֵן וּלְחֶסֶד וּלְרַחֲמִים לְחַיִּים וּלְשָׁלוֹם בְּיוֹם	Our God and God of our fathers, may there ascend, come, and reach, appear, be desired, and heard, counted and recalled our remembrance and reckoning; the remembrance of our fathers; the remembrance of the Mashiach the son of David, Your servant; the remembrance of Yerushalayim, city of Your Sanctuary; and the remembrance of Your entire people, the House of Israel, before You for survival, for well-being, for favor, kindliness, compassion, for life and peace on this day of:
לְר"ח: רֹאשׁ הַחֹדֶשׁ הַזֶּה	This *Rosh Chodesh*
לְפֶסַח: חַג הַמַּצּוֹת הַזֶּה	The Festival of *Matzos*
בשבועות: חַג הַשָּׁבֻעוֹת	The Festival of *Shavuos*
לְסֻכּוֹת: חַג הַסֻּכּוֹת הַזֶּה	The Festival of *Sukkos*
לש"ע וש"ת: הַשְּׁמִינִי חַג הָעֲצֶרֶת הַזֶּה	The Festival of *Shemini Atseres*
לר"ה: הַזִּכָּרוֹן הַזֶּה	This Day of Remembrance
זָכְרֵנוּ יְהֹוָה אֱלֹהֵינוּ בּוֹ לְטוֹבָה, וּפָקְדֵנוּ בוֹ לִבְרָכָה, וְהוֹשִׁיעֵנוּ בוֹ לְחַיִּים, וּבִדְבַר יְשׁוּעָה וְרַחֲמִים חוּס וְחָנֵּנוּ, וְרַחֵם עָלֵינוּ וְהוֹשִׁיעֵנוּ, כִּי אֵלֶיךָ עֵינֵינוּ, כִּי אֵל מֶלֶךְ חַנּוּן וְרַחוּם אָתָּה:	Remember us Lord, our God, on this day for well-being; be mindful of us on this day for blessing and deliver us for life. In accord with the promise of deliverance and compassion, spare us and favor us, have compassion on us and deliver us; for to You our eyes are directed because You are the Almighty Who is King, Gracious, and Merciful.
וּבְנֵה יְרוּשָׁלַיִם עִיר הַקֹּדֶשׁ בִּמְהֵרָה בְיָמֵינוּ: בָּרוּךְ אַתָּה	Rebuild Yerushalayim, the city of the Holy Sanctuary, speedily, in our days. Blessed are You, Lord,

יְהֹוָה בּוֹנֵה בְרַחֲמָיו יְרוּשָׁלָיִם, אָמֵן:	Builder of Yerushalayim in His mercy. Amen.[46]
ברכה רביעי	**FOURTH BRACHA[47]**
בָּרוּךְ אַתָּה יְהֹוָה אֱלֹהֵינוּ מֶלֶךְ הָעוֹלָם, הָאֵל אָבִינוּ, מַלְכֵּנוּ, אַדִּירֵנוּ בּוֹרְאֵנוּ, גּוֹאֲלֵנוּ, יוֹצְרֵנוּ, קְדוֹשֵׁנוּ קְדוֹשׁ יַעֲקֹב, רוֹעֵנוּ רוֹעֵה יִשְׂרָאֵל, הַמֶּלֶךְ הַטּוֹב, וְהַמֵּטִיב לַכֹּל, שֶׁבְּכָל יוֹם וָיוֹם הוּא הֵטִיב, הוּא מֵטִיב, הוּא יֵיטִיב לָנוּ, הוּא גְמָלָנוּ, הוּא גוֹמְלֵנוּ, הוּא יִגְמְלֵנוּ לָעַד לְחֵן וּלְחֶסֶד וּלְרַחֲמִים וּלְרֶוַח הַצָּלָה וְהַצְלָחָה בְּרָכָה וִישׁוּעָה, נֶחָמָה, פַּרְנָסָה וְכַלְכָּלָה, וְרַחֲמִים, וְחַיִּים וְשָׁלוֹם, וְכָל־טוֹב, וּמִכָּל־טוֹב לְעוֹלָם אַל יְחַסְּרֵנוּ:	Blessed are You, Lord our God, King of the Universe, the Almighty, our Father, our King, our Mighty One, our Creator, our Redeemer, our Maker, our Holy One, Holy One of Yaakov, our Shepherd, Shepherd of Israel, the King, Who is good and beneficent to all. Every single day He has done good, does good, and will do good to us. He has rewarded us, He rewards us, He will reward us forever with favor, kindness, and compassion, relief, rescue, and success, blessing, deliverance, and consolation, maintenance, sustenance, compassion, life, peace, and everything good; and of all good things may He never deprive us.[48]
If you are using a cup of wine, you may now put it down.	
הָרַחֲמָן הוּא יִמְלוֹךְ עָלֵינוּ לְעוֹלָם וָעֶד:	The Merciful One will reign over us forever and ever.

---

[46] It is unusual for one to answer Amen after his own blessing. This blessing ends with Amen because it marks the end of the three blessings, authority for which is derived from Devarim (8:10) and separates them from the next blessing which is Rabbinic in origin. (Maseches Berachos 45b)

[47] The fourth *bracha* was established in Yavneh by Rabban Gamliel the Elder on the day when the victims of the Roman massacre at Beitar were permitted to be buried. We gave thanks to HaShem for permission to bury them and that their bodies had not decayed.

[48] Many people are granted the bounties of life but are unable to enjoy them. We first invoke God's blessing for all the good things in life and then ask Him to grant us the privilege of enjoying them. (Iyun Tefillah)

הָרַחֲמָן הוּא יִתְבָּרֵךְ בַּשָּׁמַיִם וּבָאָרֶץ:	The Merciful One will be blessed in Heaven and on earth.
הָרַחֲמָן הוּא יִשְׁתַּבַּח לְדוֹר דּוֹרִים, וְיִתְפָּאַר בָּנוּ לָעַד וּלְנֵצַח נְצָחִים, וְיִתְהַדַּר בָּנוּ לָעַד וּלְעוֹלְמֵי עוֹלָמִים:	The Merciful One will be praised for all generations, He will be glorified through us forever and for all eternity; and He will be honored through us for time everlasting.
הָרַחֲמָן הוּא יְפַרְנְסֵנוּ בְּכָבוֹד:	May the Merciful One maintain us with honor.
הָרַחֲמָן הוּא יִשְׁבּוֹר עֻלֵּנוּ מֵעַל צַוָּארֵנוּ וְהוּא יוֹלִיכֵנוּ קוֹמְמִיּוּת לְאַרְצֵנוּ:	The Merciful One will break the yoke (of oppression) from our necks and lead us upright to our land.
הָרַחֲמָן הוּא יִשְׁלַח לָנוּ בְּרָכָה מְרֻבָּה בַּבַּיִת הַזֶּה וְעַל־שֻׁלְחָן זֶה שֶׁאָכַלְנוּ עָלָיו:	May the Merciful One send us abundant blessing to this house, and upon this table at which we have eaten.
הָרַחֲמָן הוּא יִשְׁלַח לָנוּ אֶת־ אֵלִיָּהוּ הַנָּבִיא זָכוּר לַטּוֹב, וִיבַשֶּׂר־לָנוּ בְּשׂוֹרוֹת טוֹבוֹת יְשׁוּעוֹת וְנֶחָמוֹת:	The Merciful One will send us Elijah the prophet, who is remembered for good, who will announce to us good tidings, deliverances, and consolations.
אם סמוך על שלחן אביו יאמר:	**When eating at your parents' table, say:**
הָרַחֲמָן הוּא יְבָרֵךְ אֶת־(אָבִי מוֹרִי) בַּעַל הַבַּיִת הַזֶּה, וְאֶת־ (אִמִּי מוֹרָתִי) בַּעֲלַת הַבַּיִת הַזֶּה, אוֹתָם וְאֶת־בֵּיתָם וְאֶת־ זַרְעָם וְאֶת־כָּל־אֲשֶׁר לָהֶם	May the Merciful One bless (my father, my teacher,) the master of this house, and (my mother, my teacher,) the mistress of this house; them, their household, their children and all that is theirs.
ואם סמוך על שלחן עצמו יאמר:	**When eating at your own table, say:**
הָרַחֲמָן הוּא יְבָרֵךְ אוֹתִי (וְאֶת־ אִשְׁתִּי/בַּעֲלִי וְאֶת־זַרְעִי) וְאֶת־ כָּל־אֲשֶׁר לִי.	May the Merciful One bless me, my spouse, my children, and all that is mine;

אוֹתָנוּ וְאֶת־כָּל־אֲשֶׁר לָנוּ, כְּמוֹ שֶׁנִּתְבָּרְכוּ אֲבוֹתֵינוּ, אַבְרָהָם יִצְחָק וְיַעֲקֹב: בַּכֹּל, מִכֹּל, כֹּל, כֵּן יְבָרֵךְ אוֹתָנוּ כֻּלָּנוּ יַחַד, בִּבְרָכָה שְׁלֵמָה, וְנֹאמַר אָמֵן:	Ours and all that is ours, just as our forefathers were blessed, Avraham, Yitzchak, and Yaakov. In all things, "From everything,"[49] and "With everything";[50] so may He bless us, all of us together, with a perfect blessing, and let us say Amen.
אם אוכל על שלחן אחרים יברך לבעה"ב. ואפילו בנים הסמוכים על שלחן אביהם, וגם האב הנסמך על שלחן בניו וגם אשתו תאמר כן:	**A guest says the following paragraph (even a son and daughter who are eating at their parent's table, a son at his parent's table. Some say that a wife at her husband's table):**
יְהִי רָצוֹן שֶׁלֹּא יֵבוֹשׁ וְלֹא יִכָּלֵם בַּעַל הַבַּיִת הַזֶּה לֹא בָּעוֹלָם הַזֶּה וְלֹא בָּעוֹלָם הַבָּא וְיַצְלִיחַ בְּכָל־נְכָסָיו וְיִהְיוּ נְכָסָיו מֻצְלָחִים וּקְרוֹבִים לָעִיר וְאַל־יִשְׁלוֹט שָׂטָן בְּמַעֲשֵׂה יָדָיו וְאַל יִזְדַּקֵּק לְפָנָיו שׁוּם דְּבַר חֵטְא וְהִרְהוֹר עָוֹן מֵעַתָּה וְעַד עוֹלָם:	May[51] it be God's will that the host should not be shamed and not humiliated not in this world nor in the World to Come. And he will be successful with all his possessions. May his properties prosper and be located close to town. May no evil force have power over his endeavors. May no opportunity present itself before him any matter of sin, nor thought of iniquity from now forever.
בַּמָּרוֹם יְלַמְּדוּ עֲלֵיהֶם וְעָלֵינוּ זְכוּת שֶׁתְּהֵא לְמִשְׁמֶרֶת שָׁלוֹם, וְנִשָּׂא בְרָכָה מֵאֵת יְהֹוָה וּצְדָקָה מֵאֱלֹהֵי יִשְׁעֵנוּ, וְנִמְצָא חֵן וְשֵׂכֶל טוֹב בְּעֵינֵי אֱלֹהִים וְאָדָם:	From on high, may there be invoked upon them and upon us, (the) merit to ensure peace, and may we receive a blessing from Lord, and kindness from the God of our deliverance; and may we

---

[49] Yitzchak said: "I have partaken from everything." Beraishis 27:33

[50] Yaakov said: "I have everything." Beraishis 33:11

[51] This blessing is quoted from the Talmud (Maseches Berachos 46a). It has been omitted in most Siddurim. The Mishnah Berura (201:5) takes issue with its omission and many are bringing it back into use. My honored father, ZT"L was particular to recite this whenever he was a guest at someone else's house or event. He even said it when he was a guest at my house.

	find favor and understanding in the eyes of God and man.
בשבת אומר:	**On *Shabbos* say:**
הָרַחֲמָן הוּא יַנְחִילֵנוּ יוֹם שֶׁכֻּלוֹ שַׁבָּת וּמְנוּחָה לְחַיֵּי הָעוֹלָמִים:	May the Merciful One let us inherit the day which will be completely *Shabbos* and rest, for life everlasting.
בראש חודש:	**On *Rosh Chodesh* say:**
הָרַחֲמָן הוּא יְחַדֵּשׁ עָלֵינוּ אֶת הַחֹדֶשׁ הַזֶּה לְטוֹבָה וְלִבְרָכָה:	May the Merciful One renew for us this month for good and for blessing.
ביו''ט אומר:	**On *Yom Tov* say:**
הָרַחֲמָן הוּא יַנְחִילֵנוּ יוֹם שֶׁכֻּלוֹ טוֹב:	May the Merciful One let us inherit that day which is completely good.
בראש השנה:	**On *Rosh HaShanah* say:**
הָרַחֲמָן הוּא יְחַדֵּשׁ עָלֵינוּ אֶת הַשָּׁנָה הַזֹּאת לְטוֹבָה וְלִבְרָכָה:	May the Merciful One renew for us this year for good and for blessing.
בסוכות:	**On *Sukkos* say:**
הָרַחֲמָן הוּא יָקִים לָנוּ אֶת־סֻכַּת דָּוִד הַנּוֹפָלֶת:	May the Merciful One raise up for us the fallen Tabernacle of David.
הָרַחֲמָן הוּא יְזַכֵּנוּ לִימוֹת הַמָּשִׁיחַ וּלְחַיֵּי הָעוֹלָם הַבָּא, מִגְדּוֹל יְשׁוּעוֹת מַלְכּוֹ, וְעֹשֶׂה חֶסֶד לִמְשִׁיחוֹ לְדָוִד וּלְזַרְעוֹ עַד עוֹלָם: עֹשֶׂה שָׁלוֹם בִּמְרוֹמָיו, הוּא יַעֲשֶׂה שָׁלוֹם עָלֵינוּ וְעַל כָּל־יִשְׂרָאֵל, וְאִמְרוּ אָמֵן:	May the Merciful One make us worthy of the days of Mashiach and life of the World to Come. He who is a tower of deliverance to His king, [52] and shows kindness to His anointed to David and his descendants forever. He Who makes peace in His high Heavens may He make peace for us and for all Israel, and say, Amen.

---

[52] During weekdays when we feel the darkness of exile we say, "God gives deliverance to His king," thus acknowledging His preparation for the time of redemption. On *Shabbos* and *Yom Tov* which are reminiscent of the time of the Mashiach, when God will be a tower of deliverance, we state it as a fact. On special occasions like a siyum, we also state it as a fact.

יְראוּ אֶת־יְהֹוָה קְדוֹשָׁיו, כִּי אֵין מַחְסוֹר לִירֵאָיו: כְּפִירִים רָשׁוּ וְרָעֵבוּ, וְדוֹרְשֵׁי יְהֹוָה לֹא־יַחְסְרוּ כָל־טוֹב: הוֹדוּ לַיהֹוָה כִּי־טוֹב, כִּי לְעוֹלָם חַסְדּוֹ: פּוֹתֵחַ אֶת־יָדֶךָ, וּמַשְׂבִּיעַ לְכָל־חַי רָצוֹן: בָּרוּךְ הַגֶּבֶר אֲשֶׁר יִבְטַח בַּיהֹוָה, וְהָיָה יְהֹוָה מִבְטַחוֹ: נַעַר הָיִיתִי גַּם־זָקַנְתִּי וְלֹא־רָאִיתִי צַדִּיק נֶעֱזָב, וְזַרְעוֹ מְבַקֶּשׁ־לָחֶם: יְהֹוָה עֹז לְעַמּוֹ יִתֵּן, יְהֹוָה יְבָרֵךְ אֶת־עַמּוֹ בַשָּׁלוֹם:	Fear Lord, (you) His holy ones, for those who fear Him suffer no deprivation. The scoffers may feel want and hunger, but those who seek Lord, will not be deprived of any good thing.[53] Give thanks to Lord, for He is good, for His kindness endures forever. [54] You open Your hand and satisfy the desire of every living being.[55] Blessed is the man who trusts in Lord, so that Lord is his security.[56] I was young and I have grown old, yet I have never seen a righteous man forsaken, nor his children begging for bread.[57] Lord will give strength to His people, Lord will bless His people with peace.[58]

Table 38 Wine After Birchas Hamazon

If you are using a cup of wine, raise it up and continue below. If not, you are finished.	
בָּרוּךְ אַתָּה יְיָ, אֱלֹהֵינוּ מֶלֶךְ הָעוֹלָם בּוֹרֵא פְּרִי הַגָּפֶן.	Blessed are You, Lord our God, King of the Universe, who creates the fruit of the vine.
Drink some of the wine and pass it around for others to partake. Afterwards, say the following *bracha*.	
בָּרוּךְ אַתָּה יְיָ, אֱלֹהֵינוּ מֶלֶךְ הָעוֹלָם, עַל הַגֶּפֶן וְעַל פְּרִי הַגֶּפֶן, עַל תְּנוּבַת הַשָּׂדֶה וְעַל אֶרֶץ חֶמְדָּה טוֹבָה וּרְחָבָה	Blessed are You, Lord our God, King of the Universe, for the vine and the fruit of the vine, and for the produce of the field; for the desirable, good and spacious land

---

[53] Tehillim 34:10 – 11
[54] II Shmuel 22:51
[55] Tehillim 136:1
[56] Yirmiyahu 17:7
[57] Tehillim 37:25
[58] Tehillim 29:11

<table>
<tr>
<td>

שֶׁרָצִיתָ וְהִנְחַלְתָּ לַאֲבוֹתֵינוּ לֶאֱכוֹל מִפִּרְיָהּ וְלִשְׂבֹּעַ מִטּוּבָהּ. רַחֶם נָא יְיָ אֱלֹהֵינוּ עַל יִשְׂרָאֵל עַמֶּךָ וְעַל יְרוּשָׁלַיִם עִירֶךָ וְעַל צִיּוֹן מִשְׁכַּן כְּבוֹדֶךָ וְעַל מִזְבְּחֶךָ וְעַל הֵיכָלֶךָ וּבְנֵה יְרוּשָׁלַיִם עִיר הַקֹּדֶשׁ בִּמְהֵרָה בְיָמֵינוּ וְהַעֲלֵנוּ לְתוֹכָהּ וְשַׂמְּחֵנוּ בְּבִנְיָנָהּ וְנֹאכַל מִפִּרְיָהּ וְנִשְׂבַּע מִטּוּבָהּ וּנְבָרֶכְךָ עָלֶיהָ בִּקְדֻשָּׁה וּבְטָהֳרָה

</td>
<td>

that You willingly gave as heritage to our ancestors, that they might eat of its fruit and be satisfied with its goodness. have compassion, Lord our God, on Israel Your people, on Yerushalayim, Your city, on Zion the home of Your glory, on Your altar and Your Temple. May You rebuild Yerushalayim, the holy city swiftly in our time, and may You bring us back there, rejoicing in its rebuilding, eating from its fruit, satisfied by its goodness, and blessing You for it in holiness and purity.

</td>
</tr>
<tr>
<td colspan="2" align="center">

On *Shabbos* add the following:

</td>
</tr>
<tr>
<td>

וּרְצֵה וְהַחֲלִיצֵנוּ בְּיוֹם הַשַּׁבָּת הַזֶּה

</td>
<td>

Be pleased to refresh us on this *Shabbos* Day.

</td>
</tr>
<tr>
<td colspan="2" align="center">

On all days continue:

</td>
</tr>
<tr>
<td>

כִּי אַתָּה יְיָ טוֹב וּמֵטִיב לַכֹּל, וְנוֹדֶה לְּךָ עַל הָאָרֶץ וְעַל פְּרִי הַגָּפֶן.

</td>
<td>

For You, God, are good and do good to all and we thank You for the land and for the fruit of the vine.

</td>
</tr>
</table>

Mazal
מזל
Tov
טוב

SECTION FOUR

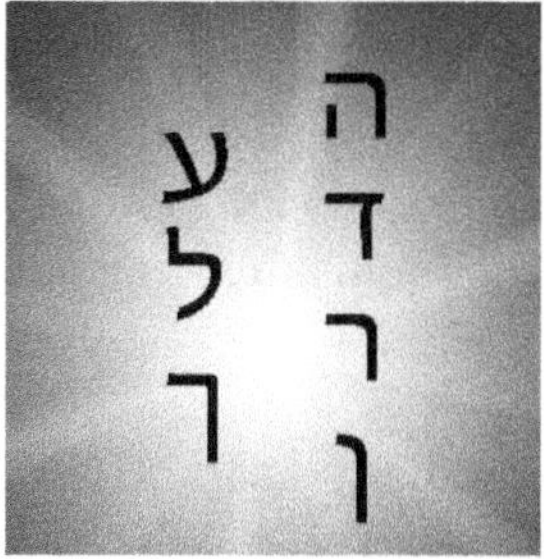

APPENDICES

APPENDIX ONE

SHEVUAH VS NEDER

Table 39 Shevuah VS Neder

What is the difference between a *neder* (vow) and a *shevua* (oath)?

A *neder* is generally described as *"issur cheftza"* vs *"issur gavra"* (*shevua*), with the practical difference being if you make one of them against a *Mitzvah*.

The Gemara[1] explicitly explains what the difference is between a *neder* and a *shevuah*:

דתנא נדרים דמיתסר חפצא עליה... לאפוקי שבועה דקאסר נפשיה מן חפצא

It explains that *nedarim* is where one forbids an object from himself, and *shevuos* is where one forbids oneself from the object.

---

[1] Nedarim 2b

This distinction follows Rambam's first two *halachos* in each of *hilchos nedarim* and *shevuos*. According to Rambam, *shevuos* are things you declare about yourself, either as past-tense declaratives, or future-tense promises. *Nedarim* are either forbidding the benefit of some object or declaring it is a dedication to something like the Temple treasury thereby also forbidding its benefit to you and obligating you to bring it to its new "owner".

Rambam[2] draws exactly this distinction, based on Nedarim 16b. He says:

ומפני מה נדרים חלים על דברי מצוה. ושבועות אין חלות על דברי מצוה. שהנשבע אוסר עצמו על דבר שנשבע עליו. והנודר אוסר הדבר הנדור על עצמו

Why do vows take effect regarding Mitzvos *and oaths do not take effect regarding* Mitzvos? *Because when a person takes an oath, he forbids himself from (partaking of the entity mentioned in the oath. When, by contrast, one takes a vow, he causes the entity mentioned in the vow to be forbidden to him.*

It is precisely a *gavra* vs. *cheftza* distinction.

In that same chapter, Rambam gives other practical differences between them. For example, *matpis* (saying "X is like Y") works only for *nedarim*, because you have declared X to be forbidden and therefore can make Y exactly like it, while that does not work for *shevuos*.

Saying that, "I will do something" which is permissible – as in "I will go to the park" – is indeed a *shevuah*. A *neder*, by definition, is either declaring something to be forbidden to oneself or taking on an obligation to bring a *korban* or give *tzedakah*.[3]

---

[2] Rambam: Hilchos Nedarim 3:7
[3] Rambam, Ibid. 1:1 – 2, Matnos Aniyim 8:1

APPENDIX TWO

MISHNAH TAMID 7:4

הַשִּׁיר שֶׁהָיוּ הַלְוִיִּם אוֹמְרִים בַּמִּקְדָּשׁ, בַּיּוֹם הָרִאשׁוֹן הָיוּ אוֹמְרִים (תהילים כ"ד:א'), לַה' הָאָרֶץ וּמְלוֹאָהּ תֵּבֵל וְיֹשְׁבֵי בָהּ. בַּשֵּׁנִי הָיוּ אוֹמְרִים (שם מח), גָּדוֹל ה' וּמְהֻלָּל מְאֹד בְּעִיר אֱלֹהֵינוּ הַר קָדְשׁוֹ. בַּשְּׁלִישִׁי הָיוּ אוֹמְרִים (שם פב), אֱלֹהִים נִצָּב בַּעֲדַת אֵל בְּקֶרֶב אֱלֹהִים יִשְׁפֹּט. בָּרְבִיעִי הָיוּ אוֹמְרִים (שם צד), אֵל נְקָמוֹת ה' אֵל נְקָמוֹת הוֹפִיעַ וְגוֹ'. בַּחֲמִישִׁי הָיוּ אוֹמְרִים (שם פא), הַרְנִינוּ לֵאלֹהִים עוּזֵּנוּ, הָרִיעוּ לֵאלֹהֵי יַעֲקֹב. בַּשִּׁשִּׁי הָיוּ אוֹמְרִים (שם צג), ה' מָלָךְ גֵּאוּת לָבֵשׁ וְגוֹ'. בְּשַׁבָּת הָיוּ אוֹמְרִים (שם צב), מִזְמוֹר שִׁיר לְיוֹם הַשַּׁבָּת, מִזְמוֹר שִׁיר לֶעָתִיד לָבֹא, לְיוֹם שֶׁכֻּלּוֹ שַׁבָּת מְנוּחָה לְחַיֵּי הָעוֹלָמִים:

The following is a list of each daily **psalm that the Levites would recite in the Temple. On the first day** of the week, **they would recite** the psalm beginning: "A psalm of David. **The earth is the Lord's and all it contains, the world and all who live in it**"[4]. **On the second** day, **they would recite** the psalm beginning: "A song; a psalm of the sons of Korach. **Great is the Lord and highly to be praised in the city of God, on His sacred mountain.**"[5]. **On the third** day, **they would recite** the psalm beginning: "A psalm of Asaph. **God stands in the divine assembly; among the judges He delivers judgment**".[6] **On the fourth** day, **they would recite** the psalm beginning: **"O Lord God, to Whom vengeance belongs, God to Whom vengeance belongs, shine forth"**.[7] **On the fifth** day, **they would recite** the psalm beginning: "For the leader; upon the Gittis, a psalm of Asaph. **Sing for joy to God, our strength; shout aloud to the God of Yaakov"**.[8] **On the sixth** day, **they would recite** the psalm beginning: **"The Lord reigns: He is robed in majesty; the Lord is**

---

[4] Tehillim, chapter 24

[5] Tehillim, chapter 48

[6] Tehillim, chapter 82

[7] Tehillim, chapter 94

[8] Tehillim, chapter 81

robed, girded with strength".[9] **On *Shabbos,* they would recite** the psalm beginning: **"A psalm, a song for *Shabbos* day".**[10] This is interpreted as **a psalm, a song for the future, for the day that will be entirely *Shabbos* and rest for everlasting life.**

---

[9] Tehillim, chapter 93
[10] Tehillim, chapter 92

APPENDIX THREE

THE TOP TEN

TANNAIM

THE WORD TANNA IS ARAMAIC for "teacher" and refers to a teacher of the Oral Law, the Mishnah. There were six generations of Tannaim for the 210 years of the Mishnah period. There are approximately 120 known Tannaim who lived in various areas of Israel, mostly in Yerushalayim.

The Amoraim (interpreters) followed immediately after the Tannaim.

Table 40 Generations of Tannaim

First Generation	10 – 80 CE
Second Generation	80 – 120 CE
Third Generation	120 – 140 CE
Fourth Generation	140 – 165 CE
Fifth Generation	165 – 200 CE
Sixth Generation	200 – 220 CE

Table 41 Top Ten Tannaim

	Name	**Times**
1	רבי יהודה	650
2	חכמים	450
3	רבי מאיר	350+
4	רבי שמעון	350+
5	רבי יוסי	350+
6	רבי אליעזר	350+
7	רבי עקיבא	300

8	בית שמאי	200+
9	בית הלל	200
10	רבי יהושע	100

There were eight generations of Amoraim who lived based on the following chart. The Amoraim were only active in Israel until approximately 370 and approximately 500 in Bavel. There are over 2,000 Amoraim who have been identified in the Gemara (both Yerushalmi and Bavli).

AMORAIM

Table 42 Generations of Amoraim

First Generation	220 – 250 CE
Second Generation	250 – 290 CE
Third Generation	290 – 320 CE
Fourth Generation	320 – 350 CE
Fifth Generation	350 – 375 CE
Sixth Generation	375 – 425 CE
Seventh Generation	425 – 460 CE
Eighth Generation	460 – 500 CE

The above charts are culled from my painstaking search of the Mishnayos. I was curious and wanted to know who were the top ten Tannaim mentioned in the Mishnayos. All numbers are approximate, and I am sorry if my numbers are incorrect, I did the best I could.

APPENDIX FOUR

SEVEN MIDDOS

THERE ARE SEVEN *MIDDOS* (DIVINE emotive attributes) — **Kindness, Severity, Harmony, Perseverance, Humility, Foundation, and Royalty**. While every soul possesses all seven of these *middos*, one of these traits is most dominant, shaping the individual soul's unique service to God. These are also called the Ten *Sefiros:* the ten attributes or emanations through which God manifests Himself. They represent specific qualities and structural forces of nature.

Table 43 Seven Middos

חסד	*Chesed*	Kindness	A soul whose service to God is characterized by a calm and flowing love. This soul is also overflowing with love for his fellows.
גבורה	*Gevurah*	Severity	A soul who serves God with awe and a flaming passion. This soul is also highly disciplined, with high expectations of himself and others.
תפארת	*Tiferes*	Harmony	The soul who has achieved a perfect synthesis of Kindness and Severity. This is accomplished through the study of the Torah. *Tiferes* is also the source of the soul's capacity for compassion.
נצח	*Netzach*	Perseverance	A soul who is constantly battling and struggling but is ultimately triumphant.
הוד	*Hod*	Humility	The soul which exemplifies self-abnegation in favor of allowing

			itself to be overwhelmed by God's goodness.
יסוד	*Yesod*	Foundation	The soul whose unique talent is establishing giving relationships, intellectually or otherwise.
מלכות	*Malchus*	Royalty	The soul who majestically serves its Creator.

The Holy Temple's *Menorah* had all seven branches hewn from a single block of pure gold. We may have different dispositions and different methods of serving God, but we are essentially one. We have one purpose and one mission, with different ways to accomplish the same goal — serving our creator and being a *Menorah* — a guiding light — for the entire world.

The depth and meaning of what I have written here are beyond the scope of this work and far above my knowledge. I will just add that Kabballah looks at the juxtaposition of letters, combinations of letters, different forms of numeric values and combinations (many forms of *gematria*), color emanations, date influences, zodiac influences, and much more.

APPENDIX FIVE

THE TEN UTTERANCES

IN THE STORY OF CREATION as narrated in the Torah,[11] there are Ten Utterances through which HaShem brought the world into existence. These are not merely rhetorical devices but profound expressions of Divine Will and Wisdom, aligning with the concept of the Ten *Sefiros* in Kabbalah. The Mishnah[12] states, "With Ten Utterances the world was created," indicating that each utterance was a distinct act of Divine Will, channeling specific energies into the fabric of reality.

Table 44 Ten Utterances

FIRST UTTERANCE			
Let there be light	Keser	Aleph	א
Keser, often translated as the "crown," is the primal source from which all Divine emanation flows. The AriZal (Rabbi Isaac Luria, "Etz Chaim") discusses Keser as the most concealed aspect of Divinity, likening it to *Ratzon*, the Divine will. *Aleph*, the first letter of the Hebrew alphabet, represents the essence of Divine unity and acts as the channel for the Ein Sof, the infinite light. Both *Aleph* and *Keser* point to the *Ohr Ein Sof*, the limitless light that is the source of all creation.[13]			
SECOND UTTERANCE			
Let there be a firmament	Chochmah	Yud	י
Chochmah or Wisdom is the first point of 'somethingness' in creation. The Talmud[14] likens it to the initial point from which a line extends. *Yud,* the smallest of Hebrew letters, epitomizes this point of wisdom			

---

[11] Beraishis chapters 1 – 2
[12] Avos 5:1
[13] Zohar, Vol. 1, 15a
[14] Chagigah 14a

that contains the potential for all else. It is the seed of ideas and concepts within the Divine mind.

THIRD UTTERANCE

Let the waters gather	Binah	Hay	ה

Binah is Understanding, often called the "mother" in Kabbalistic literature[15] It serves as the womb that gives form and substance to the spark of *Chochmah*. The letter *hay* signifies Divine breath and is the vehicle through which the formless is given form, analogous to how *Binah* gives fullness to the conceptual point of *Chochmah*.

FORTH UTTERANCE

Let the earth sprout vegetation	Chesed	Gimel	ג

Chesed, or Loving-Kindness, epitomizes the unbounded generosity of HaShem. In the Talmud,[16] *Gimel* is depicted as a rich man (*Gimel* symbolizing "*Gomel*," to bestow) pursuing a poor man, signifying the constant flow of divine grace and benevolence to the world.

FIFTH UTTERANCE

Let there be lights in the firmament	Gevurah	Dalet	ד

Gevurah, often translated as Strength or Judgment, represents the Divine attribute of constraint. The Vilna Gaon (Aderes Eliyahu, Bereshis) links *Dalet*, resembling a door, to this principle. A door can both admit and exclude, much like *Gevurah's* role in filtering and moderating the unbounded light of *Chesed*.

SIXTH UTTERANCE

Let the waters swarm	Tiferes	Vav	ו

Tiferes, or Beauty, serves as the harmonizing force between *Chesed* and *Gevurah*. In grammar, the letter *Vav* is a connector, serving a similar role in harmonizing and integrating the opposing energies, reminiscent of Aaron's role as the lover and pursuer of peace.[17]

SEVENTH UTTERANCE

Let the earth bring forth living creatures	Netzach	Zayin	ז

Netzach stands for Eternity and the ongoing influence of the Divine in our world. In Kabbalistic thought *Netzach* and *Hod* are often seen as a pair, representing the legs that move a person forward. *Zayin* symbolizes sustenance and the struggle inherent in perpetuating existence.

---

[15] Zohar 2, 84b
[16] Shabbos 104a
[17] Avos 1:12

<table>
<tr><td colspan="4">EIGHTH UTTERANCE</td></tr>
<tr><td>Let us make man</td><td>Hod</td><td>Tes</td><td>ט</td></tr>
<tr><td colspan="4">Hod embodies Glory and the aspect of surrender to Divine will. The letter Tes represents something concealed and is associated with the hidden aspects of Divinity that become manifest in the humility and submission that characterize Hod.</td></tr>
<tr><td colspan="4">NINTH UTTERANCE</td></tr>
<tr><td>Be fruitful and multiply</td><td>Yesod</td><td>Tsadi</td><td>צ</td></tr>
<tr><td colspan="4">Yesod, the Foundation, channels the flow of Divine blessing into the material realm. The Tsadi, seen as the righteous tzaddik, embodies this principle. The tzaddik is often viewed as the foundation of the world (Tehillim 10:25), a conduit for Divine blessing.</td></tr>
<tr><td colspan="4">TENTH UTTERANCE</td></tr>
<tr><td>It was very good</td><td>Malchus</td><td>Hay</td><td>ה</td></tr>
<tr><td colspan="4">Malchus represents the Kingdom, the realm where Divine energies find their expression in action and physicality. The second Hei in the Divine name Yud-Hay-Vav-Hay signifies the actualization of all preceding spiritual energies, much like Malchus signifies the completion of the Divine flow through the sefirotic structure.</td></tr>
</table>

The Zohar makes numerous connections between the *sefiros*, the Ten Utterances of creation, the Ten Utterances of the Decalogue, and the Ten Plagues brought on Egypt. There are also similarities to the requirement to have ten men for a quorum for saying *kaddish*, the ten praises in *kaddish*, and more.

BIOGRAPHICAL VIGNETTES

THE STUDY OF THIS VOLUME may be enhanced if the student is familiar with the lives of the commentaries who authored various works on the subject. For this reason, a summary of these men is included herein. Curious people who wish to study their lives in depth can find a plethora of works on the lives of these great Torah giants.

In the following section, I will give you a brief biography of some of the great Rabbis mentioned herein. This brief list also includes commentators and Rabbis who have helped me in my superficial learning in producing this volume. I hope you also benefit from this chapter.

Aitz Yosef:
Rav Chonoch Zundel of Bailystock – Died 1867.
Author of Aitz Yosef and Anaf Yosef, commentaries on the prayers, including the Siddur Otzar Tefillos.

Asaf: He was one of King David's three chief musicians. He was the son of Berachiah from the Tribe of Levi.

Avudraham, Rabbi David:
Late 13th to 14th century. Flourished around 1340.
A specialist in the laws and customs of the Jewish liturgy and the *kavanah* behind the prayers.

Berlin, HaRav Chaim:

1832 – 1912

Born in Voloshin died in Yerushalayim. He was the Chief Rabbi of Moscow from 1865 – 1889. Eldest son of the Netziv (Naftali Zvi Yehuda Berlin.

Dovair Shalom:

Rabbi Yitzchak Eliyahu Landau – 1810 – 1876.

Author of Dovair Shalom, a basic commentary on prayer, included within the Otzar Tefillos *siddur*.

Eliezer *ben* Hurcanus:

A Tanna from the first or second century in Israel.

He was a student of Rabban Yochanan *ben* Zakkai. He is the sixth most frequently mentioned sage in the Mishnah. He was also a *Kohen*. See Appendix Three on Page 215 for more on the top ten.

Elyashiv, Rav Yosef Shalom:

1910 – 2012.

Lived in Yerushalayim and was considered by many as the leading Rabbi of the generation.

Feinstein, HaRav Moshe:

1895 – 1986.

He was probably the most well-regarded and accepted leading Rabbi of his generation. He was a prolific writer on Jewish law and his opinions are widely accepted as final law.

Gerrer Rebbi:

Yehudah Aryeh Leib Alter. 1847 – 1905.

Leader of the Ger Chasidim. He was known after his main work Sefas Emes.

Hai Gaon, Rav:

939 – 1038 CE.

Last of the Geonim of Pumbedisa (a small town near Baghdad, Iraq).

BIOGRAPHICAL VIGNETTES

Hirsch, R. Samson Raphael:
1808 – 1888. Born in Hamburg, French Empire, died in Frankfurt am Main, German Empire. He was a prolific writer and deep thinker of Jewish philosophy and Written and Oral Torah.

Hutner, HaRav Yitzchak:
1906 – 1980
Born in Warsaw. Was Rosh Yeshiva of Yeshivas Chaim Berlin in Brooklyn, then moved to Yerushalayim and started Yeshivas Pachad Yitzchak which later changed its name to Chaim Berlin. He died in Yerushalayim.

Isserles, Rav Moshe:
1520 – 1572.
He wrote a major commentary on the Turim

Kanievsky, Rav Shemaryahu Yosef Chaim:
1928 – 2022
The leading authority of Jewish law was considered the Prince of Torah by Jews worldwide. Born in Pinsk, Poland, died in Bnei Brak, Israel.

Maharal:
Yehudah Loew ben Bezalel. Born between 1512 and 1526 Poznan, Poland, died in 1609 in Prague, Bohemia. Also known as the Maharal from Prague.

Maharshal:
Rabbi Shlomo Luria. 1510 – 1573
Ashkenazic leader and *posek*. Wrote Yam Shel Shlomo, Yerios Shlomo, Amuduei Shlomo, Chochmas Shlomo, and more. Born in Poznan, Poland

Mishnah Berura:
Written by Rabbi Yisrael Meir HaKohen Kagan of Radin, 1838 – 1933 also known as the Chofetz Chaim after another of his famous works. The Mishnah Berura is considered the final authority of Jewish law. He also wrote a plethora of works on Jewish law and ethical issues.

Nechunya *ben* Hakanah:
Was a Tanna of the first and second centuries. It appears from Bava Basra 10b that Nechunya was a contemporary, but not a pupil, of Yohanan *ben* Zakkai. He was the teacher of Yishmael *ben* Elisha.

Nechunya was rich and had a large retinue of servants; but he was distinguished for his meekness and forgiving nature, to which he attributed his attainment of great age; the two short prayers mentioned above[18] that he composed exhibit the same qualities.

According to Yochanan *bar* Nappacha,[19] Nechunya interpreted the entire Torah by the hermeneutic rule known as the "general and particular" (*kelal uprat*), a rule which his pupil Rabbi Yishmael made the eighth of his thirteen hermeneutic rules. Nechunya is frequently mentioned in the Talmud:

- [20]He is referred to disagreeing with Eliezer *ben* Hurcanus and Yehoshua *ben* Chananiah regarding a *halachah*.

- In a post-Talmudic text, he said that the Pharaoh of the Exodus was rescued from the Red Sea, that he repented, that he afterward reigned in Nineveh, and that it was he who in the time of Yonah exhorted the inhabitants of Nineveh to repentance.

- Nehunya is also known for his ethical saying, "Whoever accepts upon him the yoke of the Torah, from him is removed the yoke of royalty and that of worldly care; and whoever throws off the yoke of the Torah, upon him is laid the yoke of royalty and that of worldly care."

- As Rabbi Yishmael, Nechunya's disciple, is regarded by the kabbalists as their chief representative, Nechunya is considered to have been Yishmael's teacher in mysticism also. He is generally supposed to have been the author of the prayer beginning Ana BeKoach, the initials of which form the forty-two-lettered name of God. He is also supposed by some to have been the author of the *Bahir*, *sefer haTemunah*, and the *sefer ha-Peli'ah*.

Otzer Dinim U'Minhagim:
> By Rabbi Yehudah David Eisenstein 1854 – 1956.
> Prolific author, historian, and philanthropist; Polish-American.

Radak:
> Rabbi David Kimchi 1160 – 1235.
> Biblical commentator, philosopher, and grammarian.

---

[18] Page 31
[19] Shevuos 26a
[20] Chullin 129b

BIOGRAPHICAL VIGNETTES

Rambam:
Rabbi Moshe *ben* Maimon 1135 – 1204
He wrote Rambam, an encyclopedia of *halacha* in fourteen volumes; Sefer HaMitzvos, an explanation of the 613 Torah Precepts; Guide to the Perplexed, a major philosophical work; as well as many other works.

Ran:
Circa 1320 – Circa 1376
Rabaynu Nissim *ben* Reuven of Gerona flourished in Barcelona

Rashi:
Rabbi Shlomo Yitzchoky – 1040 – 1105
Author of the definitive basic commentary on Chumash and Gemara

Rabbi Yona Reiss:
Born 1966 – Contemporary
American rabbi has served as Av Beth Din of the Chicago Rabbinical Council (CRC), dean of Rabbi Isaac Elchanan Theological Seminary (RIETS), and director of the Beth Din of America.

Rif:
1013 – 1103
Rav Yitzchak Alfasi, North African Rabbi, Talmudic commentator, and legal decider.

Scheinberg, Rav Chaim Pinchas, ZT"L:
1910 – 2012
Rosh HaYeshiva Torah Ore in Yerushalayim. One of the leading authorities of Jewish law and member of the Moetzes Gedolei HaTorah.

Sefer Eshkol: The Cluster
Born between 1080 and 1085 died 1058
Avraham *ben* Yitzchak of Narbonne. Wrote many *sefarim* on the Gemara, most of which have been lost to the ravages of time.

Seforno:
Ovadia *ben* Yaakov Seforno
Born in Cesena about 1475 and died in Bologna in 1549

Shapiro, Rabbi Yehuda Meir:
1887 – 1933
Born in Shatz, Austria-Hungary (present-day Romania), died in Lublin, Poland
Rosh HaYeshiva Chachmei Lublin from 1930 – 1933
Most famously, the founder of the Daf Yomi program where Jews study one folio of Talmud a day and complete the entire Gemara in seven and a half years.

Steipler: Also known as The Steipler Gaon
1899 – 1985
Rabbi Yaakov Yisrael Kanievsky lived in B'nai Brak, Israel. Author of Kehilos Yaakov, a multi-volume commentary on the Gemara, and many other *sefarim*.

Sternbuch, Rabbi Moshe:
1926 – Contemporary
Born in London, lives in Yerushalayim

Taamei Minhagim:
1851 – 1921
Rabbi Avraham Yitzchak Sperling

Teitelbaum, Rav Yoel:
1887 – 1979
He wrote many *seforim* on Chumash, Halacha, Gemara, and more. Founder of the Satmar Chasidic group.

Teshuvot v'Hanhagot: See Sternbuch, Rabbi Moshe

Yehoshua *ben* Chananiah:
Died 131 CE
Also known as Rabbi Yehoshua, was a leading Tanna of the first half-century following the destruction of the Second Holy Temple. He was a Levi

Yishmael *ben* Elisha:
He was a third-generation Tanna, not to be confused with a First-Generation Tanna or the Baal HaBaraisa who was also a third-generation Tanna by the same name.
He was a third-generation Tanna from a wealthy priestly family from the Upper Galil.

He was born about 90 C.E. and possibly was one of the martyrs of Betar.

Yochanan *bar* Nappacha:
180 C.E. – 279 C.E.

He was among the second generation of the Amoraim. His opinions are quoted thousands of times throughout the Talmud Bavli and Yerushalmi.

The Rambam[21] says that he was one of the compilers of the Talmud Yerushalmi.

Yochanan *ben* Zakkai:
First-century CE

Also known as the Ribaz. Lived during the late Second Holy Temple period and was a main contributor to the Mishnah.

---

[21] Rambam Introduction to Talmud Yerushalmi

GLOSSARY

Aleph: The first letter of the alphabet. Has the numeric value of one.

Aggadah: Homiletical explanations of the Torah; Divine Concepts and fundamental realities which renowned men of wisdom kept hidden and which they did not want to openly reveal. This includes everything that philosophers of their generation established.[22]

Aggadic: Pertaining to *Aggadah*

Almighty: This word is a description of one of the attributes of God, namely, that He is Omnipotent. Moreover, it symbolizes His trait of Divine Judgement.[23]

Amen: The word "Amen" implies an oath, a promise, and a prayer for fulfillment.[24]

"Amen" implies an oath as stated, "The woman shall respond, 'Amen. Amen.'"[25] And even though the officiating *kohen* uttered the

---

[22] Rambam: Introduction to Mishnayos
[23] Vilna Gaon: Shulchan Aruch: Orech Chayim 5:1
[24] Shevuos 36a
[25] Bamidbar 5:22

imprecation, her response of "Amen," is effective in that the 'bitter waters' will cause her belly to explode if she had indeed been adulterous.[26]

"Amen" is indicative of a promise as stated: "May he who fails to uphold the Torah and observe (its precepts) be cursed. And the populace responded, 'Amen.'"[27] This means that Jewry made a promise to God to abide by the Torah and observe its commandments.[28]

"Amen" represents a request that one's wish be granted as stated, "The Prophet Yirmiyahu proclaims 'Amen! So may the Eternal do. May the Eternal fulfill the prophecy which you have forecast to bring back the vessels of the Eternal's House and all those who were exiled to Babylonia to this place.'".[29]

Amorah: A Talmudic authority who flourished from approximately 220 – 500 C.E.

Amoraim: Plural of Amorah

Babylonian Talmud: A commentary upon the Mishnah that was compiled by Ravina and Rav Ashi and redacted into its final form with the aid of the Sages and sealed seventy-three years after Ravina's death – approximately 500 C.E.[30]

Ba'alay batim: Any member of working-class society whose entire day is not devoted to learning or teaching Torah

Baal teshuvah:
- Any person who repents of a given sin to such a degree that he will not again fall prey to it.[31]
- A non-observant Jew who accepts upon himself the tenets and laws of the Torah and Rabbis.

Bachur: Young single man

Beis Midrash: Study Hall where Torah is learned, usually referring to a Yeshiva or Synagogue

---

[26] Rashi: Ad. loc.
[27] Devarim 27:26
[28] Shavuos Loc. cit.
[29] Jeremiah 27:6 Ibid.
[30] Rambam: Introduction to the Talmud
[31] Rambam: Hilchos Teshuva 2:1 – 2

GLOSSARY

Bamidbar: Fourth Biblical Book of Numbers

Bavli: Babylonian Talmud

Bekius: Broad superficial knowledge in many areas.
Generally speaking, Talmudic study consists of two areas:

- Deep analytical dissection of a small portion of the Gemara with the aim of developing a person's thinking ability and logic
- Superficial study of large areas of the Gemara to develop a general familiarity with the wide scope of subjects discussed therein.

The former may be likened to working implements and the latter to the material handled with these tools. Both are essential and success in learning is dependent upon both of these disciplines.[32]

Ben: The son of

Bracha: Blessing

Brachos: Blessings

Birchas hamazon: Grace after meals that is recited after a meal eaten with bread

Chanukah: Festival of Lights that lasts eight days and nights that typically occurs in December. Twenty-fifth of the Lunar month of Kislev.

Chavrusah: Study partner

Chazak: Be strong

Chazakah:
- A legal act of property acquisition
- Halachic status of permanence being established when an event repeats thrice
- An entity's assumptive state based on its nature or track record

---

[32] Kiddushin 37b; Rabbi Yisrael Salanter: Ohr Yisrael Section 27

Cheftza: An object

Chesed: Good deed

Creation: The creation of the universe which contains the secrets of the world. For most of us mortals, it is beyond our comprehension.[33]

Daf: Page (one folio)

Daf Yomi: A program started by Rabbi Meir Shapiro, ZT"L where the participants learn one *daf* of Gemara per day, finishing the entire Gemara Bavli in seven and one-half years.

Dapim: Pages (two folios)

Devarim: Biblical Book of Deuteronomy

Dinim: Laws.

Edicts: Promulgations enacted by the Rabbis for the benefit of society or to prevent a person from unwittingly sinning.[34]

Eretz Yisrael: The Land of Israel

Eternal: The One who is, was, and always will be.[35] This very name hints at His existence. If one asks how a particular item came to be in this world, he will be answered that such and such made it. And what made that, etc.? He must answer that somewhere along the line there exists an entity to whom the question of "who made it" does not apply because that entity has no beginning. Consequently, that entity does not exist within the framework of time and hence has no end. He is, was, and always will be – the Eternal.

Gan Eden: Garden of Eden

Gavra: A person, usually referring to a man

---

[33] See Rambam: Foundations of the Torah: Chapters #1 – 2
[34] See Gitten. 4:2, Avos. 3:13, Berachos 1:1
[35] Shulchan Aruch: Orach Chaim, Chagigah 5:1

GLOSSARY

Gedolay: The leading Rabbinic authorities in any given generation. (The Greatest of…)

Gemara: The Talmud

Gittis: A musical term of uncertain meaning, most likely referring to a musical instrument. It is found only three times and only in Tehillim – Psalms 8, 81, and 84.

Gog and Magog: Two world powers who will wage war against one another in the Messianic age and try unsuccessfully to conquer Israel and subjugate her.[36]

Gadol Hador: Leader of the generation

Halacha: Jewish Law

Halachic: Pertaining to Jewish Law

Halachos: Jewish Laws (plural)

Hiddur: Beautify, honor, glorify

Ibid.: (Latin) Ibidem – In the same place

Kaddish: A prayer said on behalf of the soul of a deceased individual which elevates it to a higher level in Heaven. A prayer whose entirety is a sanctification of God's name.

Kaddish deRabanan: The Rabbi's *Kaddish* recited after learning.

Kavanah: Devotion and concentration during prayer and the fulfillment of the *Mitzvos*.

Kohen: Priest, a descendant of Aaron (Shemos 28:1). He served in the Temple and received twenty-four gifts as enumerated in the Torah.[37]

Kohen Gadol: High Priest.[38]

---

[36] Yechezkel 38:1 – 39; 39:29; Daniel 11:40; 12:1
[37] See Gitten 5:8, Horayos 3:8; Tiferes Yisrael: Avos 6:5; Bamidbar 18:8 – 32
[38] Rabbi Ovadia from Bartenura: Yoma 1:3

Kohanim: Plural of *kohen*.

Kol Nidre: An Aramaic declaration that begins the Yom Kippur service that publicly declares all vows made, null and void.

Kollel: An institution, Yeshiva, where men study Torah for recompense for this time studying.

Korbonos: Parts of the daily prayers that are said in the morning that discuss the offerings in the Holy Temple.

Levites:
    a.   A member of the tribe of Levi which includes both Levites and *kohanim*.[39]
    b.   The person who gets called up second to the reading of the Torah after the *kohen*.

Lord: A term referring to God's attribute of being the Master of the Universe.[40]

Malachim: A catchall term for the ten different forms of angels

Maseches: See *Masechta*

Masecheta: Tractate of Mishnah or Gemara

Middos: Personality traits

Minyan: A quorum of ten males that is required to say certain prayers and to perform certain specific Torah *Mitzvos*.[41]

Mishnah: A Halachic commentary on the Torah written and compiled by Rabbi Yehuda Hanasi (The Prince). It was compiled approximately from 190 to 220 C.E.

---

[39] Bamidbar 3:11; 8:17, 40; Devarim 10:8
[40] Shulchan Aruch: Orech Chayim 5:1
[41] Megillah 4:3

GLOSSARY

Mishnayos: Plural of Mishnah. There are 4189 *Mishnayos* in *Shas* that are subdivided into sixty-three Tractates.

Mispar katan: (Small value) calculates the value of each letter but truncates all the zeros. It is also sometimes called *mispar me'ugal*.

Mitzvah:
- A Precept in the Torah
- A good deed

Mitzvos: Plural of *Mitzvah*

Musaf Service: The additional Prayer Services for *Shabbos*, Festivals, *Rosh Chodesh*, Intermediate days, and certain fasts.

Muvhak: *Rav Muvhak* refers to the teacher from whom a student rabbi received most of his knowledge. It could also be referring to the student who is the main student of his Rabbi.

Nedarim: Plural of *neder*

Neder: A vow or a Vow-Offering

Neshama: Soul

Nevi'im: Prophets

Ohr HaGenuzah: The special light that HaShem created and hid away during the Creation period. It is reserved for the righteous in the future world.

Olam Haba: Hereafter. The place where one who has died, but whose soul lives on, receives a reward for *Mitzvos* performed in his life for which he has not received recompense.

P'sak din: Legal decision

Paskens: Offers a legal opinion.

Pasuk: Verse in Scripture

THE HADRAN ALACH

Pesukim: Verses in Scripture

Rabaynu: Our teacher

Rishonim: Commentators who flourished and wrote their Torah works during an era which began in 1038 C.E. and extended to the era of the fifteenth century. The exact cut-off date marking the end of this era and the start of the *Achronim* is not universally agreed upon. Some say it was as early as 1460 while others contend that it was as late as 1575.

Rosh Yeshiva: Dean of students at a Torah school for boys of high school age and older.

Seder: Order

Sedra: Weekly portion of Torah reading

Sefer: Book

Sefarim: Books

Sefiros: Esoteric powers.

Segulah: A protective incantation or ritual based on Kabbalistic or Talmudic tradition.

Seudas Mitzvah: A festive meal that one eats in honor of fulfilling a Torah *Mitzvah* or in celebration of a significant occasion, *e.g.,* circumcision and the completion of a Tractate of Talmud.

Shabbos: Sabbath

Shamash: Sexton

Shas: The sixty-three tractates that make up the six orders of *Mishnayos* and comprise the Talmud.

Shas Gemara: The six orders of Gemara encompassing the entire spectrum of the Gemara.

Shevuah: An oath is where one forbids oneself from an object

GLOSSARY

Shema: The prayer reaffirming our belief in God consists of the following Scriptural Passages:
1. Devarim 6:4 – 9
2. Ibid. 11:13 – 21
3. Bamidbar 15:37 – 41

Shemos: Biblical Book of Exodus

Shevuah: Oath

Shiur: Class or lecture

Shul: Synagogue

Siddur: Prayer Book

Sifrei Torah: Torah scrolls

Siyum: Completion of a significant work

Siyumim: Plural of siyum

Tachanun: Part of the morning or afternoon prayers where one lowers his face onto his arm for part of the service. There are two formats, one long and the other short. The long one is typically said on Mondays and Thursdays. The short version is said on most other days, except *Shabbos* and holidays or special occasions.

Talmid: Student

Talmid Chacham: A Torah scholar

Talmud Yerushalmi: The Talmud of Eretz Yisrael, which is a concise explanation of the Mishnah. It contains about 1700 folios.

TaNaCH: Abbreviation for Torah, Nevi'im, and Kesuvim – The Torah, Prophets, and Writings.

Tanna: Commentators on the *Mishnayos* who flourished from 10 to 220 C.E.

Tannaim: Plural of Tanna

Tefillah: Prayer

Tefillin: Phylacteries

Teshuva: Repentance

Tzadikim: Righteous people

Vayikra: Biblical Book of Leviticus

Venischazaik: And let us become strong

Yahrzeit: Anniversary of the death of someone.

Yerushalayim: Jerusalem

Yerushalmi: See Talmud Yerushalmi

Yeshiva: A school in which Torah topics are studied

Yetzer Hara: Evil Inclination

Yom Kippur: Day of Atonement

Yom Tov: Jewish Festivals such as *Pesach*, *Shavuos*, and *Sukkos*

ZT"L: The memory of the righteous should be for a blessing

CHART OF TABLES

OTHER TITLES BY BEN JAKOB

- <u>Doomsday Bunker Book</u> – On being prepared for a disaster
- <u>Doomsday Bunker Book,</u> Underground Edition – On being prepared for a disaster
- <u>Addendums for Doomsday Bunker Book</u> – On being prepared for a disaster
- <u>Doomsday Prepper Lessons</u> – Lessons learned from Covid19 to be prepared for the future.
- <u>CADD Manual for House Location Drawings</u> – Written for a specific company, but adaptable for any company that uses CADD for house location drawings.
- <u>Viduy</u> – A translation of the *Viduy* written by the Chida, ZT"L.
- <u>The Quality of Light</u> – A manual for photographers on lighting
- <u>Kitchen Guide</u> – Tips and tricks for the kitchen
- <u>Not My People</u> – A Historic Fiction Thriller Novel 1976 – 1986
- The Late Great Who? – The Sequel to Not My People 1987 – 1999
- <u>Below the Surface</u> – The conclusion
- <u>Mishnayos Chagigah</u> – A detailed translation and explanation of Mishnayos Maseches Chagigah
- <u>The Viduy of the Chida</u> – A translation and explanation of the *Viduy* from the Chida, ZT"L Second edition
- <u>Pesach Haggadah</u> – A Haggadah for *Pesach* with translation and commentary. The Haggadah is in a format that is convenient to use at your *seder*.

הֲדְרָן עֲלָךְ מַסֶּכֶת ... וְהַדְרָךְ עֲלָן. דַּעְתָּן עֲלָךְ מַסֶּכֶת ...
וְדַעְתָּךְ עֲלָן. לָא נִתְנְשֵׁי מִינָךְ מַסֶּכֶת ... וְלָא תִתְנְשֵׁי מִינָן, לָא
בְּעָלְמָא הָדֵין וְלָא בְּעָלְמָא דְאָתֵי

יְהִי רָצוֹן מִלְּפָנֶיךָ יְיָ אֱלֹהֵינוּ וֵאלֹהֵי אֲבוֹתֵינוּ שֶׁתְּהֵא תוֹרָתְךָ
אֻמָּנוּתֵנוּ בָּעוֹלָם הַזֶּה וּתְהֵא עִמָּנוּ לָעוֹלָם הַבָּא. חֲנִינָא בַּר
פָּפָּא, רָמִי בַּר פָּפָּא, נַחְמָן בַּר פָּפָּא, אַחַאי בַּר פָּפָּא, אַבָּא
[מָרִי] בַּר פָּפָּא, רַפְרָם בַּר פָּפָּא, רָכִישׁ בַּר פָּפָּא, סוּרְחָב בַּר
פָּפָּא, אַדָּא בַּר פָּפָּא, דָּרוּ בַּר פָּפָּא

הַעֲרֶב נָא יְיָ אֱלֹהֵינוּ, אֶת דִּבְרֵי תוֹרָתְךָ בְּפִינוּ וּבְפִיּוֹת עַמְּךָ
בֵּית יִשְׂרָאֵל, וְנִהְיֶה כֻּלָּנוּ אֲנַחְנוּ וְצֶאֱצָאֵינוּ וְצֶאֱצָאֵי עַמְּךָ
בֵּית יִשְׂרָאֵל, כֻּלָּנוּ יוֹדְעֵי שְׁמֶךָ וְלוֹמְדֵי תוֹרָתֶךָ. מֵאֹיְבַי
תְּחַכְּמֵנִי מִצְוֹתֶךָ כִּי לְעוֹלָם הִיא לִי. יְהִי לִבִּי תָמִים בְּחֻקֶּיךָ
לְמַעַן לֹא אֵבוֹשׁ. לְעוֹלָם לֹא אֶשְׁכַּח פִּקּוּדֶיךָ כִּי בָם חִיִּיתָנִי.
בָּרוּךְ אַתָּה יְיָ לַמְּדֵנִי חֻקֶּיךָ אָמֵן אָמֵן אָמֵן סֶלָה וָעֶד

מוֹדִים אֲנַחְנוּ לְפָנֶיךָ יְיָ אֱלֹהֵינוּ וֵאלֹהֵי אֲבוֹתֵינוּ שֶׁשַּׂמְתָּ
חֶלְקֵנוּ מִיּוֹשְׁבֵי בֵית הַמִּדְרָשׁ, וְלֹא שַׂמְתָּ חֶלְקֵנוּ מִיּוֹשְׁבֵי
קְרָנוֹת. שֶׁאָנוּ מַשְׁכִּימִים וְהֵם מַשְׁכִּימִים. אָנוּ מַשְׁכִּימִים
לְדִבְרֵי תוֹרָה וְהֵם מַשְׁכִּימִים לִדְבָרִים בְּטֵלִים. אָנוּ עֲמֵלִים
וְהֵם עֲמֵלִים. אָנוּ עֲמֵלִים וּמְקַבְּלִים שָׂכָר וְהֵם עֲמֵלִים וְאֵינָם
מְקַבְּלִים שָׂכָר. אָנוּ רָצִים וְהֵם רָצִים. אָנוּ רָצִים לְחַיֵּי הָעוֹלָם
הַבָּא, וְהֵם רָצִים לִבְאֵר שַׁחַת. שֶׁנֶּאֱמַר: וְאַתָּה אֱלֹהִים
תּוֹרִדֵם לִבְאֵר שַׁחַת אַנְשֵׁי דָמִים וּמִרְמָה לֹא יֶחֱצוּ יְמֵיהֶם
וַאֲנִי אֶבְטַח בָּךְ